Regulating entrepreneurial behaviour in European health care systems

European Observatory on Health Care Systems Series

Series Editors

Josep Figueras is Head of the Secretariat and Research Director of the European Observatory on Health Care Systems and Head of the European Centre for Health Policy, World Health Organization Regional Office for Europe.

Martin McKee is Research Director of the European Observatory on Health Care Systems and Professor of European Public Health at the London School of Hygiene & Tropical Medicine as well as a co-director of the School's European Centre on Health of Societies in Transition.

Elias Mossialos is Research Director of the European Observatory on Health Care Systems and Brian Abel-Smith Reader in Health Policy, Department of Social Policy, London School of Economics and Political Science and Co-Director of LSE Health and Social Care.

Richard B. Saltman is Research Director of the European Observatory on Health Care Systems and Professor of Health Policy and Management at the Rollins School of Public Health, Emory University in Atlanta, Georgia

The series

The volumes in this series focus on key issues for health policy-making in Europe. Each study explores the conceptual background, outcomes and lessons learned about the development of more equitable, more efficient and more effective health systems in Europe. With this focus, the series seeks to contribute to the evolution of a more evidence-based approach to policy formulation in the health sector.

These studies will be important to all those involved in formulating or evaluating national health care policies and, in particular, will be of use to health policy-makers and advisers, who are under increasing pressure to rationalize the structure and funding of their health systems. Academics and students in the field of health policy will also find this series valuable in seeking to understand better the complex choices that confront the health systems of Europe.

Current and forthcoming titles

Martin McKee and Judith Healy (eds): *Hospitals in a Changing Europe*
Martin McKee, Judith Healy and Jane Falkingham (eds): *Health Care in Central Asia*
Elias Mossialos, Anna Dixon, Josep Figueras and Joe Kutzin (eds): *Funding Health Care: Options for Europe*
Richard B. Saltman, Reinhard Busse and Elias Mossialos (eds): *Regulating Entrepreneurial Behaviour in European Health Care Systems*

The European Observatory on Health Care Systems is a unique project that builds on the commitment of all its partners to improving health care systems:

- World Health Organization Regional Office for Europe
- Government of Greece
- Government of Norway
- Government of Spain
- European Investment Bank
- Open Society Institute
- World Bank
- London School of Economics and Political Science
- London School of Hygiene & Tropical Medicine

The Observatory supports and promotes evidence-based health policy-making through comprehensive and rigorous analysis of the dynamics of health care systems in Europe.

European Observatory on Health Care Systems Series

Edited by Josep Figueras, Martin McKee, Elias Mossialos and Richard B. Saltman

Regulating entrepreneurial behaviour in European health care systems

Edited by
Richard B. Saltman,
Reinhard Busse and
Elias Mossialos

Open University Press

Buckingham · Philadelphia

Open University Press
Celtic Court
22 Ballmoor
Buckingham
MK18 1XW

email: enquiries@openup.co.uk
world wide web: www.openup.co.uk

and
325 Chestnut Street
Philadelphia, PA 19106, USA

First Published 2002

A catalogue record of this book is available from the British Library

ISBN   0 335 20922 X (pb)   0 335 20923 8 (hb)

Library of Congress Cataloging-in-Publication Data
Regulating entrepreneurial behaviour in European health care systems / edited by Richard B. Saltman, Reinhard Busse, and Elias Mossialos.
      p. cm. — (European Observatory on Health Care Systems series)
   Includes bibliographical references and index.
   ISBN 0-335-20923-8 (hb) — ISBN 0-335-20922-X (pb)
      1. Medical care—Economic aspects—Europe. 2. Medical care—Europe—Finance.
   3. Medicine—Economic aspects—Europe. I. Saltman, Richard B. II. Busse, Reinhard, 1963– III. Mossialos, Elias. IV. Series.

R484 .R44 2002
338.4′33621′094—dc21   2001036116

Typeset by Graphicraft Limited, Hong Kong
Printed in Great Britain by Biddles Limited, Guildford and Kings Lynn

Contents

List of figures and tables

List of contributors

Wienke Boerma is Senior Researcher at Nivel, the Netherlands Institute for Health Services Research.

Reinhard Busse is Associate Professor for Epidemiology, Social Medicine and Health Systems Research at Medizinische Hochschule in Hannover, Germany, and is Head of the Madrid hub of the European Observatory on Health Care Systems.

David Chinitz is Senior Lecturer in Health Policy and Management at the Hebrew University-Hadassah School of Public Health, Jerusalem, Israel.

Jennifer Dixon is Director of the Health Care Policy Programme at the King's Fund, London, United Kingdom.

Antonio Duran-Moreno is Head of Tecnicas de Salud in Seville, Spain and a regular consultant to WHO.

Tim Ensor is Senior Research Fellow and Head of the International Programme at the Centre for Health Economics, University of York, United Kingdom.

Julien Forder is Research Fellow at LSE Health and Social Care in the London School of Economics and Political Science, United Kingdom.

Tom van der Grinten is Professor of Health Care Policy and Organization in the Department of Health Policy and Management at Erasmus University, Rotterdam, Netherlands.

Peter Groenewegen is Head of the Research Department at Nivel, the Netherlands Institute for Health Services Research, and Professor of Social and Geographical

Aspects of Health and Health Care at the Departments of Sociology and of Human Geography at Utrecht University, Netherlands.

Dorthe Holst is Professor in the Department of Community Dentistry at the University of Oslo, Norway.

Elias Mossialos is Research Director of the European Observatory on Health Care Systems and Brian Abel-Smith Reader in Health Policy in the Department of Social Policy at the London School of Economics and Political Science, United Kingdom and Co-Director at LSE Health and Social Care.

Monique Mrazek is Research Officer at LSE Health and Social Care in the London School of Economics and Political Science, United Kingdom.

Poul Erik Petersen is Professor in the Department of Community Dentistry at the University of Copenhagen, Denmark, WHO collaborating centre for community oral health programmes and research.

Jaume Puig-Junoy is Professor in the Department of Economics and Business at the Pompeu Fabra University (UPF) in Barcelona, Spain and Secretary of the Research Centre for Health and Economics at UPF.

Ana Rico is Research Fellow at the Madrid hub of the European Observatory on Health Care Systems in Spain.

Richard B. Saltman is Research Director of the European Observatory on Health Care Systems and Professor of Health Policy and Management at the Rollins School of Public Health, Emory University, Atlanta, Georgia, USA.

Ellie Scrivens is Professor of Health Policy in the Centre for Health Planning and Management and Director of the NHS Controls Assurance Support Unit at Keele University, Staffordshire, United Kingdom.

Aubrey Sheiham is Professor at the International Centre for Health and Society in the Department of Epidemiology and Public Health at University College Medical School, London, United Kingdom.

Igor Sheiman is Director of the Boston University Legal and Regulatory Health Reform Project in Moscow, Russian Federation.

Per-Gunnar Svensson is Director-General of the International Hospital Federation in London, United Kingdom.

Jürgen Wasem is Professor of Business Administration and Health Management at the Ernst-Moritz-Arndt-University, Greifswald, Germany.

Series editors' introduction

European national policy-makers broadly agree on the core objectives that their health care systems should pursue. The list is strikingly straightforward: universal access for all citizens, effective care for better health outcomes, efficient use of resources, high-quality services and responsiveness to patient concerns. It is a formula that resonates across the political spectrum and which, in various, sometimes inventive configurations, has played a role in most recent European national election campaigns.

Yet this clear consensus can only be observed at the abstract policy level. Once decision-makers seek to translate their objectives into the nuts and bolts of health system organization, common principles rapidly devolve into divergent, occasionally contradictory, approaches. This is, of course, not a new phenomenon in the health sector. Different nations, with different histories, cultures and political experiences, have long since constructed quite different institutional arrangements for funding and delivering health care services.

The diversity of health system configurations that has developed in response to broadly common objectives leads quite naturally to questions about the advantages and disadvantages inherent in different arrangements, and which approach is 'better' or even 'best' given a particular context and set of policy priorities. These concerns have intensified over the last decade as policy-makers have sought to improve health system performance through what has become a European-wide wave of health system reforms. The search for comparative advantage has triggered – in health policy as in clinical medicine – increased attention to its knowledge base, and to the possibility of overcoming at least part of existing institutional divergence through more evidence-based health policy-making.

The volumes published in the European Observatory series are intended to provide precisely this kind of cross-national health policy analysis. Drawing on an extensive network of experts and policy-makers working in a variety of academic and administrative capacities, these studies seek to synthesize the available evidence on key health sector topics using a systematic methodology. Each volume explores the conceptual background, outcomes and lessons learned about the development of more equitable, more efficient and more effective health care systems in Europe. With this focus, the series seeks to contribute to the evolution of a more evidence-based approach to policy formulation in the health sector. While remaining sensitive to cultural, social and normative differences among countries, the studies explore a range of policy alternatives available for future decision-making. By examining closely both the advantages and disadvantages of different policy approaches, these volumes fulfil a central mandate of the Observatory: to serve as a bridge between pure academic research and the needs of policy-makers, and to stimulate the development of strategic responses suited to the real political world in which health sector reform must be implemented.

The European Observatory on Health Care Systems is a partnership that brings together three international agencies, three national governments, two research institutions and an international non-governmental organization. The partners are as follows: the World Health Organization Regional Office for Europe, which provides the Observatory secretariat; the governments of Greece, Norway and Spain; the European Investment Bank; the Open Society Institute; the World Bank; the London School of Hygiene & Tropical Medicine and the London School of Economics and Political Science.

In addition to the analytical and cross-national comparative studies published in this Open University Press series, the Observatory produces Health Care Systems in Transition Profiles (HiTs) for the countries of Europe, the Observatory Summer School and the *Euro Observer* newsletter. Further information about Observatory publications and activities can be found on its web site at www.observatory.dk.

Josep Figueras, Martin McKee, Elias Mossialos and Richard B. Saltman

Foreword

Policy-makers often find themselves torn between two seemingly contradictory health sector objectives. On the one hand, shifting demography and improving technology generate strong interest in permitting innovative new procedures that can improve the ability of service providers to respond to the needs of patients. On the other hand, insufficiently tested interventions and inadequately thought-through schemes run the risk of damaging patients' health and perhaps even their chances of survival. Faced with this conflict, many policy-makers feel that the only responsible path is to adopt a strong regulatory regime. Confronted by the unknown in the form of unleashed entrepreneurialism, they prefer the known consequences of static, often bureaucratic models of service design and delivery.

Yet the art of regulating well, as this volume contends, is to develop regulatory strategies and frameworks that pursue a middle path, by allowing the carefully controlled introduction of innovative approaches without surrendering major responsibility for achieving good overall outcomes for patients. It is in this balance, in understanding regulation as a means rather than an end, that the way forward must lie. By developing these new regulatory approaches, and by working with countries as they adapt these methods to their own unique health sector circumstances, international organizations can ensure that policy combines the necessary dynamism that entrepreneurialism brings with the essential stability that good public health policy requires.

Ultimately, regulation should be understood as a major instrument in the pursuit of effective stewardship. For governments to successfully manage their health care systems in the public interest, their regulatory initiatives must accommodate a range of innovative as well as traditional objectives, and facilitate the introduction of new as well as the operation of existing activities. This fusion of regulation with entrepreneurialism, then, can serve an important role in the development of effective stewardship of the health sector. It is towards this goal that this volume makes a valuable contribution.

Marc Danzon
WHO Regional Director for Europe

Acknowledgements

This volume is one in a series of books undertaken by the European Observatory on Health Care Systems. We are very grateful to our authors, who responded promptly both in producing and later amending their chapters in the light of ongoing discussions.

We particularly appreciate the detailed and constructive comments made by Richard Alderslade, David Chinitz, Antonio Duran, Josep Figueras, Gunnar Griesewell, Nick Jennett, Martin McKee, Charles Normand, Clive Smee and Herbert Zöllner on early drafts of Part one. We should also like to thank the Observatory partners for their review of, and input to, successive versions of the manuscript.

We also thank all our colleagues in the Observatory. Our special thanks go to Wendy Wisbaum for copy-editing and project support, to Suzy Lessof for coordinating the studies, to Jeffrey Lazarus, Jenn Cain and Phyllis Dahl for managing the book delivery and production, and to Myriam Andersen for administrative support. In addition, very special thanks to Frank Theakston for pre-publication editing of the final manuscript.

Richard B. Saltman, Reinhard Busse and Elias Mossialos

part one

chapter one

Balancing regulation and entrepreneurialism in Europe's health sector: theory and practice

Richard B. Saltman and Reinhard Busse

The new regulatory challenge

The 1990s witnessed a dramatic upsurge in the scale, character and calibre of entrepreneurial initiatives within European health care systems. A wide variety of market-inspired efforts to stimulate service innovation, including increased quality and greater efficiency, have been launched in both public and not-for-profit private sectors, and in core health service activities as well as in more peripheral supplies and services. This structural ferment is visible whether one looks to the United Kingdom and the Nordic countries across northern Europe, to Spain, Portugal and Italy in the south, to the Netherlands and Germany in the European heartland or to the pre-accession countries of Central Europe. The upsurge in innovative activities, although not as great as many proponents had hoped, has been far greater than more cynical observers had expected. In practice, the last 10 years have been a period of substantial organizational reconfiguration in the health sector, and increased entrepreneurial activity has been at the core of that process of change (Saltman and Figueras 1997; Saltman *et al.* 1998; Paton *et al.* 2000).

This European experience has demonstrated that entrepreneurialism can, in practice, be a powerful lever to induce institutional restructuring in the health sector. Entrepreneurial behaviour has long been recognized as the central catalytic element in stimulating industrial innovation, defined as the process of identifying, developing, introducing and commercializing a new product or service. The most economically pure definition of an entrepreneur is attributed to the early nineteenth-century French economist Say, as someone who 'shifts economic resources out of an area of lower and into an area of higher productivity and greater yield' (Drucker 1985: 21). Nearly a century later, the German economist Schumpeter understood entrepreneurialism as inextricably tied to the waxing and waning of major business cycles, each tied to new technologies and the new industries that grew up around them (Schumpeter 1911). The role of an entrepreneur was to take advantage of a broad opportunity for structural change by introducing a 'dynamic dis-equilibrium', signalled by 'creative destruction', that could push a national economy forward to new levels of efficiency and performance. Reflecting the same central logic but from the level of the individual firm, Hamel and Prahalad (1994) view entrepreneurial behaviour not simply as developing a new product but conceptualizing and bringing into being whole new markets that never before existed (for example, Sony with the development of the video camera in the 1980s). Entrepreneurs, in this analysis, compete not for market share or profit alone, but for a more essential precursor: 'to shape the structure of future industries' (Hamel and Prahalad 1994: 25). Drucker (1985: 28) summarizes the optimistic view of entrepreneurialism's proponents by defining an entrepreneur as someone who 'searches for change, responds to it, and exploits it as an opportunity'.

Those who seek to apply the lessons of entrepreneurialism to the not-for-profit private and the public sectors adopt a similar logic, although they have a decidedly different focus on the objectives of entrepreneurial behaviour. Dees suggests that social entrepreneurship 'combines the passion of a social mission with the image of business-like discipline, innovation and determination' (Hunt 2000: 27). van der Grinten (1999) explores the concept of social entrepreneurialism, involving innovative services in not-for-profit Dutch hospitals and home care. The logic of social entrepreneurship draws upon Hood (1991), who has written more generically about the importance of freeing senior civil servants to perform much the same function as private sector entrepreneurs in the implementation of innovative social sector policies. Looking at the opposite end of the public sector hierarchy, Lipsky's (1980) classic study of 'street level bureaucrats' demonstrated that entrepreneurial innovation could often be found among front-line personnel working directly with individual clients. Hunter (1997) highlights the potential in the health sector to supplement traditional bureaucratic requirements with the managerial autonomy that forms an important component of Hood's New Public Management School. Drucker (1985: 254) concluded his own analysis by arguing that innovation and entrepreneurship are needed 'in society as much as in the economy, in public-service institutions as much as in business'.

This conceptual and practical emphasis on entrepreneurialism can have a positive impact on health systems when the changes undertaken help strengthen the ability of national policy-makers to achieve their stated policy objectives. At the organizational level, entrepreneurialism seeks to modernize and rationalize organizations to increase their operating efficiency. In the private sector, the surrogate symbols for efficiency are, typically, increased profits as well as expanded market share and, in some industries, improved quality of product and service to customers. In the public sector, the surrogate symbols are improved volume and quality of service to clients, as well as generating a financial surplus and, in some sub-sectors, enhanced market share. Increased efficiency is also seen as essential to preserving the range and scope of current benefits offered by the public sector to the citizenry.

At the societal level, some economists view entrepreneurialism as important because they believe that it necessarily expands the choice of products or services available to individuals (Rice 1998). Expanded choice can also be a valuable outcome of innovation in publicly operated health systems (Saltman and von Otter 1992). Public sector planners, somewhat differently, tend to emphasize the macro-level advantages of entrepreneurialism in achieving a better match between resources invested and output obtained, what is sometimes termed 'better value for money' (Smee 1995).

The powerful impetus to innovate generated by entrepreneurialism can have decidedly less positive effects, however, when it has not been adequately fenced in by effective state regulation. Entrepreneurs inevitably seek to segment markets so as to exploit profitable niches, while publicly accountable regulators try to ensure that the entire market is served efficiently and affordably. The potential scope for dysfunctional outcomes from unconstrained entrepreneurialism in the health sector is vast. At the extremes, it ranges on the funding side of health care systems from bankrupt insurance companies (Czech Republic, Slovakia) and massive deficit spending (Hungary, Estonia) to efforts to design service baskets that chase away undesirable (i.e. more expensive) subscribers (Netherlands) (de Roo 1995). As Sheiman and Wasem stress in Chapter 9, central and eastern European countries have learned to their chagrin that, with regard to health insurance, there is real danger in instituting new entrepreneurial mechanisms without adequate regulatory support. On the provider and production side of health systems, inadequate regulatory frameworks have been unable to restrain incompetent surgeons who operate despite regularly fatal results (paediatric surgeon in Bristol, United Kingdom), independent pharmacists who sell powerful drugs without prescriptions (Spain), private clinical laboratories that falsify test results (Sweden) or unscrupulous drug companies that dump out-of-date stock on unsuspecting patients (former Soviet Republics).

Precisely to preclude such outcomes, the scope of the regulatory apparatus that national policy-makers put in place to safeguard national policy objectives tends to be comprehensive and complex. It incorporates a wide variety of mechanisms, from legislative acts to administratively imposed reporting requirements, and from positive incentives such as subsidies to negative incentives such as legal sanctions. The unique character of health care as a social as well as a private good reinforces the importance of the regulatory role in the health sector (Saltman in press). Yet regulation is an essential element in harnessing entrepreneurialism within all sectors of a modern economy. Consumer-related industries in much of Europe operate under an extraordinary range of legislative, legal, product safety, sales, marketing, employer, occupational safety, environmental, financial, tax, construction and other regulatory responsibilities. The threat of anti-competitive rulings by the European Commission to halt potentially monopolistic mergers demonstrates that even the largest and wealthiest private sector corporations operate their businesses subject to regulatory supervision by the state. In practice, some of the more extravagant arguments in favour of deregulation need to be judged in the context of the extensive scope of existing state regulatory authority. Such an assessment suggests that even major deregulatory efforts would leave (and undoubtedly should leave) a wide-ranging body of other regulatory measures still intact. As elsewhere in the economy, in the health sector – indeed, especially in the health sector given the social character of its operating objectives – the strength of entrepreneurial incentives makes it essential to have in place adequate regulation to 'steer-and-channel' what would otherwise be only self-interested private decisions.

This concern with the social importance of regulation can serve as a useful introduction to recent experience with state regulation of entrepreneurial behaviour in European health systems during the 1990s. The most basic observation one can make about this activity is that a substantial volume of new regulation has been generated over the course of the decade. Largely in response to the needs of both intentionally and unintentionally generated entrepreneurial activities, most European countries established new types, as well as expanded the existing range, of what can be termed steer-and-channel regulation. In the United Kingdom, for example, the introduction of the purchaser–provider split, of self-governing trusts and of general practitioner fundholders, all required large new regulatory initiatives, which are currently being evaluated for consistency and coherence by the Department of Health (C.H. Smee, personal communication). In Germany, the introduction of individual choice among sickness funds, as well as the introduction of global budgets for hospitals and other cost-control measures, similarly expanded the regulatory apparatus of the state. Parallel patterns could be observed in the Netherlands, Spain, Italy and the Nordic countries. Moreover, these regulatory efforts constantly evolved over the course of the decade to meet new concerns, to reflect developments in the health sector and to reflect changes in policy due to changes in sitting governments.

Thus, as areas of entrepreneurial activity grew, they were accompanied by a parallel growth in related state regulation. As has been suggested elsewhere (Saltman 1997; Saltman and Figueras 1997), increased reliance in Western European countries on markets to make production-related decisions in the health sector has necessarily been accompanied by an increased (if more outcome-rather than input-oriented) role for the state. Precisely because the state is now expected to 'row less but steer more', its role in driving the health sector forward has in practice had to increase in scale, scope and sophistication. Indeed, the state's supervisory responsibilities have evolved to the point that the term 'stewardship' has now been applied to its overall policy and management obligations in the health sector (Saltman and Ferrousier-Davis 2000; WHO 2000). Drawn from religious and environmental roots, the concept of stewardship obliges the state to steer overall health system activity in an ethically grounded as well as a financially efficient manner. Regulation, as a central instrument of stewardship, must from this perspective similarly satisfy these two basic requirements calling for ethical and efficient state behaviour. Failing to regulate entrepreneurialism adequately in the health sector would be a serious breech of the state's role as a responsible steward.

A parallel dimension of this period of expanding regulatory responsibilities has been the growing recognition that 'good regulation', to use Chinitz's phrase from Chapter 2, is a complex and often tedious process. As Rico and Puig-Junoy suggest in Chapter 3, it is substantially more complicated to regulate a competitive market than it is to regulate a traditional private-sector monopoly such as the public utility model. The number of issues involved is greater than it initially appears, and finding an effective balance among them so as to accommodate the major concerns of key actors is inherently difficult. Avoiding the types of negative outcome expressed in antagonistic definitions of regulation put forward by many micro-economists – self-serving protectionism, regulatory capture, etc. (see section on 'Conceptualizing regulation') – further complicates the process. This complexity itself often comes as a shock to micro-economists, who have been trained to see regulation only in one narrow dimension – that is, economic – and who frequently assume that regulatory matters should be decided solely on the basis of technical efficiency.

It is partly in response to the difficulty of designing effective regulation, and to the mix of values as well as technical issues that suffuse regulatory decisions, that policy-makers have sought new strategic options during the 1990s, seeking more nuanced instruments that better fit differing national contexts. In its design and implementation, regulation no longer needs to be considered as a 'black box' that a policy-maker either adopts or avoids. Rather, the art of regulating well appears to be related to the type and form of regulation, and to the recognition that regulation is a means of achieving a desired objective rather than an end in itself. Moreover, as more conceptually minded economists from Arrow (1963) to Sen (1978) to Rice (1998) have noted, the market-style mechanisms that form the heart of entrepreneurial initiatives are inherently incapable, in themselves, of either comprehending or addressing the major normative goals that most governments posit for the health sector.

Similarly, the recent increase in entrepreneurial behaviour in European health systems need not necessarily be associated with any substantial increase in privatization in the health sector. As examined elsewhere (Saltman and von Otter 1992; LeGrand and Bartlett 1993; Saltman 1997), there is no inherent relationship between the introduction of competitive mechanisms into publicly operated health services and the transfer of these public providers to private ownership. Indeed, one can argue convincingly that the introduction of market-style mechanisms within publicly operated providers can – by bringing greater efficiency, effectiveness and patient responsiveness – preserve the future of publicly owned providers and of the social values they embody. The wisdom of this position has been demonstrated across several countries of western Europe (the United Kingdom, Sweden, Finland and parts of Spain and Italy) as well as of central Europe (in particular Hungary and the Czech Republic) (Saltman and Figueras 1997; Saltman *et al.* 1998). A parallel theme has been picked up in recent work on hospital restructuring conducted by the World Bank (Harding and Preker 2000). In practice, countries that have placed the greatest emphasis on carefully developing more market-like relationships within their publicly owned hospital sectors have experienced little privatization of publicly operated facilities over the past 10 years.

The analysis that follows explores the complex relationship between state regulation and entrepreneurial behaviour in four linked sections. The next section considers the multiple conflicting definitions of regulation utilized by different actors or academic disciplines, and examines the implications of these different definitions in the general approach that different schools of analysts take to this field. We then apply these different notions of regulation specifically to the health sector, and assess their appropriateness to the regulatory endeavour within it. Next, we review the evidence and experience with regulation as generated in the invited chapters in Part two, presenting a systematic typology for classifying different regulatory initiatives. Finally, we address the implications of this review for future policy decisions in the health sector in Europe.

Conceptualizing regulation

Regulation is one of the most contested issues in social organization. Beginning with Downs' (1957) attack on traditional Weberian bureaucracy in the middle of the century, the process by which the nation state has sought to steer behaviour in non-state sectors of society has been subjected to increasingly close scrutiny. This debate has penetrated to the most basic level of defining what regulation is, as well as determining whether and when regulation can be beneficial, who should undertake it, and which organizational structures and mechanisms should be used. Different academic disciplines have come to view these and similar questions through decidedly different conceptual lenses, resulting in a public discussion that often sheds more heat than light.

Here, we briefly review recent debates concerning the concept of regulation in general and, in particular, the appropriate role of the state as regulator. Several alternative definitions of regulation are presented, followed by a consideration of the various characterizations that different schools of thought have placed on state regulatory activities.

Differing definitions of regulation

There is no single standard definition of regulation. Rather, there are multiple, different, frequently conflicting definitions. While each definition is grounded in the academic literature, each reflects different disciplinary perspectives, different political agendas and the different value sets that underlie these agendas.

As Chinitz suggests in Chapter 2, regulation looks rather different when approached from the different disciplinary perspectives of economics, management, law and politics. Efforts to control prices, volume, market structure or the behaviour of economic actors concern economists. Measures that interest management theorists include mutual adjustment, direct supervision, standardization and decentralized decision-making. Public management focuses on the process of designing, implementing and monitoring regulatory initiatives. Legal scholars concern themselves with related questions of law and status, while political scientists emphasize the need to make trade-offs among different interests and potential outcomes. Chinitz concludes that regulation in the real world is a constantly evolving mix of these different disciplinary dimensions.

Baldwin *et al.* (1998) classify the various definitions of regulation found in the academic literature into three basic categories, tied to how wide-ranging the level of control is. The first and narrowest category defines regulation as setting forth mandatory rules that are enforced by a state agency. In this definition, regulation may be economic or social in nature, but does not include the criminal justice system or administrative or criminal sanctions unless there is a relevant court decision. The second category, typically found in the political economy literature, incorporates all efforts by state agencies to steer the economy. This considerably broader view is seen to include state ownership and contracting, as well as taxation and disclosure requirements. The third and broadest category considers regulation to include all mechanisms of both intentional and unintentional social control. Here, societal norms and values join intentional policy initiatives to construct what is in effect an environmental approach to regulation.

A similar scale of increasing comprehensiveness, but only for direct state intervention, serves as the organizing principle for the continuum of approaches to regulation set forward in Altman *et al.* (1999). Derived from work by Wallack *et al.* (1991), this approach describes a continuum of four models. Seen through the eyes of standard economic theory, regulation is understood as artificial governmental restraint on otherwise natural and unconstrained market activity. The least interventionist is the elective model, in which the state imposes regulation only to correct market failure. In the directive model, the state uses its leverage as a purchaser or regulator to stimulate certain types or standards of service. With the restrictive model, the state steps in to limit what is made available on the market. In the most interventionist, prescriptive model, the state itself defines the criteria for offering services on the market.

A quite opposite approach to regulation defines it in terms of the social goods and normative values influenced by certain types of economic activity. In this approach, normative values are the starting point and main concern, with issues of economic efficiency being of distinctly secondary importance. Presaging by some 50 years the now-emerging stewardship approach, Selznick (1985) defined regulation as 'the sustained and focused control exercised by a public agency over activities that are socially valued'. Following a similar line of logic, Colton *et al.* (1997) argue that there are two levels of state regulation of economic actors. The least restrictive or general level involves ensuring that companies satisfy state requirements regarding consumer protection, worker health and safety, and environmental protection. The more restrictive, considerably tighter level of regulation is applied – citing the legal language of this United States-based doctrine – to 'industries affected with the public interest'. These sectors (of which health is one) are subject to regulation as public utilities and must meet additional standards of public accountability, universal access and quality of service. A key point regarding Colton *et al.* (1997) is the implicit recognition that not just the health sector but all economic sectors automatically and permanently exist within a political market, in which the state defines the boundaries of permissible economic behaviour (Polanyi 1944).

Differing rationales

Much as there is no agreement among analysts on how to define regulation, there is similarly little consensus on the rationale for introducing state regulation into any particular sector of the economy. Although some schools of commentators strongly support state activity, others view any active state role as self-serving and unacceptable. Thus, while the previous section described the absence of a standard definition of regulation, this section presents what is overt contradiction between the several rationales as to the motive of states in seeking to regulate.

Baldwin *et al.* (1998) provide three broadly different – and contradictory – rationales for regulation. The first is *public interest*. This refers to the set of normative assumptions that 'good government' can be had in a democratic society, and that it can serve the best interests of the vast majority of the population. In the economic sector, the public interest position holds that the state acts as an agent for the general public interest when it intervenes to tackle market imperfections. As Baldwin *et al.* (1998) note, consistent with this view is a belief in the trustworthiness and public spiritedness of both experts and regulatory officials. Current rationales for the state as steward draw on this viewpoint, although stewardship has efficiency as well as ethical dimensions (Saltman and Ferroussier-Davis 2000).

A second, quite different understanding of the rationale for state regulation emerged from the writings of political scientists in the 1930s and 1940s (Lasswell 1936; Long 1949). These scholars put forward what has become known as the *interest group perspective*, in which the implementation of regulatory measures is seen to reflect the clash of various interested parties, with the outcome of this power struggle ranging from open pluralist competition to the absorption of the most powerful groups into a corporatist state position (Baldwin *et al.* 1998). This perspective emphasizes process over content and views regulation as just one more form of normal political activity in a pluralistic society.

The third approach draws on micro-economic theory to discern rational self-interest in the behaviour and decisions of each separate individual involved in a regulatory undertaking. Disaggregating the state into the individuals that run it, this individual *self-interest* school sees the personal preference of each separate decision-maker as the central explanation for everything that happens in the regulatory arena. In this perspective, regulation is just one more commodity, 'bought by the economically powerful and used in a manner to gain further wealth' (Baldwin *et al.* 1998: 10). Among the different variants of this position are: the capture theorists (state regulatory agencies primarily serve the interests of the regulated company or industry); the closely related 'special interest' and 'rent-seeking' theorists (individuals and companies prefer regulation since it can be used to restrict entry of new firms and increase retained profits); and the public choice theorists (public officials are primarily concerned with easier jobs, higher salaries and building empires that enhance their individual careers). In this view, state regulation inherently distorts economic efficiency and, consequently, should be minimized or eliminated.

A more market-friendly, transaction-based view of the state's regulatory role can be seen in Chapter 2, drawing on Williamson's studies of hierarchy and markets (Williamson 1975, 1985). In Chinitz's assessment, Williamson's framing of the critical strategic decision for all organizations in terms of 'make or buy', leavened by concerns about opportunism (manipulation) and bounded rationality (limits to knowledge), suggests that state regulation should act as an essentially neutral technical tool by which to ensure low transaction costs and thus greater economic efficiency. In Chinitz's phrase, the state's role should 'improve the manner in which different institutional structures allow particip-ants to see through to completion the transactions in which they are engaged'. The rationale for state regulation thus becomes that it serves as an enabler, a mechanism by which to improve the operation and efficiency of economic under-takings. Such state functions would include establishing the physical and legal infrastructure necessary to do business, a role that has become important in the transition economies of central and eastern Europe (Nunberg 1999).

One particular outcome that has emerged from the public interest rationale for state regulation can be seen in the recent history of the state in Europe (Majone 1994, 1996). From the welfare state that guaranteed and often itself provided basic services to the national population, a new 'regulatory state' is emerging that understands its role as enabling (but not necessarily providing) traditional human services as well as, in a new departure, enabling markets to exist and thrive in a variety of formerly state-run sectors (transportation, telecommunication, utilities, etc.). While there are commentators with both normative and substantive concerns about this transformation, particularly in the health sector (Dahlgren 1994; Diderichsen 1995), this new rationale places the regulatory function at the heart of the emerging new state structure.

Two additional explanations have been suggested for the specific manner in which the state engages in regulatory initiatives. Certain authors separate the influence of organizational or *institutional interest* from both interest group and self-interest, since they view institutions not purely as a group of individuals but as shaped in action, knowledge and preference by organizational rule and social environments (cf. March and Olsen 1984; Immergut 1992). 'Regulation is thus seen as shaped not so much by notions of the public interest or com-petitive bargaining between private interests but by institutional arrangements and rules' (Baldwin and Cave 1999: 27). Other commentators have argued that the content of regulation may not be primarily linked to any of the forces mentioned above, but reflect rather the *force of ideas* within civil society at a given historical moment (Hood 1995).

The mechanisms of regulation

Despite wide-ranging definitions and contradictory rationales, there is broad agreement about the source and general mechanisms of regulation. Regarding who regulates, initiatives can be instituted not just at national level but, depending on the structure of governmental arrangements, at regional and local municipal levels of administration as well. With the emergence of new pan-European agencies, European Union regulation can also be supranational. While most regulation in Europe is conducted by some form of government department, it can be undertaken by independent regulatory agencies (for example, OFTEL in the United Kingdom to regulate private telecommunication companies) or by self-regulatory bodies. Most countries (as well as the European Union) have provisions that give precedence to higher-level governments in case of a conflict between different regulatory regimes.

The mechanisms of regulation can be grouped into two basic categories, tools and strategies, which can in turn be combined in various mixes. The basic tools of regulation are straightforward. They are traditionally premised on the ability of government to require mandatory compliance with its decisions (which, in turn, flows from the sovereignty rights of the state). The major categories are legislation, administrative decree and judicial order, one for each of the three branches of government (legislative, executive and judicial). Each of these three can be generated in many different forms and formats, particularly administrative decrees, and with various degrees of finality (advisory regulations, guidelines, emergency measures, etc.). Most regulatory measures promulgated by the executive branch in a democratic society can be challenged in court by those who fear they will be adversely affected, and can be overruled if appropriate by judicial order. Litigation is expensive and time-consuming, however, and in a well-functioning system is undertaken only in the most egregious circumstances.

The use to which these basic tools are put is the realm of strategy. Here, governmental bodies have a wide and growing range of options. Indeed, one of the major changes in regulatory regimes during the 1990s has been the development of softer market-style incentives to encourage (rather than require) certain desired behaviour, particularly with regard to economic efficiency (Osborne and Gaebler 1992; Majone 1996). Baldwin and Cave (1999) put forward the following (occasionally overlapping) framework of potential regulatory strategies: (1) command and control; (2) self-regulation and enforced self-regulation; (3) incentive-based regimes (taxes and subsidies); (4) market-harnessing controls (competition laws, franchising, contracts and tradable permits); (5) disclosure regulation; (6) direct governmental action; (7) legal rights and liabilities; and (8) public compensation/social insurance schemes. As discussed on pp. 20–1, categorizing command and control as a form of regulation generates several difficult questions, which are considered below in the discussion of who is regulated. It also seems wise to consider the concept of incentives (as above) to have both positive and negative dimensions (Saltman, in press). The implications of these different strategic alternatives for regulating the health sector are considered on pp. 19–24.

In thinking about the logic of these various strategies, regulation clearly can have two quite different orientations: it can seek either to achieve compliance and/or disclosure, or to achieve deterrence and/or institute sanctions. Furthermore, the outcome from different regulatory strategies can be fluid as well as static in character, in that the boundaries between state and market, and the focus of specific regulatory initiatives, can shift over time. These changes can be unintentional as well as intentional in terms of how they affect the outcome achieved. Lastly, as implied earlier about the emerging 'regulatory state', regulation can be designed to be either pro-competitive or anti-entrepreneurial in its impact.

Beyond tools and strategies, there lies the difficult but essential process of implementation. As every regulator is aware, it is one thing to develop a good regulatory regime on paper, but it is quite another to put that regime into operation successfully. Implementation involves its own separate set of strategic assessments and political skills (Pressman and Wildavsky 1973; Walt 1998), which have evolved to differing degrees within health systems in Europe (Rathwell 1998). Successful implementation also requires a cadre of trained regulators and of competent managers inside regulated institutions, both capable of ferreting out (rather than succumbing to) bureaucratic inertia and institutionalized corruption. Recent experience in the countries of central and eastern Europe suggests how important and complicated each of the additional aspects of implementation can be (see Chapter 5) (Nunberg 1999).

Regulating the health sector

Bringing the general approach of regulation to bear on the specific characteristics of health care systems is an inherently complex process. As explored in the previous sections, regulation is a wide-ranging set of activities comprising a considerable array of specific tools and strategies. Similarly, the health sector is a sprawling mix of programmes and services ranging from acute to preventive, from individual to population, and from inpatient to primary care, dental, mental and occupational health services. Melding these two unwieldy entities into a clear and internally consistent package is not easy. Not surprisingly, in the health sector as in other human service sectors (education, for example), policy-makers typically settle for reasonable approximations and imperfect solutions, knowing that even these will be hard to implement and sustain over time. This section considers how the general models, strategies and tools just described can be applied within the specific conditions of the health sector.

Two dimensions of health sector regulation

In thinking about the application of the available range of regulatory tools and strategies to the health sector, it is useful to separate out two different public purposes for taking regulatory action: these can be termed 'policy objectives' and 'managerial mechanisms'. Each has its own specific function and rationale, but each needs to be connected closely to the other to achieve its goals. This section considers how the general concept of regulation applies to these two different dimensions of policy-making in the health sector.

The first dimension of regulatory activity can be termed *social and economic policy objectives*. It is normative and value-driven in nature, concerned with specific policy goals – with ends and objectives – and with the broad public interest (which may be seen differently in different countries). Core policy goals are typically expressed in the national constitution (or societal consensus to the same end), in key legislative acts and in the overall organization of socially sentinel sectors such as health care. These societal decisions are reflected, for example, in the choice to create a national health service or a system based on statutory health insurance. Such value-driven decisions tend to change only infrequently, typically as a consequence of major historical events such as wars (the foundation of the British National Health Service (NHS) in 1948), the end of dictatorships (the change from social insurance to NHS-type systems in Portugal and Spain) or as a result of political revolutions (as in central

Table 1.1 Social and economic policy objectives

- *Equity and justice*: to provide equitable and needs-based access to health care for the whole population, including poor, rural, elderly, disabled and other vulnerable groups
- *Social cohesion*: to provide health care through a national health care service or to install a social health insurance system
- *Economic efficiency*: to contain aggregate health expenditures within financially sustainable boundaries
- *Health and safety*: to protect workers, to ensure water safety and to monitor food hygiene
- *Informed and educated citizens*: to educate citizens about clinical services, pharmaceuticals and healthy behaviour
- *Individual choice*: to ensure choice of provider, and in some cases insurer, as much as possible within the limits of the other objectives

European countries after 1990). Within this core dimension of health sector policy-making, however, certain policy expectations can also evolve and mature in normal political times. In Europe in the 1990s, for instance, a variety of health sector reforms sought to address more explicitly broad policy objectives regarding the overall health of the population (WHO 1999a).

The broad societal focus of this first dimension of regulatory activity in the health sector emphasizes a series of common concerns that influence both western European and the countries of central and eastern Europe (CEE) and the former Soviet Republics that are now loosely linked in the Commonwealth of Independent States (CIS) alike. Examples of the more common concerns are presented in Table 1.1. The central distinguishing characteristic of these objectives is that they are population-wide and that they typically lead to mandatory national requirements on all actors, including the private not-for-profit and for-profit sectors. To achieve their stated objectives, these broad policies also need to influence government decisions in other sectors such as education, transport, employment, housing and agriculture (WHO 1999a).

The second dimension of regulatory activity can be termed the *health sector management mechanisms*. This level is practical and operational and is concerned with the specific regulatory mechanisms through which decision-makers seek to attain the type of policy objectives set out in Table 1.1. These means are largely technical in nature, emphasizing efficient and effective management of both human and material resources. They may or may not have a direct impact on the ability of the overall health system to achieve its broad policy objectives. These managerially oriented mechanisms may have a mixed public/private character, reflecting the complex profusion of different provider arrangements across the health sector. Their managerial focus means that they tend to emphasize micro-level activities at sub-sector or even at facility/institution level.

The tightly defined institutional character of this second, management dimension of regulation can be seen in the types of activity that fall within its purview. These comprise a familiar litany to Ministry of Health and parliamentary social committee decision-makers, including the topics listed in Table 1.2. As that list suggests, these are predominantly mechanisms that affect health care

Table 1.2 Health sector management mechanisms

- *Regulating quality and effectiveness*: assessing cost-effectiveness of clinical interventions; training health professionals; accrediting providers
- *Regulating patient access*: gate-keeping; co-payments; general practitioner lists; rules for subscriber choice among third-party payers; tax policy; tax subsidies
- *Regulating provider behaviour*: transforming hospitals into public firms; regulating capital borrowing by hospitals; rationalizing hospital and primary care/home care interactions
- *Regulating payers*: setting rules for contracting; constructing planned markets for hospital services; developing prices for public-sector health care services; introducing case-based provider payment systems (e.g. diagnostic-related groups); regulating reserve requirements and capital investment patterns of private insurance companies; retrospective risk-based adjustment of sickness fund revenues
- *Regulating pharmaceuticals*: generic substitution; reference prices; profit controls; basket-based pricing; positive and negative lists
- *Regulating physicians*: setting salary and reimbursement levels; licensing requirements; setting malpractice insurance coverage

management capabilities, and typically include measures associated with greater operating efficiency and effectiveness. Some of these regulatory instruments – such as the development of planned markets for hospital services and the concomitant transformation of public hospitals into public firms; or the rationalization of relations between hospitals and primary care providers – lie at the core of recent health reforms across western as well as central Europe (Saltman and Figueras 1997; Saltman *et al.* 1998). These and several other recent regulatory mechanisms adapted from private-sector instruments have been part of a concerted effort to implement the 'new public management' movement within the health sector (Hunter 1997).

The specific choice of mechanisms as well as the balance among them differs between countries, depending on the precise configuration of broad policy objectives as expressed in the overall design of the health sector. For example, anti-trust concerns are substantially greater in the more competitively structured post-1997 health system in the Netherlands than in the predominantly corporatist arrangements found in Germany. How policy-makers define regulation, and which rationale they adopt to justify or reject specific regulatory mechanisms, also plays an important role in the overall regulatory design adopted. The key point here, however, is that, while policy objectives and management mechanisms differ from each other conceptually, they must be designed to fit together if a government is to have a coherent and sustainable regulatory framework in its health sector.

This two-part framework – policy objectives and managerial mechanisms – describes the role of regulation within the health sector in a manner consistent with the general role of regulation set out earlier. The emerging 'regulatory state', for instance, has clear responsibilities within both the social policy and institutional management dimensions found in the health sector. Several of the general definitions of regulation are visible within the health sector as well. Selznick's (1985) stress on controlling 'socially valued activities' and the emphasis of Colton *et al.* (1997) on 'industries affected with the public interest' are captured by the concept of social and economic policy objectives. Similarly, the dominant focus of regulation in the health sector incorporates the first two of three definitions of Baldwin *et al.* (1998) (e.g. the narrow rule-setting and enforcement approach, together with the wider notion encompassing all state efforts to steer the economy). One could also choose to apply to the health sector any of the three main characterizations presented as the rationale for introducing regulation (public interest, self-interested groups and rational self-interest). In all these regards, the conceptualization of regulation developed earlier fits with the approach presented here for application to the health sector.

Lastly, while health care is the major societal sector charged with pursuing the objective of improving the health of the population, the overall design of other sectors such as education, transport or agriculture should also reflect this objective. Regulation to ensure health gain necessarily addresses actors outside as well as inside health care. The types of intersectoral regulatory concerns involved are presented in Table 1.3.

Allocating regulatory roles in the health sector

Within the health sector, a wide range of different public sector bodies can be involved in regulation. The three major pillars of a democratic state – the legislature (parliament), the executive (government and government administration) and the judiciary (the courts) – each play a clearly delineated role. Other governmental, quasi-governmental and non-governmental actors may also be expected or designated to act as regulators. Some countries rely on devolved public responsibility to either regional (county, *Land*, autonomous community) or local (municipal) authorities, while others delegate 'self-regulatory' authority to various private-sector entities (licensure to medical associations, insurance to sickness fund associations). Some countries utilize independently managed national agencies (National Board of Health, Office of Prices and Tariffs, National Insurance Fund, etc.). Who will be responsible for what is contingent upon a range of factors, including the type of activity being regulated, the segment of the health system being regulated (hospitals, physicians, etc.), the capacity of various actors within that segment and a variety of national factors including institutional structure and cultural traditions.

Regulatory activity itself, in the health sector as elsewhere, consists of legislation, implementation, monitoring and evaluation, enforcement and judicial supervision. Although legislation often focuses on social and policy objectives, setting out the broad health system institutional framework, once a health system is well established, legislation can also mandate mechanisms of health sector management. Once legislation is enacted, the variously designated public, mixed public–private or private agencies issue administrative regulations that seek to implement the relevant regulatory provisions. This is formally termed 'promulgation' and is particularly time-consuming in the health sector, with its confluence of strong yet divergent interests along with the need to accommodate the inherent complexities of the medical decision-making process.

Table 1.3 Intersectoral dimensions of health-related regulation

Broad policy objectives	Intersectoral regulatory responses					
	Tax system	Employers in general	Health care (details in tables on sub-sectors)	Education	Transport	Agriculture
Equity and justice	Minimization of tax evasion	Mandatory equal job opportunities for the physically disabled, minorities, etc.	Access and treatment only according to need[a]	Access and educational offers according to ability	Provision of public transport	—
Social cohesion	Progressivity of income taxes	Taxes for enterprises (in addition to income tax)	Contribution relating to income/wealth, not health status[b]	Paying for education from taxes	Public subsidies for public transport	—
Informed and educated citizens	Tax exemptions for educational material or institutions	—	Patient information and health education[c]	Effectiveness/quality of educational system	—	Customer information labelling
Health and safety	Higher taxes on products/services damaging health	Workers' health and safety: working hours; occupational health service; protective equipment (e.g. helmets)	Protection of health care personnel; effectiveness/quality of health care[d]	Safety on way to school; mandatory vaccination programmes; school nurses	Industry: mandatory installation of seat-belts and airbags Drivers: mandatory use of seat-belts; speed limits	Hygiene requirements for food production, inspection and quality

Table 1.3 *Cont.*

Broad policy objectives	Intersectoral regulatory responses					
	Tax system	*Employers in general*	*Health care (details in tables on sub-sectors)*	*Education*	*Transport*	*Agriculture*
Sustainability/ protection of the interests of future generations	Matching taxes and public expenditure	Environmental protection requirements	Sustainability of financing and capital[e]	Sustainability of financing and capital	Industry: limits for exhaust pollution	Restrictions on pesticide use
Individual choice	—	—	Choice of provider, payer, etc.	Choice of school or university	—	—
Rising standard of living/ economic growth	Post-tax profits	Anti-trust/pro-competition laws	Ensuring investment; increasing efficiency[f]	—	—	—

[a]A in column 3 of Tables 1.6–1.10. [b]C in column 3 of Tables 1.6–1.10. [c]P in column 3 of Tables 1.6–1.10. [d]P (first item) and Q (second item) in column 3 of Tables 1.6–1.10. [e]S in column 3 of Tables 1.6–1.10. [f]Columns 1 and 2 of Tables 1.6–1.10.

Different health sector actors bring different strengths and weaknesses to the structuring, implementation, evaluation and enforcement of regulatory measures. In a useful summary of the characteristics of different regulatory actors generally, Baldwin and Cave (1999: 72) suggested the following:

> self-regulators tend to be strong on specialist knowledge but weak on accountability to the public; local authorities strong on local democratic accountability, weak on coordination; parliament strong on democratic authority, weak on sustained scrutiny; courts and tribunals strong on fairness, weak on planning; central departments strong on coordination with the government, weak on neutrality; agencies strong on expertise and combining functions, weak on neutrality; directors general strong on specialization and identification of responsibility, weak on spreading discretionary powers.

A further issue concerns the appropriateness of allowing the same actor simultaneously to set the rules as well as to supervise their implementation. Once again, institutional structures and national traditions often have an influential role in the allocation of regulatory authority among different competing groups.

Strategies for health sector regulation

When the general framework of strategies and tools developed above is applied to the health sector, it quickly becomes apparent that European policy-makers have many strategic options with which to structure health-related regulation. The scope of these options has expanded during the 1990s, reflecting the inclusion of approaches adapted from other sectors of the economy – for example, the notion of independent regulatory agencies for public utilities. These potential strategies now span considerable territory and, while they are formally designed to achieve the same basic social and economic objectives, they have notably different internal logics, secondary consequences and – once implemented – mechanisms.

The range of choice that these various strategies represent is already visible in how state authority is currently exercised in the health sector. Present-day options can be arranged in a continuum from the strongest to the weakest degree of regulatory involvement. As Table 1.4 indicates, however, the strongest form of state intervention is not in fact regulation at all, but rather a military-style command-and-control model of authority. In practice, health sector entities that are wholly owned and operated by the state (or devolved to regional or local government on the same operating basis) are subject to a top-down form of administrative control that is qualitatively different from that found elsewhere in the health sector. Command-and-control in the health sector, as in the military, demands obedience rather than negotiation and/or litigation. This understanding of command-and-control is the one adopted by Baldwin *et al.* (1998), who note that, as one example, the United Kingdom's Competition Commission (the former Monopolies and Mergers Commission) did not concern itself with anti-competitive practices by utilities until they were privatized. It is also consistent with the approach to regulation set forward in the concept of the 'regulatory state' (Majone 1994, 1996).

Table 1.4 Continuum of state authority in the health sector

Degree of state authority and supervision

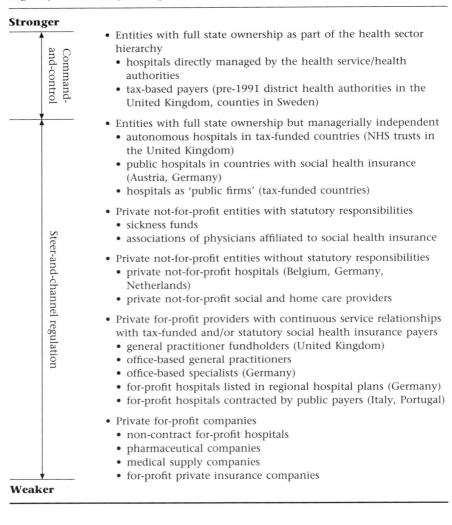

Stronger

- Entities with full state ownership as part of the health sector hierarchy
  - hospitals directly managed by the health service/health authorities
  - tax-based payers (pre-1991 district health authorities in the United Kingdom, counties in Sweden)

- Entities with full state ownership but managerially independent
  - autonomous hospitals in tax-funded countries (NHS trusts in the United Kingdom)
  - public hospitals in countries with social health insurance (Austria, Germany)
  - hospitals as 'public firms' (tax-funded countries)

- Private not-for-profit entities with statutory responsibilities
  - sickness funds
  - associations of physicians affiliated to social health insurance

- Private not-for-profit entities without statutory responsibilities
  - private not-for-profit hospitals (Belgium, Germany, Netherlands)
  - private not-for-profit social and home care providers

- Private for-profit providers with continuous service relationships with tax-funded and/or statutory social health insurance payers
  - general practitioner fundholders (United Kingdom)
  - office-based general practitioners
  - office-based specialists (Germany)
  - for-profit hospitals listed in regional hospital plans (Germany)
  - for-profit hospitals contracted by public payers (Italy, Portugal)

- Private for-profit companies
  - non-contract for-profit hospitals
  - pharmaceutical companies
  - medical supply companies
  - for-profit private insurance companies

Weaker

(Left margin labels: Command-and-control; Steer-and-channel regulation)

In Table 1.4, the critical break occurs between 'entities with full state owner-ship as part of the health sector hierarchy' and 'entities with full state owner-ship but managerially independent'. As this break suggests, once one introduces planned market mechanisms into a publicly owned and operated health sector, one no longer has a command-and-control structure of authority (Saltman and von Otter 1992). Instead, when for instance publicly owned hospitals are transformed into public firms, hospital-level managers acquire substantial decision-making autonomy on such issues as service provision, staffing mix and levels, and some aspects of salary levels. As Table 1.4 indicates, once such managerial autonomy exists, then those publicly owned institutions become subject to what can be termed 'steer-and-channel' regulation. This distinction reflects the basic consideration that independent decision-making capacity at institutional level in turn generates a need for state regulation to ensure that those decisions remain consistent with broader social and economic policy objectives.

An additional point about Table 1.4 concerns the regulation of for-profit companies or providers, where state authority is weakest. Consistent with the argument made by Colton *et al.* (1997), weak state authority still involves a relatively wide range of regulatory measures (at least in western Europe). Beyond the basic industrial measures applicable to all sectors of the economy (worker health and safety, etc.), even the least regulated elements of the health sector must comply with a variety of social and economic policy objectives. Hence, 'less regulated' in the health sector may still be considerably more regulated than in sectors of the economy that are not 'affected with the public interest.'

This existing distribution of state authority, and in particular the important distinction between military-style command-and-control as against a regulatory steer-and-channel approach, defines the context within which various potential regulatory strategies can be applied. As Table 1.5 suggests, after excluding command-and-control, there are five general types of steer-and-channel options: decentralization (four variants), enforced self-regulation, accreditation, independent regulatory agencies and intersectoral cooperation. As with all public policies, each general type has its distinct advantages and disadvantages. Moreover, these different strategies can be used in combination as well as singly, for example by requiring accreditation of hospitals that, as public firms, are also subject to other extensive steer-and-channel mechanisms.

The four different variants of decentralization are also typically conjoined with other regulatory strategies, in that they reflect changes in organizational structure as well as in the distribution of decision-making authority. Deconcentration, devolution, delegation and (quite differently) privatization are commonly considered strategic options for health system reform (Hunter *et al.* 1998). Deconcentration refers to passing the power to set regulatory acts from the national government to independent government agencies. Devolution applies to passing regulatory power to regional or local authorities (who may choose to further deconcentrate or delegate those powers). In the case of delegation, power is typically granted to non-governmental actors, often with legal backing. The delegation of regulatory authority to either funders (insurers) or providers is typically described as 'self-regulation' or (when supplemented by state supervision) 'enforced self-regulation'. While tax-funded health care systems tend to rely on deconcentration and devolution, delegation is more commonly found in systems funded by social health insurance. Privatization involves a fundamental shift from predominantly public-sector to predominantly private-sector authority. Although rarely used, it has been adopted for primary care provision in the transition countries of central and eastern Europe (see Chapter 10) (Saltman and Figueras 1997).

Self-regulation refers to a state-generated mandate that allows certain professionals or enterprises to set standards for the behaviour of its membership

Table 1.5 Strategies for health sector regulation

Social and economic policy dimension

Strategies	(Military command-and-control)	Steer-and-channel	Decentralization	– deconcentration	– devolution	– delegation	– privatization	Enforced self-regulation	Accreditation	Independent regulatory agencies	Intersectoral cooperation

Institutional management dimension

(Baldwin and Cave 1999). These arrangements vary considerably in Europe in the extent of governmental delegation (see, for example, Graham 1994). Self-regulation can be viewed as a continuum from the purely private (with no governmental delegation) to various forms of publicly mandated delegation. Private self-regulation can be found within some professional organizations or within voluntary organizations, but the lack of state-enforced compliance renders this form of self-regulation too weak to sustain most policy objectives. Typical examples of publicly mandated regulation in health care are professional self-regulation by physicians, dentists and pharmacists, and in some countries also nurses, by health insurance funds in countries with social health insurance and, at least to a certain degree, by the pharmaceutical industry (e.g. in the United Kingdom).

The major advantages of self-regulatory delegation have been summarized as follows: high commitment to own rules; well-informed rule-making; low cost of government; close fit of regulatory standards with those seen as reasonable by actors; greater comprehensiveness of rules; potential for rapid adjustment; more effective enforcement and complaints procedures; and potential to combine with external supervision (Baldwin and Cave 1999). Conversely, self-regulation also has potential weaknesses: self-serving rules; meddling in management decisions; complex rules; high cost of approving rules; closed rule-making procedures; weak enforcement; lack of public trust; problematic legal supervision; and potential desire of the public for governmental responsibility (Baldwin and Cave 1999).

Ayres and Braithwaite (1992) have further differentiated between 'enforced self-regulation' and 'co-regulation'. In enforced self-regulation, the promulgation of the rules is delegated to non-governmental actors, while the enforcement can be done either (1) publicly or (2) privately but publicly mandated and monitored. In the case of 'co-regulation', typically the government ratifies privately written regulation. Although health care systems across Europe have some examples of private self-regulation without state enforcement, publicly mandated self-regulation is more common – normally coupled with the threat of public enforcement.

Accreditation and licensing are specifically quality-oriented strategies. They are both constructed on two main components: external review and fixed standards. However, as Scrivens discusses in Chapter 4, these two approaches differ in that accreditation traditionally focuses on a higher standard and has been voluntary and self-funding (e.g. the institution seeking accreditation pays the costs), while licensure typically focuses on minimum standards and has been mandatory and state-funded. The establishment of mandatory accreditation within several European health systems, including those of Belgium and France, has blurred these distinctions, transforming accreditation into a formal dimension of state regulation. This has become particularly important as publicly operated health systems in these countries have allowed more entrepreneurial activity, particularly in the hospital sector, which in turn has raised concerns about consistent quality of care. As a strategic option, however, accreditation and licensure have typically been used as only one component of a multi-pronged set of regulatory initiatives.

The deconcentration of governmental regulatory power to independent regulatory agencies is not widely utilized in health service sectors in Europe. These independent agencies are unique in the public sector in that they combine specialized expertise and fact-finding with a judicial decision-making function (Baldwin *et al.* 1998). Most state health-related regulatory activity at the national level, including food and drug safety, are handled by departments within the Ministry of Health or, in the Nordic countries, by semi-autonomous national boards still subject to ministry management. There are some exceptions, however, such as the establishment of the European Medicines Evaluation Agency (EMEA) or the Agence Nationale d'Accréditation et d'Evaluation en Santé (ANAES) in France, which is charged with the accreditation of hospitals.

Policy-makers can also adopt extrasectoral (what WHO calls intersectoral) strategies in pursuit of policy objectives. One common strategy has been to rely on taxation mechanisms to promote better health. A prime example is special taxes on tobacco to deter people from smoking (Pekurinen and Valtonen 1987; WHO 1999b).

Assessing recent experience with regulating entrepreneurial behaviour

Recent regulatory initiatives in European health systems have sought to balance reform-driven efforts to stimulate greater entrepreneurialism with legislatively mandated requirements to maintain existing social and economic policy objectives. Policy-makers have had to accommodate the differing rationales and expectations that various health sector actors bring to the regulatory process, seeking strategies and tools with which to establish effective yet not overly restrictive frameworks to steer institutional decision-making. Previous sections have explored different types of regulatory measure and different purposes to which they might be applied. This section builds on those conceptual distinctions to examine recent practical experience in Europe in devising a workable balance between regulation and entrepreneurialism.

We pursue this objective through two related but different analytical approaches to the available evidence. First, we lay out a systematic four-part framework through which to conceptualize recent regulatory measures in terms of their relative impact on entrepreneurial and innovative behaviour across the entire health care system. This is followed by an assessment of the current status of entrepreneurial activity in six key sub-sectors of the health system (hospitals, general practice, social care, dental care, pharmaceuticals and insurance) and the likely impact of recent regulatory measures in enhancing or retarding the range and scope of that activity. Examples utilized in both analytical approaches draw considerably on the chapters in Part two.

Assessing recent experience through a systematic framework

In thinking about the relationship between regulation and entrepreneurialism, one can place recent experience within four distinct categories. The first, regulation that stimulates entrepreneurial opportunities, needs to be differentiated from a second, regulation that promotes competition but restricts the entrepreneurial freedom of individual actors. This differentiation is, however, not as clear-cut as it may initially appear. A considerable degree of regulation restricts individual entrepreneurs in the short term in order to facilitate sustainable competitive markets in the long term. Pro-competitive regulation can thus either stimulate or restrict short-term entrepreneurial behaviour. A third category of regulation restricts entrepreneurial decisions as a way to safeguard the social and economic policy objectives discussed above. A fourth category concerns regulation restricting entrepreneurial freedom that cannot be directly associated with specific social and economic policy objectives.

These four categories provide a conceptual template with which to organize existing and potential regulatory measures that affect entrepreneurial activity in the health sector. Many of these measures, shown in detail in Tables 1.6–1.10, are drawn from the chapters in Part two. Others reflect broader social and economic policy objectives in society at large, and are indicated in the tables under the heading 'GE', for general economy. Lastly, a few measures (particularly in the first category) represent conceptual possibilities that would in theory encourage entrepreneurialism, but which no European government has chosen to implement.

As noted above, a health sector actor needs to have some managerial autonomy to be an appropriate candidate for state regulation. Health care entities that are an indivisible part of the state hierarchy (cf. Table 1.4), such as those without any decision-making independence, are part of a command-and-control structure of authority and thus cannot be considered to be regulated.

Consequently, for health care organizations that are fully incorporated into state administration, the most basic initiative to stimulate entrepreneurial opportunity would be to grant these health care actors some managerial independence – in effect, to restructure these organizations into suitable subjects for state regulation. While recent evidence suggests that many publicly operated health care systems have sought to introduce this type of partial managerial independence among providers on the supply side of their health care systems (Saltman and Figueras 1997; Saltman *et al.* 1998), policy-makers in some countries where health care is funded by social insurance have sought to convey limited autonomy to publicly accountable funders on the demand side as well.

Turning to the four different categories of regulation, the first, regulation that stimulates entrepreneurial opportunities in the health sector, concerns efforts to develop a more competitive environment among health sector institutions and professionals. Regulation specific to the health sector that fits within this first analytical category (see Tables 1.6–1.10) typically mandates certain types of funding and reimbursement arrangement. These include replacing fixed budgets with volume- or performance-based reimbursements, granting provider institutions the possibility to retain surpluses, and tax subsidies or exemptions for certain services. More radically, regulation could allow institutions to set their own fees, allow patients to choose their hospital, ambulatory care provider or third-party payer, and let subscribers elect certain peripheral benefits.

The second analytical category, regulation to facilitate sustainable competitive markets (which includes measures that may restrict short-term entrepreneurial behaviour), incorporates an array of anti-trust/competition laws taken on board from the general economy. Regulation specific to the health sector mainly addresses issues of organizational structure and pro-competitive behaviour. Organizational structure issues include: setting minimum standards, such as through requirements for licensing, accreditation or certification (see Chapter 4); ownership of health care institutions; and preventing monopolies through restrictions on horizontal and vertical mergers. Regulation addressing pro-competitive behaviour includes measures to reduce adverse selection by health care payers and providers, such as mandatory redistribution of contributions between payers as well as requirements that health insurance funds accept all applicants.

In the third analytical category, regulation to achieve normative/social objectives (such as access, social cohesion, public health and sustainable financing), regulation applicable to the broader general economy reflects restrictions on entrepreneurial behaviour adopted to protect employees, consumers and the environment (Colton *et al.* 1997). Regulation specific to the health sector addresses issues of capacities, entitlements, funding and reimbursement arrangements. To ensure access to health services, regulatory measures set minimum service hours for hospitals and ambulatory care providers, mandate the delivery of services to all citizens, and call for the planning of needs-based and equitably distributed capacities. The social cohesion objective is addressed by a variety of measures, such as a mandate to deliver services to all citizens, a waiting time guarantee, health care funding through community-rated or income-related contributions (instead of risk-related premiums) and the setting of a uniform catalogue of benefits. Public health and safety concerns drive regulation in the pharmaceutical sub-sector in particular, mandating customer information and limiting advertisements for drugs. Ensuring the quality of health services leads to regulations in the hospital as well as ambulatory care sub-sectors, such as mandating health technology assessments for services to be included in the benefits catalogue; requiring regular or continuous quality assurance for health care providers; and allowing treatment only according to protocols and guidelines to ensure the appropriate use of technologies. Finally, the objective of sustainable financing leads to regulations affecting all sub-sectors. Typical measures are the setting of uniform or maximum prices (or maximum profit margins in the case of the pharmaceutical industry), regulations stipulating minimum and maximum reserve levels for health insurers, and acceptable types of investment for surplus revenues.

An additional dimension of regulation restricting entrepreneurial behaviour to ensure that social objectives are achieved is that it can incorporate (in countries where adopted) elements of professional as well as joint self-regulation that supplement or substitute for governmental regulation. This is particularly true for the objectives of access, quality and sustainable funding, while it is typically not the case for the 'public health and safety' objective.

Regulation weakly tied to social objectives that may be unnecessary includes restrictions on providing certain services by certain providers (such as not allowing hospitals to offer ambulatory services) and limitations on maximum practice hours. These regulations arguably are not directly linked to social and economic policy objectives in the health sector and thus can be considered potential candidates for elimination.

Assessing recent experience across different sub-sectors

The chapters in Part two review the relationship across Europe between regulation and entrepreneurialism in six separate health system sub-sectors: hospitals, general practice, social care, dental care, pharmaceuticals and insurance. Over the course of the 1990s, developments in each of these sub-sectors reflected its particular clinical, organizational and professional characteristics, as well as its centrality to national social and economic policy objectives. Moreover, consistent with the region's diversity, there are important differences across countries and types of health system within each sub-sector – a point reinforced in its own way in each of the chapters.

Beyond this diversity, however, it is possible to discern clearly evolving patterns among the various sub-sectors in terms of the regulatory/entrepreneurial balance within them. One pattern concerns the relative strength of entrepreneurial incentives within each sub-sector. A second concerns the extent to which the present balance has been shifting in particular sub-sectors over the past decade (if it has been shifting). A third pattern concerns the extent to which such shifts have been associated with measurable changes in either the efficiency or effectiveness with which services have been delivered in that sub-sector. Drawing on evidence collected in the chapters in Part two, this section addresses the present status of each pattern in turn.

First, with regard to the relative strength of entrepreneurialism, the scope and range of such activities are considerably more widespread in peripheral than in core clinical areas of health systems. The greatest entrepreneurial opportunities can be found in dental care (where the predominant reimbursement mechanism continues to be fee-for-service, as Holst *et al.* remind us in Chapter 11) and in pharmaceuticals (where development and production of new drugs is the province of global private for-profit corporations). In addition, in a recent development, Forder (Chapter 8) describes increasing experimentation with entrepreneurial mechanisms in the provision of social and home care services. Conversely, one finds that entrepreneurial initiatives have made the smallest inroads in the two most important and most expensive delivery (supply-side) sub-sectors of health systems (e.g. hospitals and primary care), as well as in what is, in policy-making terms, perhaps the most controversial and sensitive sub-sector – the funding structure (demand side).

Having drawn these conclusions, we must immediately qualify them with three caveats. The above assessments do appear to hold for most of western Europe, in tax-funded (TF) as well as in social health insurance (SHI) funded countries. Groenewegen *et al.* (Chapter 10), for example, make the point that even though Dutch general practitioners are technically private entrepreneurs, they have in recent years moved 'in the direction of more professional control (e.g. recertification) rather than more entrepreneurship'. Concerning hospitals, Busse *et al.* show in Chapter 6 that, even in SHI health systems, independent private not-for-profit and (fewer) for-profit hospitals are tightly reined in by various types of budget and reimbursement restrictions on operating funds, as well as by a variety of capital controls.

In central and eastern Europe, however, although the main premise of these conclusions is valid, it carries somewhat different characteristics. Certainly dental care and pharmaceuticals are strongly entrepreneurial. Dental care ('stomatology') was often the first service delivery component of former Soviet health systems to change once the economic transition began, shifting rapidly to a fee-for-service basis. Pharmaceuticals are similarly highly entrepreneurial – perhaps too much so, when one considers that, in countries such as Hungary, pharmaceuticals absorbed 25.7 per cent of all official health care expenditures in 1997 (Gaál *et al.* 1999). Conversely, most hospitals remain publicly owned and operated, although often devolved to local, regional or municipal governments (Gaál *et al.* 1999). Yet social and home care is only in its formative phase (not having been a part of the prior Semashko approach) and, in several central and eastern European countries, some outpatient policlinics have been transformed into predominantly fee-for-service operations (Gaál *et al.* 1999; Busse *et al.* 2000).

An additional caveat is that applying this broad pattern of the regulatory/ entrepreneurial balance to CEE/CIS countries takes account only of official revenues in the health care system. As Ensor and Duran point out in Chapter 5, informal payments can comprise a considerable proportion of real health system revenue in countries like Bulgaria and Georgia. Even in central Europe, where informal payments are estimated to comprise a lower proportion of total health sector revenues, a substantial degree of black- and grey-market entrepreneurialism still exists, particularly in the hospital sector. Hence, the conclusion that entrepreneurialism is not strong in hospitals must be adjusted for CEE/CIS countries to refer exclusively to official or above-the-table revenues.

A final caveat concerning the relative strength of entrepreneurialism is that sub-sectors with greater amounts of entrepreneurialism do not necessarily have less regulatory activity. Indeed, as Tables 1.6–1.10 suggest, in western Europe increased entrepreneurialism is typically accompanied by rapid growth in state regulatory efforts (Saltman and Figueras 1997). The third column in Tables 1.6–1.10 suggests why that is the case: policy-makers seek to channel entrepreneurial innovations in directions that are consistent with, and supportive of, the broader social and economic objectives that guide national policy for the health sector overall. The further fact that, until recently, the growth of entrepreneurialism in many CEE/CIS countries has not been accompanied by a similar growth in regulatory activity reflects far more the conceptual, organizational and administrative dilemmas of the ongoing economic transition than any new and convincing approach to the structuring of efficient and effective health care systems (see Chapter 5) (Nunberg 1999).

The second visible pattern with regard to the regulatory/entrepreneurial balance concerns how that balance has shifted during the 1990s. Drawing on the experience cited in the chapters, the central observation is that the most important shift has been in the three largest and most central service delivery areas in health systems. Interestingly, these are also precisely those areas where, in general, entrepreneurialism has been the weakest in the past. The most notable area of increase has been among hospitals. As Busse *et al.* document in Chapter 6, the broad general approach to hospital governance in tax-funded health systems in northern and southern Europe has shifted from command-and-control to steer-and-channel. Similar (if structurally somewhat different) efforts to loosen the decision-making reins on hospitals are noted in the SHI-funded countries of continental Europe. The central notion that underlies this reform process to grant individual hospitals a substantial measure of decision-making autonomy, either as 'public firms' (Saltman and von Otter 1992) or, in SHI systems, as not-for-profit private enterprises (see Chapter 6), has now been amplified and refined by the World Bank (Harding and Preker 2000) for use in (among others) CEE countries, where little of this shift has yet occurred.

A second area where there has been increased entrepreneurialism over the past decade has been among primary care providers in tax-funded systems. In Nordic and, to a limited extent, in some Mediterranean tax-funded systems (Spain and Portugal), primary care physicians have acquired greater administrative autonomy even as they continue to be publicly paid civil servants. In Sweden, some primary health centres are now being independently run for the county councils by physician groups; one district in Stockholm County (Söder) has announced a tendering process that by 2001 will place all 16 of its primary health care centres under various forms of independent management (G. Berleen, personal communication). In the United Kingdom, many general

Table 1.6 Regulating the entrepreneurial behaviour of sickness funds and other statutory third-party payers

| | Pro-competitive regulation | | Restricting (individual) entrepreneurial behaviour | |
	Regulation that stimulates entrepreneurial opportunities	Regulation to facilitate sustainable competitive markets	Regulation to ensure achieving social objectives	Regulation weakly tied to social objectives that may be unnecessary
GE				
HS	Allow the insured choice of third-party payer	Install risk-related adjustments of contributions between third-party payers (to reduce market distortion due to risk selection)	A: Require contracts with all willing providers	Require contracts with all willing providers (if in area of oversupply)
	Allow new/additional services to be included in benefit catalogue	Require payers to accept all applicants (to lower chance of market distortion due to risk selection)	C: Require payers to accept all applicants (to enforce right to health insurance)	
	Allow differing levels of premiums/co-payments/co-insurance/deductibles	Mandate annual open enrolment period	C: Mandate community rating or income-related contributions (i.e. not risk-related)	
	Require financial responsibility of fund (i.e. no retrospective cost cover by government or association of funds)	Restrict or define conditions for (horizontal) mergers between payers	C & Q: Set uniform benefit catalogue/mandate the setting of a uniform benefit catalogue through self-regulatory bodies	Restrict acquisitions and operating of non-health-care institutions
	Allow/mandate selective contracting	Restrict (vertical) mergers, acquisitions and running of other health care institutions	S: Regulate maximum expenditure for administrative and overhead costs	
		Install supervisory agency(ies) to approve contracts/supervise financial behaviour and stability	S: Impose actuarial controls, i.e. regulate minimum and/or maximum reserves and types of acceptable investment	

Abbreviations: GE = general economy, HS = health sector, A = access, C = social cohesion, P = public health and safety, Q = quality, S = sustainable financing.

Table 1.7 Regulating the entrepreneurial behaviour of hospitals

	Pro-competitive regulation		Restricting (individual) entrepreneurial behaviour	
	Regulation that stimulates entrepreneurial opportunities	*Regulation to facilitate sustainable competitive markets*	*Regulation to ensure achieving social objectives*	*Regulation weakly tied to social objectives that may be unnecessary*
GE	European Union regulations on free movement of services	General anti-trust/competition laws	P: National and international (EU/ILO) regulations to protect employees (e.g. working hours or lifting of weights)	
	Preferable tax rates/tax exemptions for not-for-profit enterprises		P: General regulations for enterprises (environmental, worker safety, consumer protection, etc.)	
HS	Replace activity-unrelated/input-oriented budgets with volume/case-mix-adjusted budgets or contract-based performance-related reimbursements	Include case-mix adjusters into flexible reimbursement system (i.e. restrict adverse selection)	A: Stipulate required service hours (e.g. for emergency care)	Set uniform or maximum price/reimbursement for privately paid services, i.e. for those outside the public benefit catalogue or those for privately paying patients
	Explicit reimbursement for formerly cross-subsidized services (e.g. services for uninsured)	Restrict (horizontal) mergers and acquisitions of other hospitals (e.g. United Kingdom)	A: Mandate that reimbursement covers costs	Restrict the purchase of non-health-care businesses
	Allow retention of surplus/profit (beyond a single calendar year)	Restrict (vertical) mergers, acquiring and operating other health care institutions	A & C: Mandate delivery of services to all patients (i.e. independent of insurance status or potential profitability)	Disallow bringing operating surplus forward to next budget year

Allow easy access to capital for infrastructure

Allow patients to choose their hospital (with or without the guidance of the general practitioner)

Let money follow patient's choice of hospital (e.g. Sweden, Germany)

Allow/stimulate contracting of public hospitals to (private) management, possibly based on competitive bidding (e.g. Portugal; Stockholm County, Sweden)

Allow horizontal and/or vertical mergers

Direct governmental accreditation, approval of contracts and/or supervision of financial behaviour/stability

Install supervisory agency(ies) for accreditation (e.g. ANAES in France), approval of contracts and/or supervision of financial behaviour/stability

A & S: Allow (new) hospitals only according to government planning criteria (Germany, Netherlands)

C: Disallow services to private patients

C & Q: Waiting time guarantee (e.g. Sweden, Denmark)

P & S: Disallow advertising of services offered (Germany)

P & S: Require patient co-payments (but exempt poor and vulnerable groups)

Q: Mandatory accreditation/quality assurance/health technology assessment

Q: Allow service delivery only according to guidelines and protocols

Restrict types of service offered (e.g. ambulatory care in Germany)

Table 1.7 Cont.

Pro-competitive regulation		Restricting (individual) entrepreneurial behaviour	
Regulation that stimulates entrepreneurial opportunities	*Regulation to facilitate sustainable competitive markets*	*Regulation to ensure achieving social objectives*	*Regulation weakly tied to social objectives that may be unnecessary*
		Q: Mandate public disclosure of performance ('league tables')	
		Q: Set (minimum) standards for staffing numbers and staffing mix (Germany)	
		Q & S: Require referral by lower-level provider (primary and/or secondary ambulatory provider and/or lower-level hospital)	
		S: Set uniform or maximum price/ reimbursement, or require providers and payers to agree on uniform reimbursement schedules (i.e. prohibit price competition)	
		S: Mandate co-payments (which hospitals may not keep)	
		S: Disallow borrowing capital from banks (without public approval); disallow charging for capital costs in reimbursement	

Abbreviations: GE = general economy, HS = health sector, A = access, C = social cohesion, P = public health and safety, Q = quality, S = sustainable financing.

Table 1.8 Regulating the entrepreneurial behaviour of ambulatory care professionals

	Pro-competitive regulation		Restricting (individual) entrepreneurial behaviour	
	Regulation that stimulates entrepreneurial opportunities	Regulation to facilitate sustainable competitive markets	Regulation to ensure achieving social objectives	Regulation weakly tied to social objectives that may be unnecessary
GE	European Union regulations to ensure equal work opportunities for equally qualified non-nationals (free movement of persons) European Union regulations on free movement of services			
HS	Allow unregulated establishment of new practices	Direct government accreditation, approval of contracts and/or supervision of financial behaviour/stability	A: Require minimum practice hours (Germany, Netherlands)	Restrict types of service offered by certain types of provider, or create service monopolies for certain types of provider
	Allow additional activities/income besides government/statutory health-insurance-financed services	Install supervisory agency for accreditation, approval of contracts and/or supervision of financial behaviour/stability	A & C: Issue practice permits exclusively/primarily for underserved areas	Regulate maximum practice hours
	European Union regulations to ensure mutual recognition of diplomas of health professionals	Restrict (horizontal) mergers and acquisitions of other practices; allow professionals to own/run one practice only (Germany)	A & S: Restrict new providers according to governmental planning criteria	Set uniform or maximum price/reimbursement for privately paid services

Table 1.8 *Cont.*

Pro-competitive regulation		Restricting (individual) entrepreneurial behaviour	
Regulation that stimulates entrepreneurial opportunities	*Regulation to facilitate sustainable competitive markets*	*Regulation to ensure achieving social objectives*	*Regulation weakly tied to social objectives that may be unnecessary*
Clinical autonomy (ability to choose which services to provide)	Require referral by general practitioner (gatekeeping) if specialist is paid fee for service	P & S: Disallow advertising of services offered (Germany)	
Allow patients to choose their physician/health care professional		P & S: Require patient co-payments (but exempt poor and vulnerable groups)	
Let money follow patient choice of physician/health care professional		Q: Allow service delivery only according to guidelines/protocols	
Encourage/mandate market pricing for services paid privately (United Kingdom)		Q: Mandatory accreditation/ quality assurance/health technology assessment	
		Q & S: Require referral by primary care provider (gatekeeping)	
		S: Set uniform or maximum price/ reimbursement, or require providers and payers to agree on uniform reimbursement schedule	
		S: Mandate co-payments (which providers may not keep)	

Regulation addressing general practitioners specifically (in addition to regulation of ambulatory providers)

Rent public facilities to private general practitioners (below cost if in remote or underprivileged area, e.g. Croatia)

P & S: Require patients to register with a general practitioner (to make general practitioner accountable to defined population)

Q & S: Require referral by general practitioner to specialist (gatekeeping)

Regulation addressing dentists specifically (in addition to regulation of ambulatory professionals)

Allow dentists to set their fees (Norway)

A: Include dental care in publicly financed and/or mandated health care benefits

A & P: Include dental care for vulnerable populations (e.g. poor, children) into publicly financed and/or mandated health care benefits

---

Abbreviations: GE = general economy, HS = health sector, A = access, C = social cohesion, P = public health and safety, Q = quality, S = sustainable financing.

Table 1.9 Regulating the entrepreneurial behaviour of the pharmaceutical industry and of pharmacies

	Pro-competitive regulation		Restricting (individual) entrepreneurial behaviour	
	Regulation that stimulates entrepreneurial opportunities	*Regulation to facilitate sustainable competitive markets*	*Regulation to ensure achieving social objectives*	*Regulation weakly tied to social objectives that may be unnecessary*
GE	European Union regulations on freedom of goods	European Union Price Transparency Directive General anti-trust/competition laws		
HS	Subsidize/exempt from taxes the development of orphan drugs Allow open market pricing for pharmaceuticals Prohibit parallel trade	Mandatory governmental licences for pharmaceutical manufacturers Restrict (vertical) mergers, acquisitions and operating of other health care institutions Stimulate parallel trade	A & S: Allow new pharmacies only according to government planning criteria P: Require customer information; regulate labelling P & S: Require patient co-payments (but exempt poor and vulnerable groups)	Set uniform or maximum price/reimbursement for privately paying customers, i.e. for drugs outside the public benefit catalogue or to privately paying patients

Release technical data to generic manufacturers before a drug's patent expires	Encourage consolidation among drug wholesalers	P & S: Prohibit drug advertising for drugs and/or pharmacy services to the general public
	Require that pharmacies can be owned only by pharmacists	S: Restrict marketing costs for pharmaceuticals
	Restrict (horizontal) mergers; allow pharmacists to own/run one pharmacy only (Germany)	S: Regulate maximum profit margins for pharmaceutical manufacturers (United Kingdom)
		S: Set uniform maximum price or reference prices for drugs
		S: Require substitution of generic for brand-name pharmaceuticals
		S: Require hospital formularies
		S: Require office-based physicians and/or drug manufacturers to reimburse insurers for expenses above budget ceilings (Germany)

Abbreviations: GE = general economy, HS = health sector, A = access, C = social cohesion, P = public health and safety, Q = quality, S = sustainable financing.

Table 1.10 Regulating entrepreneurial behaviour in social care

	Pro-competitive regulation		Restricting (individual) entrepreneurial behaviour	
	Regulation that stimulates entrepreneurial opportunities	*Regulation to facilitate sustainable competitive markets*	*Regulation to ensure achieving social objectives*	*Regulation weakly tied to social objectives that may be unnecessary*
GE	Preferable tax rates/tax exemptions for not-for-profit enterprises	General anti-trust/competition laws	P: National and international (EU/ILO) regulations to protect employees (e.g. working hours or lifting of weights) P: General regulations for enterprises (environmental, worker safety, consumer protection, etc.)	
HS	Create a new financing system for social care, possibly replacing means-tested financing through entitlements	Include case-mix adjusters into flexible reimbursement system (restrict adverse selection)	A & S: Allow new providers only according to government planning criteria	Set uniform or maximum price/reimbursement for privately paid services

Replace activity-unrelated/input-oriented budgets with volume/case-mix-adjusted budgets or contract-based performance-related reimbursements	Restrict horizontal mergers	Q: Make accreditation/quality assurance/health technology assessment mandatory	Restrict the purchase of non-health-care businesses
Allow patients to choose their provider	Restrict vertical acquisitions by hospitals	Q: Set minimum standards for staffing numbers and/or mix	
Let money follow patient's choice of provider (indirectly through contract model or directly by giving cash benefits)		S: Set uniform or maximum price/reimbursement, or require providers and payers to agree on uniform reimbursement (prohibit price competition)	
Allow provider to retain surplus/profit			
Allow horizontal and/or vertical mergers among providers			

practitioners became fundholders, and the new arrangement of primary care groups is expected to consolidate the decision-making influence of all general practitioners. In several central European countries, as already noted, much of first-line medical care has become fully private.

Two areas where entrepreneurial forces are relatively strong – social and home care, and pharmaceuticals – have also experienced notable change. Social and home care is, as Forder demonstrates in Chapter 8, perhaps the most dynamic area in the western European health sector at present, with a dramatic increase in experimentation through a large number of entrepreneurial approaches. Most developments appear to involve making public payments of various types (from public funds in Denmark, from social insurance funds in the Netherlands and Germany) that individuals can then use to pay variously vetted public, not-for-profit or, in some instances (Germany), fully for-profit service providers. Pharmaceuticals, not surprisingly given their emergence in the second half of the 1990s as one of the most vexing expenditure issues that national policy-makers confront, have been the subject of both greater entrepreneurialism but also enhanced regulatory efforts to restrict overly aggressive behaviour. As Mossialos and Mrazek demonstrate in Chapter 7, countries are currently moving in a wide variety of often contradictory directions as they attempt to restrain growing pharmaceutical costs in their public and/or publicly reviewed budgets. Yet here, too, an area of European health systems that already has relatively strong entrepreneurial characteristics also saw considerable change during the 1990s.

Interestingly, the sub-sectors with fewer changes in the regulatory/entrepreneurial balance have been those, such as dental care, where entrepreneurial incentives are very strong and those, such as funding, in which, overall, entrepreneurial incentives have been intentionally kept quite weak. Holst *et al.* (Chapter 11) note that most recent health reforms are not germane to the dental sector, in that many of the proposed entrepreneurial measures are weaker than those already existing in dental care, and they find that there has been little thinking as to whether existing entrepreneurial measures might (or should) be extended further. Funding represents an intriguing case where, quite the opposite from dental care, there is a complex pattern across countries but in which, at least in western Europe, only weak entrepreneurial incentives are tolerated. While tax-funded systems intentionally eschew most entrepreneurial notions regarding funding, SHI-based health systems have found that – for the predominant statutory portion of their funding arrangements – entrepreneurialism directly confronts core social and political policy objectives in ways that make it difficult to accommodate. The major case in point is the Netherlands' inability to implement the proposals of the 1987 Dekker Report for United States-style managed competition (de Roo 1995; van de Ven and Schut 1995), although a similar if less extreme version can be found in recent German experience (Busse 2000). Sheiman and Wasem, in Chapter 9, strongly suggest that CEE/CIS countries could benefit from adopting this more studied western European approach to introducing entrepreneurialism in their health care funding arrangements.

The upshot seems to be that the extent of change in the regulatory/entrepreneurial balance appears not to be related to the existing entrepreneurial activity in a particular sub-sector. Rather, it is apparently correlated with particular characteristics of each sub-sector, in particular the extent to which it is perceived to provide a core function and thus should conform closely to broader social and economic policy objectives regarding solidarity, access and cost. Policy-makers in western Europe appear to approach change in these core sectors with both caution and a suitable measure of trepidation.

Having considered the level of entrepreneurial activity as well as the recent extent of change in that level, it remains to explore what is in many ways the most important of the three questions posed. This is the impact of recent changes in entrepreneurial behaviour on productivity and outcomes in the affected health system area. Or, as political scientists put it rather more bluntly, this is the 'So what?' question: 'So what if there's increased entrepreneurial behaviour?'

Responses to this question typically lag considerably behind, given the necessary lead time required to conduct validated academic studies. If, as noted above, conceptualizing regulation is one of the more controversial substantive issues in social theory, certainly the inability of social science to pronounce rapidly on the consequences of new policy departures has to be one of the most frustrating methodological issues in social policy. As the British economist Tony Culyer (personal communication) has put it, the evaluation mantra runs 'too early, too early, . . . oops, too late'. There is, furthermore, the dilemma that regulatory interventions often have a preventive purpose, yet it is difficult to calculate how much undesirable behaviour such measures have in fact stopped.

A further set of vexing issues concerns the criteria for assessment. While most commentators consider greater economic efficiency to be valuable, there is less consensus as to whether service effectiveness, access, quality or health gain ought to receive equal consideration. Thus, typically, a study that hails improvements in financial efficiency will ignore the consequences of enhanced entrepreneurial activity along those other dimensions – again complicating objective assessment efforts. Such less-than-complete studies have recently led to hotly contested public debates, not least in the United Kingdom (Bosanquet 2000; Pollock 2000).

Despite these caveats, there is a substantial if not unequivocal body of evidence of the impact of increased entrepreneurial behaviour in the six reviewed health system sub-sectors. Regarding those areas that have seen more change – hospitals and, to a lesser extent, social and home care as well as primary care – the chapters in Part two generally find that the changes associated with increased entrepreneurial behaviour within tax-funded systems have brought greater economic efficiency. Busse *et al.* (Chapter 6) cite a Swedish study showing that technical efficiency in hospitals improved by 9.7 per cent (Gerdtham *et al.* 1999). Recent studies in Spain (Andalusia) and Italy are cited that show at least initial improvements in economic efficiency with the establishment of hospitals that are various types of public firms. While, as already noted, evidence about economic efficiency in the United Kingdom has been hotly contested, there are some grounds to suspect a trade-off in that increased productivity generated by hospital-sector reforms may have been largely consumed by greater transaction costs.

Forder's (Chapter 8) review of social and home care concludes that, although the reform process is still at an early stage, there is 'some recent evidence that market arrangements generate lower production costs'. They have also reduced perverse incentives to elect more expensive residential care rather than home care. In primary care, Groenewegen *et al.* (Chapter 10) conclude that, in tax-funded systems, general practitioners have had more freedom to purchase services and to make budgetary savings.

More broadly, the introduction of entrepreneurial incentives within tax-funded health systems has had considerable impact when it has been combined with patient choice of provider within that system. Anecdotal evidence suggests that, in the hospital sub-sector in Sweden (where patients can choose their hospital) and in the (differently configured) primary care sub-sector in Sweden and the United Kingdom, providers have felt constrained to focus their attention more directly on meeting patient concerns about logistical/scheduling and clinical treatment issues. Put bluntly, publicly operated hospitals and primary care centres in Sweden, and the (now abolished) general practitioner fundholders in the United Kingdom, began to improve publicly provided and/or funded services by treating patients at a higher personal standard. In effect, these reforms introduced the possibility that public-sector and publicly funded institutions can operate at the same high standards typically associated with the private sector, while still maintaining universal access.

The evidence presented in Part two concerning increased entrepreneurial activity is not all positive. Sheiman and Wasem (Chapter 9), addressing funding arrangements in the Russian Federation (and by extension a number of other CIS countries), describe a situation in which entrepreneurialism was unleashed too rapidly and without the necessary countervailing regulation to ensure that core social and economic policy objectives were being met. Ensor and Duran-Moreno (Chapter 5) note that entrepreneurialism without adequate regulation has led, in the CEE/CIS countries in transition, to widespread instances of informal payments and official corruption. Scrivens (Chapter 4) concludes that one reason why governments tend to shift from voluntary high-standard accreditation to mandatory minimal-standard licensure is a strong concern that uncontrolled entrepreneurial freedom will be likely to lead to opportunistic behaviour. Both Groenewegen *et al.* (regarding primary care) and Forder (regarding social and home care) raise concerns about allowing unbridled entrepreneurial incentives to operate, either because it is incompatible with delivering good service to all citizens (primary care) or because of the skewed character of essential information (social and home care). Similar concerns have been raised by some economists (as noted above) as long ago as Arrow (1963) and as recently as Rice (1998).

The chapters in Part two contain one additional source of evidence about the impact of changes in the regulatory/entrepreneurial balance. In Chapter 3, Rico and Puig-Junoy argue by analogy, reviewing recent experience in deregulating utilities and telecommunications. They conclude that there are two main lessons to be learnt from recent experience in public utility sectors, both of which directly affect the choice of regulatory strategies appropriate to the health sector. One is the importance of moving beyond large-scale or macro-level contracts to more nuanced institutional-level approaches. This is essential to ensuring that the equity and quality of the delivery system are not negatively affected by the shift from command-and-control to contract-based regulatory arrangements. The second valuable observation concerns timing; specifically, the need to move incrementally in the introduction of newly developed regulatory systems. Both lessons clearly reflect the importance of carefully tailoring new regulations to the emerging entrepreneurial environment as previous command-and-control arrangements are dismantled. This lesson has been reinforced by recent experience with the process of energy deregulation in the United States. Federal data released in mid-2000 show that, in California, one of the country's largest and most deregulated electricity markets, average wholesale power prices had doubled in the past 3 years (Smith and Fialka 2000). More dangerously, the unwillingness of producers to invest in new capacity has raised the possibility of rolling blackouts during peak mid-summer periods (Berenson 2000). Experts attribute these negative consequences to the problems of transition from regulation to competition, and believe they reflect significant inadequacies in the residual regulatory capabilities of the state.

Policy-making lessons

Finding an appropriate and sustainable balance between regulation and entrepreneurial behaviour is a complicated and contentious undertaking. Conceptually, there are strongly divergent opinions among analysts as to what the proper definition of regulation should be and the suitability of regulation as a tool of public policy. Operationally, implementing effective regulatory mechanisms that can help achieve core social and economic objectives requires sophisticated policy-making skills capable of accommodating the multiple intended and unintended consequences that flow from the introduction of restrictive regulatory requirements. Moreover, as Tables 1.6–1.10 demonstrate, regulatory intentions specifically focused on entrepreneurial behaviour can pursue a variety of different, sometimes contradictory, outcomes.

Drawing lessons for future policy-making from recent European experience with the regulatory/entrepreneurial balance is an equally multifaceted endeavour. Opinions diverge and caveats abound. Here, we approach the question of lessons along three related but separate tracks. First, we entertain possible strategies for introducing competition-enhancing regulation, as set out in Chapter 3 by Rico and Puig-Junoy and as put forward in European Union requirements. Subsequently, we present a set of basic 'rules of the road', incorporating suggestions from Chinitz (Chapter 2), that attempts to operationalize a broadly 'public interest' approach to regulation in the health sector. We then consider the potential impact of several technological advances on future regulatory issues, notably the Internet and the mapping of the human genome, and conclude with comments on the potential future role of social entrepreneurialism.

Lessons from other sectors

Rico and Puig-Junoy conclude that the design of pro-competitive regulation must reflect both the unique characteristics of each sector and the extent to which that sector produces a social good. They present a three-point methodology to tailor such regulation to an economic sector, focusing on: (1) the particular type of competition to be generated (output competition, competitive tendering, franchise competition and/or competition in capital markets); (2) the contractual issues involved in facilitating the transition from monopoly to competitive production; and (3) regulating prices. The overall message is that, while the process of encouraging entrepreneurialism in the delivery and funding of health services can benefit from experience in other sectors, the content may be too different for any direct transfer to be made.

Rico and Puig-Junoy's views are contrary to several strong tendencies within the European Union to treat the question of encouraging competitive behaviour within the health sector on the same footing as that in any other economic sector. The Treaty of Rome, which established the European Community and was last modified by the Treaty of Amsterdam in October 1997, constructed a 'single market' in the European Community. This market encompasses what is termed the four freedoms of persons, goods, services and capital. Single market regulation clearly has the aim of promoting entrepreneurial opportunities throughout the Union by diminishing or abolishing economic barriers. Article 152 of the Treaty, however, specifically respects 'the responsibilities of the Member States for the organization and delivery of health services and medical care'. This view of a separation between the single market on the one hand and national health systems on the other is complicated, in that the freedom of persons includes the freedom of health care professionals to work in other member states under the same requirements as nationals; the freedom of goods includes the freedom to sell pharmaceuticals or medical devices; and the freedom of services now includes substantial freedom for patients to choose services by health care professionals in another European Union member state (Wismar and Busse 1998, 1999). Pharmaceutical companies, for example, placed substantial pressure on the European Commission in the late 1990s to force member states to accept market-set prices for all drugs sold within their borders (Wold-Olsen 1998).

A particularly vexing dimension of this tension between the single market and the subsidiarity rights of national governments regarding the health sector concerns the legal status of sickness funds and of health sector contracting. Faced with 1990s reforms that sought to encourage competition among sickness funds, the Dutch National Competition Authority has ruled that sickness funds in the Netherlands must be viewed as enterprises (Sheldon 2000). A recent report by the Dutch Raad voor de Volksgezondheid en Zorg has also suggested that regulations in the Netherlands that restrict open-market pricing of premiums by private health insurers, by mandating cross-transfers to the statutory scheme, may 'not stand the European test'. The report then recommended a redefinition of the role of the European Union and that of its member states in health care to allow 'setting one's own course for the system' (Raad voor de Volksgezondheit en Zorg 2000). Similarly, a recent report written for the European Commission by members of the European Health Management Association raised the possibility that member states with publicly funded or operated health systems may find themselves forced to jettison reforms that introduce entrepreneurial behaviour to preserve their systems' existing funding and delivery structure (Paton *et al.* 2000).

Lessons from recent experience

Disputes over the applicability of deregulation and the European Union single market to the health sector underline the increasingly important role that steer-and-channel regulation is likely to play in the short and medium term. Returning to Baldwin's tripartite discussion of the rationale for regulating, the traditional concern of 'public interest' regulation – to guide competitive behaviour into directions consistent with core social and economic objectives that animate national policy – fits well into this picture. For a 'public interest' approach to have regulatory teeth, however, it must take on board the insights of the 'interest group' perspective as well. Given the evidence and experience presented above about the interconnections between regulatory and entrepreneurial endeavours, as well as the four recommendations made by Chinitz (Chapter 2) regarding 'good and bad' regulation, national policy-makers might benefit from considering the four-part 'rules of the regulatory road' in Table 1.11 as they select the mix of strategies and tools to apply.

Regulate strategically

Good regulation in the health sector should always have a clear long-term purpose. Just as all large private for-profit corporations use strategic planning to maximize their ability to achieve their objectives, so should public regulators, particularly in dealing with a sector as complex and with as many powerful actors as the health sector (Walt 1998). If regulation is to successfully stimulate entrepreneurial behaviour while still sustaining core social and economic policy objectives, it should be thought through and adopted on a long-term basis.

Regulate complexly

The health sector is one of the most complicated areas that the modern state seeks to regulate. National policy-makers realize that each sub-sector has intricate direct and indirect linkages to other sub-sectors, requiring multiple initiatives to achieve a set policy objective. The perverse consequences of narrowly drawn regulatory efforts in the health sector are the stuff of political science legend. Moreover, powerful health-sector actors arrayed against regulation thrive by seizing on individual regulations one at a time. Setting out a broad integrated

Table 1.11 Rules of the regulatory road

Regulate strategically
- Regulation is part of strategic planning
- Regulation is a means rather than an end
- Regulation should further core social and economic policy objectives
- Regulation is long-term not short-term

Regulate complexly
- Regulation involves multiple issues simultaneously
- Regulation can combine mechanisms from competing disciplines
- Regulation requires an integrated approach that coordinates multiple mechanisms
- Regulation should fit contingencies of each health system
- Regulation requires flexible public management

No deregulation without re-regulation
- Deregulation requires a new set of regulatory rules
- Re-regulate before you deregulate

Trust but verify
- Regulation requires systematic monitoring and enforcement
- Self-regulation requires systematic external monitoring and enforcement

---

framework of regulations makes opponents deal with the wider pattern and the policy objectives they seek to achieve.

No deregulation without re-regulation

Any industry leaving behind command-and-control authority for a new life of managerial autonomy will test the permissible policy boundaries. In another context, Williamson (1985) referred to these tendencies as the temptation of opportunism and the limits of rationality. The consequences of such tendencies can be particularly acute in a sector of the economy engaged in providing a complex social good such as health care. The chapters by Rico and Puig-Junoy (concerning deregulation in public utilities) and by Sheiman and Wasem (concerning entrepreneurial incentives in the funding of health care) both describe the importance of putting in place a clear new regulatory framework before dismantling the old command-and-control structure. Smith and Fialka (2000) provide chilling stories about the consequences of inadequate, ineffective and untimely deregulation in the delivery of a far less complex service (i.e. electricity) in California. In recent European experience, Poland found that overly impatient hospital deregulation produced large capital debts, which, subsequently, the Polish state itself has had to discharge (T. Palu, personal communication).

Trust but verify

Regulation without systematic monitoring and enforcement may well be worse than no regulation at all, in that it engenders disrespect and ultimately delegitimizes state authority. Particularly in an environment with substantial entrepreneurial incentives, inadequate or absent controls invite disdain for the core social and economic policy objectives that regulation seeks to attain. In practice, this suggests that policy-makers should only promulgate regulations that they know they have the administrative capacity to monitor properly. This requires a balance that preserves adequate cooperation between actors without sacrificing public accountability. This holds equally true in a self-regulatory context, reflecting Baldwin and Cave's (1999) emphasis on the term 'enforced self-regulation'. In the CEE/CIS countries, regulation is thus not only a question of designing good regulation but of administrative capacity-building to ensure that those regulations are respected and enforced – a point implicit within Ensor and Duran-Moreno's own recommendations to reduce corruption.

Lesson-breakers?

Beyond lessons learned from deregulated public utilities and from the health sector, there are two rapidly emerging technological forces that some observers expect to disrupt the existing distribution of authority within health systems. These are, first, the Internet and evolving information technology and, second, the emergence of bioengineering and genomics, especially in the areas of pharmaceuticals and transplantable body parts grown in animals. Although both raise complicated regulatory issues, particularly for the future balance between regulation and entrepreneurialism in health systems, it is unlikely that the regulatory rules of the road just considered will change very much.

The argument that the Internet will force a fundamental restructuring of health care systems is, on the face of it, the more credible. Tremblay (2000) concentrates on the role of the patient, who will have access to vast new sources of information about health and disease treatment, information that will alter what patients expect from their physician and from their health system. The impact of this new information is already apparent, as patients in Wales appear at their general practitioners' doors carrying pages of computer printout, and English-reading Europeans have access to the advertisements for brand-name pharmaceuticals placed on the Internet by United States drug companies. A broader and potentially even more difficult question concerns the capacity of so-called business-to-business ('B2B') websites to make fully transparent all contracting and service delivery costs. If a third-party payer (sickness fund, primary care group or county council purchasing unit, to name three) were able, through the Internet, to purchase hospital services from a wide range of providers across Europe and North America, how would that affect both local providers and the regulatory arrangements that national governments use to constrain unacceptable entrepreneurial behaviour? How would such 'e-commerce' in health services be dealt with under European Union legislation and judicial decisions?

The probable impact of human genetics on health systems – the second possible lesson-breaker – is less of an unknown. This is because bioengineered pharmaceuticals are already on the market and state regulatory systems have already had to cope with their impact. In this instance, the challenge is not to the structure and authority of the health system but to its available funding. Bioengineered pharmaceuticals also tend to emphasize the curative and individual-focused rather than the preventive and population-based aspects of health policy-making. While the recent rise in pharmaceutical costs associated with the introduction of new ethical compounds has strained health sector budgets all across Europe, the response by national governments has been instructive. As Mossialos and Mrazek suggest in Chapter 7, regulations are becoming increasingly sophisticated in the range of tools they are applying. Far from overwhelming the existing regulatory apparatus, the recent upsurge in cost has given new life to the regulatory enterprise across Europe. Whether and to what extent the regulatory response will be successful in containing rising costs is less important here than the fact that this new challenge has not overwhelmed the existing regulatory ramparts.

This observation regarding human genetics brings us back to the challenge of the information economy. Solutions with regard to the new role of patients will probably reflect two realities. One is that publicly employed physicians can also search out new clinical information on the net, so as to be as well informed as their patients about new treatments. The second is that, as health systems become more flexible by increasingly decentralizing decision-making both to funders and to providers (for example, the purchaser–provider split in tax-funded countries), these new decision-makers will be able to move more rapidly to incorporate new procedures and treatments.

The challenge presented by the emergence of B2B e-commerce in the health sector is a more difficult one for existing, nationally based regulatory authorities. Perhaps the most useful observation that can be made at the time of writing (September 2000) is that it is still highly likely that, when the cyberdust settles, the same regulatory rules of the road will apply. Their mode of application is likely to change, but their focus and methodology will probably be strikingly familiar. The only alternative is to imagine a future in which governments can no longer insist that health-sector actors are bound by the state's core social and economic policy objectives. To make such a case, one is no longer suggesting that the health sector will be fundamentally changed, but rather that the existence of the state as a political creature will be fundamentally changed. Suffice it to say that such a debate extends beyond the framework of this volume.

Concluding observations

There is little doubt that the test of wills between regulators and entrepreneurs in the health sector will intensify in the future. There will probably also be a slower but steady growth in the number of social entrepreneurs, operating inside the boundaries of the public sector but importing a variety of private-sector concepts and incentives. As policy-makers become more comfortable with the probable outcomes that they can achieve by balancing specific market-oriented mechanisms with targeted regulatory requirements, they are likely to be more willing to allow those mechanisms to play a greater role within publicly operated and publicly accountable health systems. Much as Drucker (1985) desired and, in the health sector, van der Grinten (1999) has proposed, there should be a noticeable increase in what the latter has termed 'social entrepreneurialism'. This middle territory between purely bureaucratic public and purely for-profit private may itself blur the public–private boundaries by incorporating, as in the Netherlands, elements of not-for-profit private in partnership with independently managed public-sector organizations. Here, too, the regulatory challenges will be considerable, and successful outcomes will be contingent on the evolution of systems of subtly targeted regulatory arrangements.

One potential regulatory framework that has yet to be adequately explored in the health sector is the application of the notion of independent regulatory agencies. Although, as currently configured, these are not as yet appropriate to play a substantial role in regulating health-related entrepreneurial behaviour, the generally positive experience with them in reconfiguring the balance of stability and competition in the regulation of public utilities and telecommunications suggests that this may be an area for future creative thinking.

One can also anticipate that, as the overall entrepreneurial level increases within health systems, the range, scope and capacity of state regulation will have to increase with it. The chapters in Part two may help policy-makers to consider which health system sub-sectors are currently over-regulated and which may be under-regulated. Once again, as noted elsewhere (Saltman and Figueras 1997), an increase in market-oriented activity in the health sector necessarily generates an increase in the state-based regulatory response. It appears safe to predict that, while the methodology of regulation will be improved and refined and new regulatory tools will be developed, tested and adopted, the basic process of regulating – the regulatory rules of the road – will remain as important as ever. The challenge to policy-makers will thus be to concentrate their energies on designing a better framework with which to conduct that supervision.

References

Altman, S.H., Reinhardt, U.E. and Shactman, D. (eds) (1999) *Regulating Managed Care*. San Francisco, CA: Jossey-Bass.

Arrow, K. (1963) Uncertainty and the welfare economics of health care, *American Economic Review*, 53(5): 940–73.

Ayres, I. and Braithwaite, J. (1992) *Responsible Regulation*. Oxford: Oxford University Press.

Baldwin, R. and Cave, M. (1999) *Understanding Regulation: Theory, Strategy and Practice*. Oxford: Oxford University Press.

Baldwin, R., Scott, C. and Hood, C. (eds) (1998) *A Reader on Regulation*. Oxford: Oxford University Press.

Berenson, A. (2000) California on edge of failing to meet electricity needs, *New York Times*, 3 August.

Bosanquet, N. (2000) Public/private partnership: change for today's patients – not tomorrow's, *Eurohealth*, 6(3): 41–2.

Busse, R. (2000) *Health Care Systems in Transition: Germany*. Copenhagen: European Observatory on Health Care Systems.

Busse, R., Struk, P., Marshall, T., Pyrmula, R. and Petrakova, A. (2000) *Health Care Systems in Transition: Czech Republic*. Copenhagen: European Observatory on Health Care Systems.

Colton, R., Frisof, K.B. and King, E.R. (1997) Lessons for the health care industry from America's experience with public utilities, *Journal of Public Health Policy*, 18: 389–400.

Dahlgren, G. (1994) *Framtidens Sjukvårdsmarknader*. Stockholm: Naturoch Kultur.

de Roo, A. (1995) Competition and solidarity in health insurance, in R.B. Saltman and C. von Otter (eds) *Implementing Planned Markets in Health Care*. Buckingham: Open University Press.

Diderichsen, F. (1995) Market reform in health care and sustainability of the welfare state: lessons from Sweden, *Health Policy*, 32: 141–53.

Downs, A. (1957) *An Economic Theory of Democracy*. New York: Harper & Row.

Drucker, P.F. (1985) *Innovation and Entrepreneurship*. New York: Harper & Row.

Gaál, P., Rékassy, B. and Healy, J. (1999) *Health Care Systems in Transition: Hungary*. Copenhagen: European Observatory on Health Care Systems.

Gerdtham, U.G., Lothgren, M., Tambour, M. and Rehnberg, C. (1999) Internal markets and health care efficiency: a multiple-output stochastic frontier analysis, *Health Economics*, 8: 151–64.

Graham, C. (1994) Self-regulation, in G. Richardson and H. Genn (eds) *Administrative Law and Government Action*. Oxford: Clarendon Press.

Hamel, G. and Prahalad, C.K. (1994) *Competing for the Future*. Boston, MA: Harvard Business School Press.

Harding, A. and Preker, A.S. (2000) Organizational reform in the hospital sector: a conceptual framework, in A.S. Preker and A. Harding (eds) *Innovations in Health Care Reform: The Corporatization of Public Hospitals*. Baltimore, MD: Johns Hopkins University Press.

Hood, C. (1991) A public management for all seasons, *Public Administration*, 69: 3–19.

Hood, C. (1995) *Explaining Economic Policy Reversals*. Buckingham: Open University Press.

Hunt, A.R. (2000) Social entrepreneurs: compassionate and tough-minded, *Wall Street Journal*, 13 July.

Hunter, D.J. (1997) *Desperately Seeking Solutions*. London: Addison-Wesley Longman.

Hunter, D.J., Vienonen, M. and Wlodarczk, W.C. (1998) Optimal balance of centralized and decentralized management, in R.B. Saltman, J. Figueras and C. Sakellarides (eds) *Critical Challenges for Health Care Reform in Europe*. Buckingham: Open University Press.

Immergut, E. (1992) *Health Politics: Interests and Institutions in Western Europe*. Cambridge: Cambridge University Press.

Lasswell, H. (1936) *Politics: Who Gets What, When, How*. New York: McGraw-Hill.

LeGrand, J. and Bartlett, W. (eds) (1993) *Quasi-markets and Social Change*. London: Macmillan.

Lipsky, M. (1980) *Street Level Bureaucrats*. New York: Russell Sage.

Long, N. (1949) Power and administration, *Public Administration Review*, 9: 257–69.

Majone, G. (1994) The rise of the regulatory state in Europe, *West European Politics*, 17: 77–101.

Majone, G. (1996) *Regulating Europe*. London: Routledge.

March, J. and Olsen, J. (1984) The new institutionalism: organisational factors in political life, *American Political Science Review*, 78: 734–49.

Nunberg, B. (1999) *The State After Communism*. Washington, DC: World Bank.

Osborne, D. and Gaebler, T.A. (1992) *Reinventing Government: How the Entrepreneurial Spirit is Transforming the Public Government*. Reading: Addisson-Wesley.

Paton, C., Bellanger, M., Berman, P.C., Busse, R. and Hunter, D.J. (2000) *Scientific Evaluation of the Effects of the Introduction of Market Forces into Health Systems – Final Report*. Dublin: European Health Management Association.

Pekurinen, M. and Valtonen, H. (1987) Price, policy and consumption of tobacco: the Finnish experience, *Social Science and Medicine*, 25: 875–81.

Polanyi, K. (1944) *The Great Transformation*. New York: Rinehart.

Pollock, A. (2000) In defence of the NHS: a response to Nick Bosanquet, *Eurohealth*, 6(3): 43–5.

Pressman, J. and Wildavsky, A. (1973) *Implementation*. Berkeley, CA: University of California Press.

Raad voor de Volksgezondheid en Zorg (2000) *Europa en de Gezondheidszorg* [*Europe and Health Care*]. Zoetermeer: Raad voor de Volksgezondheid en Zorg.

Rathwell, T. (1998) Implementing health care reform: a review of current experience, in R.B. Saltman, J. Figueras and C. Sakellarides (eds) *Critical Challenges for Health Care Reform in Europe*. Buckingham: Open University Press.

Rice, T. (1998) *The Economics of Health Reconsidered*. Ann Arbor, MI: Health Administration Press.

Saltman, R.B. (1997) Balancing state and market in health system reform: editorial, *European Journal of Public Health*, 7: 119–20.

Saltman, R.B. (in press) Regulating incentives: the past and future role of the state in health care systems, *Social Science and Medicine*.

Saltman, R.B. and Ferroussier-Davis, O. (2000) The concept of stewardship in health policy, *Bulletin of the World Health Organization*, 78: 732–9.

Saltman, R.B. and Figueras, J. (1997) *European Health Care Reform: Analysis of Current Strategies*, WHO Regional Publications, European Series No. 72. Copenhagen: WHO Regional Office for Europe.

Saltman, R.B. and von Otter, C. (1992) *Planned Markets and Public Competition*. Buckingham: Open University Press.

Saltman, R.B., Figueras, J. and Sakellarides, C. (eds) (1998) *Critical Challenges for Health Care Reform in Europe*. Buckingham: Open University Press.

Schumpeter, J. (1911) *Theorie der Wirtschaftlichen Entwicklung*. Leipzig: Dunker & Humblot.

Selznick, P. (1985) Focusing organizational research on regulation, in R.G. Noll (ed.) *Regulatory Policy and the Social Sciences*. Berkeley, CA: University of California Press.

Sen, A. (1978) *Inequality*. Cambridge, MA: Harvard University Press.

Sheldon, T. (2000) EU law makes Netherlands reconsider its health system, *British Medical Journal*, 320: 206.

Smee, C.H. (1995) Self-governing trusts and GP fundholders: the British experience, in R.B. Saltman and C. von Otter (eds) *Implementing Planned Markets in Health Care*. Buckingham: Open University Press.

Smith, R. and Fialka, J.J. (2000) Electricity firms play many power games that jolt consumers, *Wall Street Journal*, 4 August.

Tremblay, M. (2000) Welcome to the new world, *Eurohealth*, 6(3): 4–7.

van de Ven, W.P.M.M. and Schut, F.T. (1995) The Dutch experience with internal markets, in M. Jerome-Forget, J. White and J.M. Weiner (eds) *Health Care Reform through Internal Markets*. Washington, DC: Brookings.

van der Grinten, T.E.D. (1999) Maatschappelijk ondernemen in de zorg, *Zorgmanagement Magazine*, 15(4): 2–5.

Wallack, S., Chen, M., Nanda Kumar, A. and Rodwin, M. (1991) *Consumer Protection and Long-Term Care Insurance: A Framework for Analysis and Policy Options*. Waltham, MA: LifePlans.

Walt, G. (1998) Implementing healthcare reform: a framework for discussion, in R.B. Saltman, J. Figueras and C. Sakellarides (eds) *Critical Challenges for Health Care Reform in Europe*. Buckingham: Open University Press.

WHO (1999a) *HEALTH21: The Health for All Policy Framework for the WHO European Region*, European Health for All Series No. 6. Copenhagen: WHO Regional Office for Europe.

WHO (1999b) *The World Health Report 1999: Making a Difference*. Geneva: World Health Organization.

WHO (2000) *The World Health Report 2000. Health Systems: Improving Performance*. Geneva: World Health Organization.

Williamson, O.E. (1975) *Markets and Hierarchies: Analysis and Anti-Trust Implications*. New York: Free Press.

Williamson, O.E. (1985) *The Economic Institutions of Capitalism*. New York: Free Press.

Wismar, M. and Busse, R. (1998) Freedom of movement challenges European health care scenery, *Eurohealth*, 4(2): 13–15.

Wismar, M. and Busse, R. (1999) Effects of the European Single Market integration on the German public health system, in B.M. Bellach and H. Stein (eds) *The New Public Health Policy of the European Union*. Munich: Urban & Vogel.

Wold-Olsen, P. (1998) A single market for pharmaceuticals: from contradiction to reality, *Eurohealth*, 4(2): 22–4.

part two

Conceptual issues

chapter two

Good and bad health sector regulation: an overview of the public policy dilemmas

David Chinitz

Introduction

This chapter examines regulation in the health sector in the context of the broader literature on regulation and public policy in modern industrial democracies. The first part presents some basic perspectives on public policy regulation, and regulation in the health sector in particular, with a view to developing a conceptual framework for assessing different modes of regulation. This section concerns the relationship between economic theories of regulation, based mainly on notions of market failure, and a broader set of considerations that might explain patterns of regulation found in different cultural settings. The second part of the chapter seeks to align this conceptual framework with what is known about different forms of regulation in the health systems, such as regulation of capacity, of prices, of market structure and of entitlements. In the conclusion, the common threads running through the various examples are integrated in the light of the overall conceptual framework.

The main lessons to be drawn from this assessment are that: (1) regulation should fit the contingencies of each health system; (2) regulation can take and combine lessons from a number of (ostensibly) competing disciplinary perspectives; (3) regulation is a continuing process of public management requiring flexibility; (4) successful regulation requires an integrated approach and cannot be based solely on the application of specific regulatory tools (no matter how successful in and of themselves) in specific areas of the health sector in an uncoordinated fashion; and (5) regulation should seek to enhance, and not replace, social cohesiveness as a means of control in the health system.

Three perspectives on regulation in the health sector

Regulation in economic theory

According to economists, regulation is defined as the intervention of government to correct market failures. There are many reasons why markets may fail to produce optimal outcomes, such as the existence of externalities, monopoly and a lack of adequate information. When government succeeds in, or engages in actions aimed at, capturing the costs (or benefits) of externalities, controlling the pricing behaviour of monopolies, limiting the degree of concentration in the market, or improving the diffusion of information in the market, it is regulating (Fischer *et al.* 1988).[1]

This view of regulation may be considered too limited for a number of reasons. First, it assumes the prior existence of markets, in which governments intervene only when the above failures are encountered. In many instances, however, government is the primary actor in the area of activity under question and government, as an alternative to its own ownership and action, sometimes creates markets. Thus, markets may come into existence to correct the failures of government as much as vice versa (Wolfe 1979).

Second, the non-governmental, non-profit sectors have received less attention in theories of regulation than companies, assumed to behave as maximizers of profit. Yet, these sectors account for a considerable portion of activities in the economies of many European states, and government regulation of these sectors is likely to involve a different set of tools than those typically associated with pure economic regulation. This is particularly true in the health sector.

Third, as some economists would argue, regulation is a political as much as an economic activity. Governments may decide for political reasons to intervene in areas of social and economic activity not necessarily justified by the logic of market failure. Politics and power, as well as concern about public welfare, affect regulation as much as economic considerations (Fischer *et al.* 1988).

Fourth, some societies may have a greater affinity for organizing activities through government rather than market action. Some cultural groups, for historical, internal organizational and anthropological reasons, may prefer a more centralized, hierarchical manner of organizing various realms of social interaction. Regulation is a matter of social culture as much as one of technical economics.

Finally, smoothly running markets may not lead to a distribution of income broadly considered acceptable by society (Stone 1997). Typically, government needs to intervene to provide an adequate safety net for those at the low end of the income scale or to ensure that all individuals have a fair chance in the marketplace. However, it is not usually possible for government to separate its intervention to correct market failures from its intervention to change income distribution. The two are often linked, so that government regulation affects both at the same time.

Williamson (1975, 1985) has proposed a comparative institutional approach for understanding economic activities. In his model, markets or hierarchies (such as government) arise based on the relative ease (or cost) with which the relevant transactions are accomplished. In this view, governments and markets each pose their own transactional difficulties as modes of organization in different areas of social and economic activity. The choice of how to organize a given activity will depend on how different modes of organization perform in smoothing out transactions. Transactional ease depends on the economic, political and cultural dimensions of the activity in question. For example, if transactions are subject to high levels of uncertainty, bounded rationality of the parties poses difficulty for contractual relations. If there is room for opportunistic behaviour, and parties to a particular transaction are given to such behaviour, again transactions may be difficult to carry out.

Viewed this way, regulation is not simply an alternative to the market, but a tool for improving the manner in which different institutional structures allow participants to complete the transactions in which they are engaged. One important aspect of any transaction is the extent to which each partner involved can be held accountable by the others. Where one transactional partner has an undue information advantage, or where viable sanctions or rewards are not available to mitigate opportunism, we might say that that partner cannot be held accountable for his or her actions. On this view, regulation is aimed, in part, at increasing accountability.

The ways in which different regulatory tools function is likely to depend on a number of contextual characteristics. For example, in relation to health systems, is there a cultural preference for markets? Is there a strong social egalitarian ethos regarding access to health services? What is the history of the system? Is it very technologically advanced? In the language of Mintzberg (1989), what is the configuration of the system? That is, what combinations of organizational structure and methods of control characterize it? Are existing institutions capable of handling new regulatory challenges or is it necessary to create a new institutional structure (Altenstetter 1998)? These considerations are key in assessing the advantages and disadvantages of different modes of regulation.

Given this background, it is appropriate to consider different possible forms of regulation in the health sector, many of which have been tried in different countries, and to assess the extent to which they have the potential to ease transactions and contribute to accountability. Through such an exercise we can gain an inventory of regulatory tools, consider the way in which different tools might fit in different sociopolitical cultures, and draw some conclusions about the advantages and disadvantages of different approaches to regulation in the health sector.

Regulation viewed as management, law and politics

As just described, much of the literature on regulation is grounded in the discipline of economics. Clearly, when government seeks to control prices, determine market structure or alter the behaviour of economic agents by providing a set of incentives and constraints, it is engaged in economic activity that is analysed using the tools of economics. As suggested above, however, the considerations involved in choosing a regulatory regime (Maor 1998) go beyond economics. This section adds management, law and politics to the economic perspective on regulation.

Some argue that resources are managed, while competition is regulated (Marmor 1997). Nonetheless, management theory is relevant to regulation, in the sense that regulation is a form of control. Management theory posits that there are different types of control mechanisms. Mintzberg (1989) proposes a number of different kinds of control, including mutual adjustment, various forms of direct supervision and different types of standardization. In seeking to regulate an area of social activity such as health care, government could issue directives to the actors in the system and engage in close supervision to ensure that these are being implemented. On the other hand, government could take a more 'hands-off' approach by relying on the preconditioned norms and values of actors – for example, the training of physicians – to bring the system into line with the goals of government (Irvine 1997). Another alternative is control through standardization, in which the regulator sets standards for performance and monitors whether they are being met.

A related dimension is the degree of centralization of the system. Central government may seek to retain direct control over the system, requiring decisions to be approved by a central authority. Alternatively, government may decentralize decision-making to lower levels in the system. One prominent possibility in this regard is to devolve authority to regional or local government. Further devolution of authority may take the form of giving discretion to individual provider institutions, such as hospitals, to decide how to allocate resources without having to seek prior approval from government regulators at any level. Again, the regulating body could set standards by which to measure the behaviour of the agents to whom authority has been devolved.

The discussion of standards leads to the role of law and the legal system in regulation. Regulation may take the form of laws and statutes by which agents in the system in question must abide. Courts of law may be called on to determine if the laws have been upheld. The legal system may also frame the basis on which regulations are determined; the laws may delineate the process through which regulation takes place. The imposition of regulations not in accordance with due process of law has a high risk of being overturned by the courts.

An important aspect of the legal approach to regulation is that it is relatively inflexible. Special legal considerations that call for a deviation from legal standards are often not recognized by the courts. A prominent example is the refusal of the courts to consider the social costs and benefits of keeping strictly to rigid regulatory standards as, for example, in the case of dangerous substances (e.g. saccharin) that also benefit defined population groups (Fischer *et al.* 1988). In the view of some, one role of the judiciary is to resolve transactional problems that arise among legislators, regulators and interest groups (Dixit 1995). Resorting to the courts, however, is not itself devoid of costs, and the question arises as to whether the judicial system is a safeguard of a viable regulatory regime or, in essence, a replacement for a failing one.

Making this type of trade-off is usually not a legal or managerial task, but rather a political one. Social values are involved. Much current thinking on public policy and management suggests that the determination of social values should be kept separate from implementation of the policies aimed at achieving those values. From this point of view, regulation should be 'de-politicized' (Chinitz 1999). In many instances, however, it is impossible to keep politics out of the implementation process. Laws and standards cannot take into account all contingencies, so some discretion has to be left to the regulator. Thus, regulators sometimes make decisions that are at least partly political, and politicians may be continually drawn into the regulatory process. Indeed, politicians may seek to reassert their control over regulators (Maor 1999).

When looked at from the perspective of public management, it becomes clear that regulation is not a 'one time' designing of rules, incentives and constraints. Rather, as Wildavsky (1979) has emphasized, it is more likely to be a continuing process of reacting to developments in the regulated sector. The management of public policy is, according to Wildavsky, as much or more an issue of dealing with problems that emerge during the implementation stage than it is a matter of policy design. Regulation is a matter of ongoing interaction between regulators and regulated, and not simply the construction of a regulatory policy. Others have emphasized the importance of the 'regulatory regime', namely the institutional structure of the regulatory system (Maor 1998).

These perspectives converge with the transaction cost approach discussed above. Institutional structures for regulation will evolve depending on how well any given set-up deals with transaction costs. As observed by Dixit (1995), however, the process is unlikely to become static, because each shift to a new institutional arrangement will be accompanied by a dynamic set of interactions among the actors involved. Regulation is concerned with the management of this game: adjusting information asymmetries where necessary, setting clear rules and standards to which all parties must conform, and creating lasting institutional modes within which competing interests can cope with new obstacles to complete the relevant transactions.

The implication of this analysis is that regulation is likely to involve a blend of approaches grounded in different disciplines. Unfortunately, these different disciplinary approaches may also imply different, and possibly conflicting, normative attitudes about what constitutes good and bad regulation. Economists, for example, are quite keen to limit regulation strictly to the correction of market failure. They prefer regulatory interventions that limit free competition as little as possible. In their view, for example, when it is necessary to set prices for natural monopolies, this should be done as close to marginal cost pricing as possible. If regulators are forced into the position of requiring minimum quality levels for natural monopoly vendors, these should be based on welfare economics or, for example, quantitative analysis of the costs and benefits of increasing output or requiring minimum levels of quality of service. Although economists recognize that the data on social preferences necessary to perform such analyses are not always readily available, they are suspicious of standards set by government bureaucrats who do not take into account the rigour of the price system (Fischer *et al.* 1988; Viscusi *et al.* 1995). Political scientists, on the other hand, place importance on the political process by which prices and standards are set. They emphasize the importance of elements such as transparency and accountability (Maor 1999). Finally, the legal approach demands, first and foremost, that all cases be treated equally before the law. While these approaches can complement each other, they may also conflict. Too much emphasis on economic analysis may not give enough focus to the type of due process sought by political scientists and lawyers. Too much emphasis on open democratic processes may compromise the cost–benefit analysis encouraged by economists. Keeping strictly to the 'letter of the law' in each case coming before the court may not permit the types of trade-offs that economists and political scientists are seeking, each with their own preferred mechanism for making such trade-offs.

The particular blend among these disciplinary emphases that emerges in a given country, as well as its degree of success or failure, will depend on the nature of its managerial, legal and political culture. These considerations are particularly important for regulation in the health sector.

Regulation in European health systems

Health systems throughout Europe are undergoing changes that have put the question of regulation in a prominent position on the policy agenda (Saltman and Figueras 1997; Saltman *et al.* 1998). In terms of the conceptual framework outlined above, it could be said that health systems have been moving from control by standardization of professional norms, to various forms of command-and-control, and on to attempts to standardize outputs and evaluate outcomes.

During the early part of the twentieth century, control over the health system in many western societies was entrusted to the medical profession (Starr and Immergut 1987; Aune 1999; Berg 1999). After the Second World War, national governments made large commitments in the provision of health services to their populations, and a struggle for control over the health system ensued among medical professionals, business, insurance carriers and the state (Starr and Immergut 1987). In the course of these struggles, in many countries health insurance funds became part of the state bureaucracy. Yet, at the same time, medical professionals significantly limited the state's control over the health field. Later, in the 1970s and in particular in the 1980s, in the interests of equity as well as of the economy, governments introduced a variety of regulatory and financial mechanisms aimed at improving access to health services and containing costs. In the late 1980s, health systems in the midst of the 'access versus efficiency' trade-off began seeking new ways of controlling the health system. Perhaps in concert with general trends in civil society and public administration (Saltman and Von Otter 1989; Morgan *et al.* 1996; Maor 1999), health system leaders sought to introduce various forms of planned or regulated market mechanism. This was the health system strain of the so-called 'third way', aimed at finding a middle ground between rigid command-and-control systems on the one hand and unbridled private competition on the other (Saltman and Von Otter 1989; Saltman 1994).

Moving away from command-and-control, however, did not necessarily mean less regulation. Where governments moved from direct provision to contractual relations between purchasers and providers, significant resources were devoted to contracting (Ham 1998; Klein 1998). Where medical providers were given incentives to be more efficient, governments sought to develop better indicators of quality of health care and health outcome to guard against overemphasis on financial restraint at the expense of patient well-being (Epstein 1998; Simchen *et al.* 1998). This type of regulation has implications for regulation of the medical profession, for example, by driving a wedge between physicians who seek to play a managerial role in changing health systems and those who cling to more traditional models of self-regulation (Irvine 1997).

Unfortunately, however, the pursuit of outcome and quality measures turns out to be a kind of 'technocratic wish' that remains largely unfulfilled and does not appear to be capable of removing uncertainty from the medical care system. Every measure of quality is subject to controversy over validity. For example, hospitals in several countries responded to the publication of mortality data by questioning whether the data took adequate account of hospital case-mix. Controversy persists over the appropriate role to be played by measures of consumer satisfaction in evaluating the outcomes of health services.

The evolution of regulation in the health sector, therefore, is not a matter of a linear progression from one mechanism of control to the next, but rather a constant mixing and remixing of regulatory tools that have accumulated throughout the years of a health system's development. To concur with Wildavsky (1979), regulation is a constant intervention on the part of policymakers and managers that responds to new challenges resulting from implementation of the previous round of regulations. Moreover, it does not appear that health systems are converging towards a similar regulatory model, but rather that they are sharing in new regulatory innovations while maintaining their own 'cultural embeddedness' (Saltman 1998).

Thus, in considering good and bad health sector regulation, it is crucial to note the particular stage of development of a given health system, as well as the country-specific contingencies that affect the mix of available regulatory tools and their success.

Regulatory approaches in the health sector

Given the above background, I now discuss a number of regulatory approaches that have been applied to different elements of health systems. Various regulatory tools, such as regulation of capacity, of prices and of levels of service, have been applied to hospitals, health insurance arrangements and other health sector actors with varying success. These different forms of regulation will be examined in the light of the preceding conceptual framework. While the following examples appear to assume convergence among countries in regulatory approaches, this is not necessarily the case. The particular parameters of the examples and dilemmas mentioned below certainly may vary across different cultures. Moreover, the list of examples is clearly not exhaustive, although the tentative lessons that emerge are likely to be relevant to other forms of regulation as well.

Regulating capacity

Many countries have adopted some form of regulation aimed at limiting the capacity of the health system. The underlying rationale for such regulation is that uncontrolled expansion of health system capacity can lead to supplier-induced oversupply and a waste of precious resources. Typically, governments enact legislation and create agencies with the statutory administrative power to approve or block proposals for the creation of new health infrastructures.

In many countries, health system capacity is regulated by rules regarding the criteria for expansion. No matter how clear the relevant standards, however, they can be subject to controversy. For example, if hospitals are economically and politically important at the local level, it may be difficult for central government to limit growth in this sector or reduce the number of hospitals or beds. For economic or prestige reasons, individual hospitals may seek to expand in ways that conflict with government attempts to regulate the sector.

If the basis for capacity limitation is direct government fiat, the issue is thrown into the political realm and may encounter resistance from providers and other interested parties (Schut 1995; de Kervasdoue *et al.* 1997; Rodwin 1997). In countries with powerful central governments, it may be easier to use capacity-limiting tools. In other settings, attempts by central government to plan the hospital system according to 'technocratic' directives may be thwarted by local interests that encourage hospital expansion (Berg 1999). A lack of integrated control over health system financing and planning, as well as the strong hegemony of the medical profession, can make regulation of capacity difficult (Saltman and de Roo 1989; Schut 1995). The success of such mechanisms as special planning boards depends not only on their technical expertise but also on the political and economic strength of the regulating body.

The same issues arise if central government tries to use its leverage as a payer in the system to influence capacity. In systems where central government determines the entire health budget, which, in turn, is controlled by regional or local branches of central government, government has a great deal of control over capacity. But if financial leverage must be exerted through the rules of reimbursement – for example, through attempts in social insurance systems such as budget capping – opposition from local or regional interests may succeed in thwarting capacity regulation. This may be even more of a factor if the financing of the health system infrastructure is fragmented among different levels of government (Wilsford 1995). Even where global budgets and caps succeed in restraining the growth of expenditure, this may come at the expense of limiting the capacity of health facilities to innovate and respond dynamically to changes in health care technologies (de Kervasdoue *et al.* 1997; Rodwin 1997). On the other hand, if capacity regulation is aimed at only part of the system, such as at hospitals but not outpatient clinics, or only at the private sector, this may lead to a tendency for the unregulated parts of the system to expand in a way that is not consistent with the aims of the regulation.

Regulating prices

Regulation can also be aimed at prices in the health system, for example by using centrally determined fees or differential payments such as the diagnosis-related group (DRG) method. If the goal is to limit overall expenditure, pricing alone is usually insufficient and must be supplemented by some effort at volume control (Berg 1999). On the other hand, price-setting by government can be an important tool, even in competitively oriented systems. For example, hospitals competing for contracts with health purchasers (such as health maintenance organizations or health districts) may respond to competitive pressures by cost-shifting. Cost-shifting is basically eliminated when all purchasers face the same price structure created when government regulates hospital prices (Anderson *et al.* 1993; Wallack *et al.* 1996). This example shows that regulatory tools can be blended, sometimes with each other and sometimes with competitive incentives (Weill and Battistella 1998).[2]

Government can also use 'price' regulation in the health insurance sector by regulating contributions, premiums and risk-adjustment mechanisms (cf. Chapter 98), as well as the terms under which such insurance is provided. Regulations may pertain to not-for-profit health insurance plans, private plans and various forms of supplementary insurance (Cohen and Barnea 1992; Fox *et al.* 1995; Shmueli 1998). But such regulations can create incentives on the part of health plans to 'cream skim' the market (select the healthiest population) and obtain healthy clients who will not stress revenues that have been limited by government regulation. Thus, regulation of premiums usually leads to the need for regulation of 'cream skimming'.

Another area in which prices are regulated in many countries is pharmaceuticals (cf. Chapter 7). Reference prices for various groups of drugs may be imposed by government, determined, for example, by joint committees of physicians and sickness funds in consultation with the pharmaceutical industry. This type of policy rarely has a straightforward effect across all groups of drugs, but rather tends to vary in terms of reductions in price and utilization. Prices and overall expenditure may decline for the reference-price drugs, but this may be compensated for by increased expenditure on drugs not subject to reference pricing. Reference pricing may contribute to 'transparency' by erasing price differentials between similar products but, on its own, it is unlikely to contain expenditures on drugs (Giuliani *et al.* 1998).

The effectiveness of a strategy to cap pharmaceutical expenditures may depend on compliance by physicians. Expenditure targets, relying to some extent on voluntary compliance, can prove more effective than rigid, fixed drug budgets, with sanctions for non-compliance. The latter can negatively affect the quality of prescription behaviour (Busse and Howorth 1996).

Another way to regulate pharmaceuticals is to make a positive list – those drugs covered under public insurance schemes. This gives payers, such as sickness funds, a legal basis to claim that they are not required to cover drugs not included on the list. However, consider the case where the list does not apply to hospitals. Hospitals often receive limited supplies of pharmaceuticals from drug companies as part of marketing ploys. Hospitals may begin by supplying drugs that are not on the list. Pressure may ensue, amounting sometimes to lawsuits, on payers to cover the drug in question. The courts, in cases such as these, tend to support the patient. The lesson is that restriction of access in only one sector is usually not the end of the story. To successfully control the utilization of drugs, it is necessary to bring hospitals into compliance with the package of services.

A lesson learned about regulation from these experiences seems to be that it is necessary to apply a number of tools simultaneously. Price regulation creates intended incentives, but other unintended outcomes also have to be considered. Moreover, it may be necessary to link regulation of pharmaceuticals to regulation in other sectors to achieve overall expenditure control without distorting prescription patterns undesirably.

Regulating quality

Government can also regulate the health sector through the collection and dissemination of information on provider performance. Dissemination of information on performance should lead citizens and insurers to seek services from hospitals providing higher quality. The success of such a regulatory strategy depends on the extent to which such data are available. There is also the question of whether medical organizations and personnel cooperate in the collection and dissemination of the data. In a number of countries, providers have argued that comparative data on hospital or physician performance are problematic in that they fail adequately to account for case mix (Edwards *et al.* 1998). Even where methodology is not subject to such criticisms, providers may be too threatened to cooperate and may seek to undermine quality monitoring. This can limit the extent to which this tool can be used by regulators (Simchen *et al.* 1998).

A different aspect of quality of care that can be regulated is implementation of patients' rights. Several countries, or political jurisdictions within countries, have enacted a patient's bill of rights, or have issued some type of patients' charter. In some contexts, such clear statements of patients' rights may raise consciousness of these issues, even in the face of initial scepticism. In other organizational cultures, patients' rights bills may function more effectively in guarding citizens' rights if sanctions can be applied to institutions that do not measure up to standards. The range and specificity of entitlements, such as the right to receive a copy of a provider's billing rates or the right to be provided with an interpreter if necessary, may increase the compliance with patients' rights bills. Implementation of patients' rights bills may suffer if they are 'neither enforced by statute, externally regulated, nor, as yet, monitored in any official way' (Silver 1997: 213) or if accountability regarding the charter is confusing and slow. Compliance can be encouraged by allowing institutions to determine their own specific standards, while retaining the authority to sanction providers failing to meet their own internal standards. The legal status and specificity of possible sanctions, as well as the cultural context in which patients' rights are articulated, influence the extent to which they are implemented in reality.

Regulating market structure and levels of service

Regulation often takes the form of establishing the 'rules of the game' for the participants in the health system. Most prominently, this involves establishing conditions for entry into health markets and setting levels of service. A key aspect of level of service relates to conditions of access, such as the conditions under which individuals become insured by different carriers. Government may seek to eliminate sectoral sick funds and combine them into larger national funds, to which most citizens belong automatically (de Kervasdoue *et al.* 1997). Alternatively, choice of sick fund could be left up to the citizen. These policies are based on the idea that competition among sick funds for citizen enrolment, combined with the financial incentives of purchasing care under fixed budgets, will lead to the purchase of efficient medical care. If citizens are to have a free choice of sick fund, government must introduce pro-competitive legislation, requiring sick funds to accept all those desiring to enrol. Open enrolment policies do not relieve government of the need to be vigilant to ensure that sick funds do not try to engage in 'cream skimming'. Health insurers have a natural economic incentive to try to avoid bad risks. If they succeed in doing so, they can undermine the social basis of health insurance (Hall 2000).

One method of regulating the incentive to 'cream skim' is to offer health insurers per capita payments (e.g. capitation) adjusted for the risk of each enrolled citizen. Much work has been done in Israel, the Netherlands and the United States on developing risk adjustment formulae for this purpose. Formulae are based on parameters such as age, sex, region and previous utilization. Some of these adjustment methods require the collection and analysis of large amounts of data, and some are controversial. Evidence on 'cream skimming' is not readily available. The prevalence of such practices depends on the incentive structure offered by government and, in particular, on the level of actual risk-sharing. On the other hand, governments may have less success monitoring so-called 'quality skimping', in which chronically ill and elderly patients fail to receive adequate care (Schut 1995).

The structure of the health market and, for example, the sheer number of health insurance plans may also be a target for government regulation. For example, insurers can avoid competition by merging. This raises the need for government regulation to respond to the possibility of cartel-like behaviour among insurers. Control of cartel behaviour among sick funds is difficult because it is not always easy to assess the similarities and differences in levels of service, or to determine whether there are economies of scale in various sick fund functions. On the other hand, government may prefer having a limited number of insurers, or at least having them organized as an umbrella organization, for the purpose of negotiating on issues such as premium rates and benefits packages. Determining the number of insurers that will strike a desired, or acceptable, balance between competition and cooperation is clearly a regulatory challenge.

Regulating entitlements

Once citizens are covered, the entitlements available to them may be subject to government regulation. Many countries are struggling with the issue of determining a package of health services that sick funds are obliged, by the national health insurance programmes, to provide. In addition, various supplementary insurance policies may be available for services not covered under national health insurance. This raises perplexing problems of differentiating between what is provided and how it is provided under the different schemes. This is another example of how difficult it can be to develop and apply regulations aimed at supplementary insurance. In the United States, so-called Medigap policies, which supplement the publicly available Medicare coverage, have come under significant regulation in terms of the services they offer, in order to protect consumers from purchasing unneeded coverage (Fox *et al.* 1995).

Regulation of the benefits to which citizens are entitled under national health insurance schemes is one of the most difficult challenges facing almost every health care system. The task essentially amounts to setting priorities among different health services. A variety of regimes may be considered. Government might mandate a standard package of services. Alternatively, central government might require that all subsystems, such as health plans or districts, provide the same level of service without specifying the services to be included. In another example, central government might delegate decisions about benefits to lower levels of the health system. This decentralization could lead to comparisons of coverage across the health system and complaints about inequity.

Updating entitlements to health services is perhaps the crux of the problem of regulating the benefits available to the population. Research and development produce a steady stream of new treatments and drugs. Some of these are still considered in an experimental stage when demands to utilize them are felt by patients and providers. Many ways of making benefits and rationing decisions are developing in different systems and have been described elsewhere (Ham 1998). There are no clear answers to the challenges posed by priority-setting. In a number of countries, the regulatory efforts of governments in this regard appear to have led to a greater willingness on the part of citizens to accept limits to access (Ham and Honigsbaum 1998; Jacobs *et al.* 1999; Leichter 1999). Regulation, aside from constituting a specific intervention at various points in the health system, can also serve a more diffuse educational role. Regulatory issues that reach the public agenda may alter behaviour in the system even if no regulations are ultimately put in place or actually implemented (Chinitz 1999).

Importance of the regulatory framework

Regulations are not simply 'disembodied' rules on the books, but are determined and carried out within a certain institutional framework (Altenstetter 1998). For example, the goals of government regulation of health insurance pricing vary across countries and may be heavily influenced by the organizational framework, or by what some have called the 'regulatory regime'.

The role and structure of regulatory bodies, such as ministries of health, regulatory boards and public commissions, are crucial aspects of the regulatory regime. In some health systems, ministries of health are confronted with the need to shift roles from direct provision of care to regulation of more decentralized systems, such as public or internal markets. Balancing and integrating various forms of regulation, such as monitoring the financial performance of health payers and providers (Gross *et al.* 1998) with the assessment of quality of health services provided by sick funds and other providers are key challenges. If financial regulation and quality assurance are not integrated, both are undercut and increased stress is caused between the regulated and the regulators. At the same time, detailed regulation may violate the decentralization inherent in the idea of internal markets. Detailed regulation does not necessarily imply success in exerting control over the system. It may reflect what Saltman and de Roo (1989) have labelled 'pre-centralization', namely formalized control from the centre that does not truly regulate the system or achieve desired outcomes (Kaye and Wood 1998; Rosen 1998).

To complicate matters, regulation of the private sector may be carried out within a different institutional framework. In Israel, for example, insurance policies for long-term and nursing care can be provided only by private insurance carriers. Private insurers, as opposed to sick funds, are subject to regulation by the National Insurance Regulator, whose main concern is to protect the financial solvency of the insurers, which is not in concert with the goal of universal coverage. Indeed, the tendency of the regulator is to forbid insurers to charge older and younger clients the same premium, because this is considered cross-subsidization across risk groups, normally not permitted in most insurance schemes. In the Netherlands, on the other hand, government has increasingly applied social insurance principles even in the private health insurance sector, requiring private insurers to offer a legally standardized policy to any person who applies. This requirement led 40 per cent of private health insurance business to be brought under a mandatory risk pool arrangement (Schut 1995).

The examples presented here have covered some key challenges facing regulators in the health sector, echoing concerns raised by the institutional and interdisciplinary approaches discussed at the outset. First, health sector regulation is typically not a straightforward matter of setting standards and enforcing them. Standards, and the determination of whether they have been achieved, are likely to be subjected to challenges in terms of their validity, leading to costly problems of enforcement. Second, regulatory tools applied to one aspect of the health system cannot be viewed or dealt with in isolation. For example, standards such as capacity limits, quality measures or price regulations that are imposed on one part of the system alter incentives and behaviour in other parts of the system. Third, the regulatory regime matters. The institutional structure of regulation – for example, which level of government is doing the regulating – has an important impact on the implementation of regulation. Finally, regulation is perhaps best seen as an ongoing balancing of competing forces and interests to enable smoother completion of transactions in the health system.

Conclusion

As noted earlier, lessons about 'good and bad regulation' need to take into account the specific contingencies of the country in question. Are there strong common values and norms that make direct supervision less necessary? Are there information systems and data available to monitor outcomes, and are there measures of outcomes to hold actors in the system accountable? Are planning and regulation linked to financial control over the system? Is government equipped to engage in regulation, and which level of government is best positioned to regulate the health system?

While answers to these questions are likely to vary across countries, both the conceptual framework and the examples of health sector regulation discussed above suggest some general lessons. These lessons take something from each of the normative frameworks discussed in the conceptual section above; indeed, they imply a blending of these frameworks, notwithstanding the ostensible conflicts among them. Furthermore, health sector regulation is unlikely to work well if it is carried out piecemeal with respect to different sectors of the health system and without coordination of different regulatory interventions. Regulation of capacity, prices, market structure and entitlements needs to be coordinated if incentives and constraints imposed by different forms of regulation are not to interact in a dysfunctional way. The design and implementation of several coordinated, well-integrated regulatory tools sounds, and may very well be, utopian. The point is that, as health system managers, regulators need to be sensitive to the linkages between various regulations and the new problems that may arise during the implementation process.

Regulation in the health sector is ultimately not only a matter of technical tools but a question of ongoing managerial intervention. Management involves not only setting rules and monitoring adherence, but leadership and the achievement of a consensus about health system goals and implementation that relies on trust and social cohesiveness. It is important to consider whether regulation encourages the regulated to cooperate more or to seek ways of evading the rules. Regulation should rely on, or at least not harm, tendencies for cooperation, and should try to build on these (Braithwaite 1993; Kagan and Skolnick 1993).

At the same time, the goal probably should not be the development of a regulatory framework that aims at a perfect sort of world in which problems of transactions costs do not exist (Dixit 1995). In the Talmud, it states that rabbis should refrain from establishing laws 'by which the community is unable to abide'. Realistic recognition of the constraints on policy processes placed by conflicting pressures and interests can only contribute to improved regulation in the health sector.

Notes

1 Some economists might argue that this description fails to distinguish between economic regulation, aimed primarily at regulating the prices of natural monopolies, and so-called social regulation, aimed at such issues as health, safety and environmental quality. However, even economists admit that the distinction is not always clear (Viscusi et al., 1998). This chapter chooses to mute the distinction, since health proves to be an area where the economic and social aspects of regulation are closely linked.

2 Some health economists in the United States argue that competition in the hospital sector is preferable to government regulations that attempt to force cross-subsidization,

such as requiring hospitals to provide uncompensated care to indigent patients, or seek to limit excess bed capacity by fiat (Keeler and Ying 1996; Banks *et al.* 1999). They also point out that, *vis-à-vis* the position taken by Wallack *et al.* (1996) alluded to above, most US states have opted not to regulate hospital prices. Although such arguments for deregulation may have some relevance and even merit, in the current US context they beg the question of what types of government regulation might be needed after deregulation has had the anticipated effect of eliminating overcapacity and 'rationalizing' hospital prices. In European systems, overcapacity is less evident and uncompensated care is not an issue, since most have some type of national health insurance. It is worth citing these arguments, however, if only to demonstrate that, at least in the context of European health systems, US-style arguments about deregulation are likely to be of limited usefulness.

References

Altenstetter, C. (1998) Implementing the EU regulatory policy on medical devices, in D. Chinitz and J. Cohen (eds) *Governments and Health Systems*. Chichester: John Wiley.

Anderson, G., Heyssel, R. and Dickler, R. (1993) Competition *vs* regulation: its effect on hospitals, *Health Affairs*, 12: 70–80.

Aune, H. (1999) Self-regulation and government regulation: implementation control, in O. Molven (ed.) *The Norwegian Health Care System*. Oslo: University of Oslo.

Banks, D.A., Foreman, S.E. and Keeler, T.E. (1999) Cross-subsidization in hospital care: some lessons from the law and economics of regulation, *Health Matrix*, 9: 1–35.

Berg, O. (1999) The organization of the Norwegian health care sytsem: the rise and decline of a public iatrocracy, in O. Molven (ed.) *The Norwegian Health Care System*. Oslo: University of Oslo.

Braithwaite, J. (1993) The nursing home industry, in *Beyond the Law*. Chicago, IL: University of Chicago Press.

Busse, R. and Howorth, C. (1996) Fixed budgets in the pharmaceutical sector in Germany: effects on costs and quality, in F.M. Schwartz, H. Glennerster and R.B. Saltman (eds) *Fixing Health Budgets: Experience from Europe and North America*. Chichester: John Wiley.

Chinitz, D. (1999) The basic basket of services under national health insurance: technocracy *vs* democracy revisited, *Social Security*, 59: 53–68 [in Hebrew].

Cohen, M.A. and Barnea, T. (1992) Private outlets for public limitations: the rise of commercial health insurance in Israel, *Journal of Health Politics, Policy and Law*, 17: 783–807.

de Kervasdoue, J., Meyer, C., Weill, C. and Couffinhal, A. (1997) The French health care system: inconsistent regulation, in C. Altenstetter and J.W. Bjorkman (eds) *Health Policy Reform, National Variations, and Globalization*. London: Macmillan.

Dixit, A. (1995) *The Making of Economic Policy: A Transaction Cost Politics Perspective*. Princeton, NJ: Princeton University Press.

Edwards, N., Hensher, M. and Werneke, U. (1998). Changing hospital systems, in R. Saltman, J. Figueras and C. Sakellarides (eds) *Critical Challenges for Health Care Reform in Europe*. Buckingham: Open University Press.

Epstein, L. (1998) The role of government in the promotion of quality in health care, in D. Chinitz and J. Cohen (eds) *Governments and Health Systems*. Chichester: John Wiley.

Fischer, S., Dornbusch, R. and Schmalense (1988) *Economics*. New York: McGraw-Hill.

Fox, P.D., Rice, T. and Alecxih, L. (1995) Medigap regulation: lessons for health care reform, *Journal of Health Politics, Policy and Law*, 20: 32–47.

Giuliani, G., Selke, G. and Garatinni, L. (1998) The German experience with reference pricing, *Health Policy*, 44: 73–85.

Gross, R., Rosen, B. and Chinitz, D. (1998) Evaluating the Israeli health care reform: strategy, challenges and lessons, *Health Policy*, 45: 99–117.

Hall, M. (2000) The geography of health insurance regulation, *Health Affairs*, 19: 173–84.

Ham, C. (1998) Health care reforms in the UK: lessons from experience, in D. Chinitz and J. Cohen (eds) *Governments and Health Systems*. Chichester: John Wiley.

Ham, C. and Honigsbaum, F. (1998) Priority setting and rationing health services, in R.B. Saltman, J. Figueras and C. Sakellarides (eds) *Critical Challenges for Health Care Reform in Europe*. Buckingham: Open University Press.

Irvine, D. (1997) The performance of doctors. 1: professionalism and self regulation in a changing world, *British Medical Journal*, 314: 1540–42.

Jacobs, L., Marmor, T. and Oberlander, J. (1999) The Oregon Health Plan and the political paradox of rationing, *Journal of Health Politics, Policy and Law*, 24: 161–80.

Kagan, R.A. and Skolnick, J.H. (1993) Banning smoking: compliance without enforcement, in R.L. Rabin and S.D. Sugarman (eds) *Smoking Policy: Law, Politics and Culture*. Oxford: Oxford University Press.

Kaye, R. and Wood, F. (1998) Economic accountability in health systems. Paper presented at the Conference on the Changing Face of Health Systems, Jerusalem, December.

Keeler, T. and Ying, J.S. (1996) Hospital costs and excess capacity: a statistical analysis, *Review of Economics and Statistics*, 78: 499–510.

Klein, R. (1998) Why Britain is reorganizing its National Health Service – yet again, *Health Affairs*, 17: 111–25.

Leichter, H.M. (1999) Oregon's bold experiment: whatever happened to rationing?, *Journal of Health Politics, Policy and Law*, 24: 147–60.

Maor, M. (1998) *Choosing a Regulatory Regime: The Experience of the Israeli Electricity Market*. Draft report to the Korett Foundation.

Maor, M. (1999) The paradox of managerialism, *Public Administration Review*, 59: 15–18.

Marmor, T.R. (1997) Global health policy reform: misleading mythology or learning opportunity?, in C. Altenstetter and J.W. Bjorkman (eds) *Health Policy Reform, National Variations, and Globalization*. London: Macmillan.

Mintzberg, H. (1989) *Mintzberg on Management*. New York: Free Press.

Morgan, D., Bacon, K.G., Bunch, R., Cameron, C.D. and Deis, R. (1996) What middle managers do in local government: stewardship of the public trust and the limits of reinventing government, *Public Administration Review*, 56: 359–66.

Rodwin, V.G. (1997) Managed care in the US: lessons for French health policy, in C. Altenstetter and J.W. Bjorkman (eds) *Health Policy Reform, National Variations, and Globalization*. London: Macmillan.

Rosen, B. (1998) Financial accountability: issues raised by the Israeli health care reform. Paper presented at the Conference on the Changing Face of Health Systems, Jerusalem, December.

Saltman, R.B. (1994) A conceptual overview of recent health care reforms, *European Journal of Public Health*, 4: 287–93.

Saltman, R.B. (1998) Convergence, social embeddedness, and the future of health systems in the Nordic region, in D. Chinitz and J. Cohen (eds) *Governments and Health Systems*. Chichester: John Wiley.

Saltman, R.B. and de Roo, A.A. (1989) Hospital policy in the Netherlands: the parameters of structural stalemate, *Journal of Health Politics, Policy and Law*, 14: 773–95.

Saltman, R.B. and Figueras, J. (1997) *European Health Care Reform: Analysis of Current Strategies*, WHO Regional Publications, European Series No. 72. Copenhagen: WHO Regional Office for Europe.

Saltman, R.B. and Von Otter, C. (1989) Voice, choice and the question of civil democracy in the Swedish welfare state, *Economic and Industrial Democracy*, 10: 195–209.

Saltman, R.B., Figueras, J. and Sakellarides, C. (eds) (1998) *Critical Challenges for Health Care Reform in Europe*. Buckingham: Open University Press.

Schut, F.T. (1995) *Competition in the Dutch Health Care Sector*. Ridderkerk: Ridderprint.

Shmueli, A. (1998) Supplemental health insurance ownership in Israel: an empirical analysis and some implications, *Social Science and Medicine*, 46: 821–9.

Silver, M.H. (1997) Patients' rights in England and the United States of America: the Patient's Charter and the New Jersey Patient Bill of Rights: a comparison, *Journal of Medical Ethics*, 23: 213–20.

Simchen, E., Galai, N. and Chinitz, D. (1998) Interaction between the Ministry of Health and cardiac surgeons in Israel to improve coronary artery bypass grafting, in D. Chinitz and J. Cohen (eds) *Governments and Health Systems*. Chichester: John Wiley.

Starr, P. and Immergut, E. (1987) Health care and the boundaries of politics, in C.S. Maier (ed.) *Changing Boundaries of the Political*. Cambridge: Cambridge University Press.

Stone, D. (1997) *Policy Paradox: The Art of Political Decision Making*. New York: Norton.

Viscusi, W.K., Vernon, J.M. and Harrington, T.E. (1995) *Economics of Regulation and Anti Trust*. Cambridge, MA: MIT Press.

Wallack, S., Skalera, K.C. and Cai, J. (1996) Redefining rate regulation in a competitive environment, *Journal of Health Politics, Policy and Law*, 21: 489–520.

Weill, T.P. and Battistella, R.M. (1998) A blended strategy using competitive and regulatory models, *Health Care Management Review*, 23: 37–45.

Wildavsky, A. (1979) *Speaking Truth to Power: The Art and Craft of Policy Analysis*. Boston, MA: Little, Brown.

Williamson, O.E. (1975) *Markets and Hierarchies*. Glencoe, IL: Free Press.

Williamson, O.E. (1985) *The Economic Institutions of Capitalism*. Glencoe, IL: Free Press.

Wilsford, D. (1995) States facing interests: struggles over health care policy in advanced industrial democracies, *Journal of Health Politics, Policy and Law*, 20: 571–614.

Wolfe, C. (1979) A theory of non-market failure, *Journal of Law and Economics*, 22: 107–39.

three

What can we learn from the regulation of public utilities?

Ana Rico and Jaume Puig-Junoy

Introduction

During the 1990s, both public utilities and the welfare state were subjected to substantial pro-competitive state regulation. Nevertheless, there are not many comparisons of the dynamics and results of regulation between these two policy fields.

We first briefly outline the objectives of recent entrepreneurially oriented regulation in the public utilities sector. Next, we summarize the main economic preconditions for successful pro-competitive regulation. Then, we examine the extent to which these conditions apply to different sectors and activities within public utilities, and the degree to which regulatory objectives were achieved in each field. Finally, we consider lessons from utilities regulation for the health care sector and vice versa.

Regulating to deregulate? Aims and constraints of pro-competitive reform

Comparisons between regulatory reforms introduced in public utilities and those introduced in health care have received little attention. One recent study of experience in the United States offers rather pessimistic conclusions: 'the lessons of utility regulation, which rely increasingly on allowing efficient prices to operate, have by their very nature a limited message for the regulation of medical care' (Abbott and Crew 1995: 36). In contrast, adopting a broader perspective, Colton *et al.* (1999) contend that such a comparative exercise is pertinent in the case of the United States. Several British health care researchers also point to the usefulness of a comparison, but they do not develop a full analysis (Propper 1995; Goddard *et al.* 1997).

This chapter concentrates on the case of British utilities and on the lessons that can be learned for pro-competitive regulation of tax-funded health care systems. The United Kingdom has been a pioneering country in Europe in developing an entrepreneurial utility sector; hence relatively extensive experience and evaluations already exist. Moreover, the United Kingdom experience has had an important impact on European regulation (Boscheck 1994) as a model to be followed elsewhere (Stern and Davis 1998). The advantage of focusing on tax-funded health care systems is that previously nationalized public utilities have institutional characteristics similar to health systems dominated by public providers (e.g. conditions of monopsony and monopoly, a weak and under-regulated private sector). This is a crucial factor for the design of regulatory policies (see Chapter 2).

The point of departure of the British utility reforms is the recognition that some sectors showed elements of natural monopoly, hindering the prospects for competition. For this reason, the policy agenda consisted of:

- breaking down formerly nationalized sectors into activities with elements of natural monopoly and activities with potential for competition;
- introducing competition in suitable sectors with the aim of lowering prices without decreasing quality (through regulation for competition); and
- progressively reducing regulation in competitive activities, while maintaining and refining regulation in the remaining sectors (through regulation of monopoly).

Apart from this checklist, few attempts were made in advance to design either the detailed regulations needed in each particular sector (Burton 1997) or the resulting type of competition (Helm and Jenkinson 1997). The lack of specification partly derived from the belief among regulators that competition is a spontaneous, self-sustained process of innovation and learning based on the assumptions of the Austrian school of economics. The main policy implication of this theoretical model is that general competition policy (e.g. removing entry barriers and changing ownership and market structure patterns) should be preferred over detailed, tailor-made regulatory action (Burton 1997).

Preconditions for successful pro-competitive regulation

The structural properties of production vary widely across economic sectors. This imposes a need to diversify the content of regulatory policies according to the specific impact of market failures in each sector: the degree of natural monopoly, the advantages of vertical and horizontal integration and the availability of competitive supply.

A second set of concerns refers to what has been termed 'contract failures' (Domberger and Jensen 1997), which constitute a key issue within the new institutional economics. Unfortunately, mainstream economics does not take sufficient account of contractual issues such as: the degree of asset specificity; the degree of market and regulatory uncertainty; the extent to which quality is difficult to identify and define; and the specific difficulties of monitoring and enforcing contracts that derive from opportunism and from stakeholders' divergent interests.

The third set of relevant issues concerns the extent to which the products and services provided are considered merit goods, addressing basic social needs. Although there is wide agreement on, for instance, the social dimension of water and sewerage provision, some other public utilities, such as mobile phones and cable television, are not considered merit goods. The social dimension of production usually implies a political commitment to providing services and goods with low or no market profitability to guarantee universal accessibility. This, in turn, imposes some economic constraints on production itself, such as the need to apply cross-subsidization across different activities, consumers or geographical markets.

The differences mentioned above pose important economic constraints for regulatory policy. Such policy implications can be grouped within three broad categories: (1) the design of competition initiatives, (2) the design of contracts and (3) the regulation of prices. A brief review of these three analytical levels provides insight into the economic prerequisites for successful market-oriented regulation.

The design of competition initiatives

The design of competition initiatives depends on specific market failures that are found in each industry or that affect the different parts of an industry. For example, some components of utilities have elements of natural monopoly and output competition is not possible. As mentioned above, this explains the vertical and horizontal disintegration forced at the initial stages of the regulatory process. In turn, such intended modification of the market structure may harm efficiency through a reduction of economies of scale or scope, an increase in transaction costs, or a loss in the opportunity to apply redistributive cross-subsidization of consumers.

Thus, to maximize efficiency, the choice of the appropriate type of competition is fundamental. Helm and Jenkinson (1997) identified the following kinds of competition that can be applied to the regulated industries: (1) output competition, (2) franchise competition (competitive bidding for time-limited monopoly licences), (3) competitive tendering applied to inputs and (4) competition in the capital market.

Contractual issues

The regulatory framework for public utilities is analogous to a contract between the regulator and the regulated firms. In addition, state pro-competitive regulation often modifies the contracts among firms involved in the production of a particular service, or the relationships between firms and consumers. If those sets of contracts are well defined, they might promote efficiency and avoid some problems associated with cost inflation. A general problem is that the adequate design and implementation of contracts might be a costly undertaking in itself.

In addition to price, every transaction involves costs known as transaction costs, represented by the writing of specifications and contracts, evaluation of tenders, negotiation of the final contract with the winning contractor and monitoring of outcomes. Potential efficiency gains attributable to market-oriented regulation could be offset by the costs of contracting. Such costs vary in each sector according to the nature of the service and the required assets, by the uncertainties surrounding market and regulatory dynamics, and by the interests and attitudes of the parties involved in each transaction.

General contracting problems: relation-specific assets, contestability and quality

Contracting is likely to confront difficulties when the magnitude and specificity of the physical assets required to provide the service are large, the availability of supply competition in the market is small, and quality characteristics that are non-contractible are relevant (Domberger and Jensen 1997).

The first condition refers to what is known as the 'hold-up problem', which is directly related to asset size and specificity. The risk of investing may be high when the initial investment required is large, asset lives are long and a large proportion of investment is sunk (i.e. relationship-specific investments), as is usually the case with public utilities. Under these circumstances, long-term contracts are needed to reduce the incentive to under-invest. Nevertheless, as explained below, this type of contract generates problems for competition.

The second condition refers to the existence of low contestability in the market (i.e. small likelihood of displacement of the incumbent by new entrants). Inadequate treatment of the hold-up problem, particularly when price regulation is tight to guarantee cost-containment, might well squeeze profits to the extent of preventing entry. The issue of merit goods points in the same direction, because it is usually linked with markets affected by low profitability.

The third condition, about quality, points to the degree of contractual in-completeness. When quality characteristics of a service are difficult to specify before service delivery (ex-ante), they become non-contractible. Incomplete contracts, in turn, increase the likelihood that further reductions in costs are made at the expense of quality. This has been termed the quality-shading hypothesis (Domberger and Jensen 1997). As Hart *et al.* (1997) show, the incentive to progressively reduce quality as a response to cost-containment pressures will be stronger in the case of private for-profit firms than in the case of public firms.

Specific problems of the transition stage

In the transition to competitive markets, privatization and the regulatory scheme increase uncertainty, generating some distribution problems that may ultimately hinder efficiency. In particular, the new owners of the privatized utilities may suffer unexpected losses (stranded assets) if the market and regulatory environment changes too quickly. This problem emerges when long-term, detailed contracts are used to create incentives for new entrants and prevent the hold-up problem. The contractual conditions agreed on may change quickly as competition evolves and, for example, either input or output prices may fall rapidly. The incumbent might then face more unfavourable conditions than those that currently apply to new entrants in the market, which will ultimately be translated into reduced profits. The problem is often derived from a previous unfulfilled commitment by the state to maintain monopoly conditions for a certain time (Helm and Jenkinson 1997).

If there are no prior arrangements to finance stranded costs (e.g. risk-sharing schemes with new entrants or government compensation), those holding these assets may attempt to block pro-competitive policies, as has happened in many European countries. Alternatively, decisions to introduce such arrangements have to address who should finance the stranded costs: the state, the shareholders, the customers or the competitors.

A critical point here is that the under-specification of the allocation of risks derived from stranded assets may help to promote contestability. In fact, the incumbent is usually in a rather strong position, due to ownership of the basic service network and to its longer experience within the market. This very strength usually deters entry. In the presence of stranded assets, however, the apparent ability of newcomers to reduce costs will have less to do with their superior efficiency than with their ability to write contracts based on current conditions in the market.

Regulating prices: design alternatives

The main alternative schemes to regulate prices are rate of return regulation (mainly applied in United States) and price cap regulation (extensively used in the United Kingdom). Rate of return regulation allows the firm to make a fair rate of return on its assets or rate base. A fair rate of return on investment is earned if gross revenue minus operating expenses is sufficient to compensate the firm for its investment in plant and capital. Rate of return regulation has been widely criticized because:

- cost recovery lowers incentives for cost reduction because increasing capital input implies an increase in the allowed profit; and
- high information requirements are needed by the regulator (depreciation policy, joint cost allocation, etc.).

In contrast, under price cap regulation, privatized utilities may maximize profits by minimizing costs during a defined period (often 5 years) for which a price limit is established. The price is fixed in relation to the retail price index (RPI) plus or minus some number, X, to represent the future efficiency gains. The formula RPI minus X was proposed as a superior alternative to rate of return regulation on the grounds that it provided greater incentives for cost containment, was simpler to operate (i.e. it reduces transaction costs) and was less vulnerable to 'capture' (corruption). Nevertheless, price cap regulation has the following disadvantages compared with traditional rate of return regulation:

- it introduces incentives to reduce quality as a response to cost-containment pressures; and
- incentives to promote technological innovation as a means of minimizing future costs might be reversed if price controls are too tight, or if regulatory discretion increases the risk of hold-up.

The impact of regulation: the case of British public utilities

This section summarizes public utilities regulation in the United Kingdom to date, focusing on two key analytical questions. Why did the same model of regulation achieve different results across sectors? Why were some of the objectives of regulation easier to achieve than others? The answers to these questions depend on the extent to which the conditions described in the previous sections apply to the different public utilities sectors.

Market structure and competition initiatives

Market reforms started in 1981 with the splitting off of British Telecom (BT) from the Post Office, the introduction of a single competitor (Mercury) in the fixed-link telecommunications network in 1982, and the subsequent privatization of BT as a vertically and horizontally integrated dominant player within the sector in 1984. The subsequent transition period can be divided into two main phases. The first (1981–91) was characterized by a duopoly policy aimed at avoiding further restructuring and entry, clearly favouring the incumbent at the expense of the newcomer. The second stage incrementally promoted unrestricted competition in most parts of the industry through 'entry assistance policies' to more than 200 telecommunication operators who entered the market between 1991 and 1998 (Burton 1997; Baldwin and Cave 1999).

The dynamics of regulation in other public utilities have followed a similar pattern. The main differences across sectors are related to (1) the extent of vertical and horizontal disintegration and (2) the type and degree of competition.

1 While British Gas was not broken up into smaller units (Manners 1996), structural reorganization was promoted in electricity, water and railway provision to different extents, based on both vertical and horizontal split-ups (Baldwin and Cave 1999). In addition, British Gas voluntarily broke up in 1997, following a recommendation of the Monopolies and Mergers Commission that was rejected by the government in 1993. As a result of the de-merger, supply was separated from distribution and extraction, which remained combined (Baldwin and Cave 1999). As has been stated, however, in this as in other cases 'from a regulative perspective, the way the company was split was not ideal' (Helm and Jenkinson 1997: 5).

Table 3.1 Competitive potential by public utility sectors

Industry	Scope for competition
Telecommunications	
Local network	Moderate
International network	Good
Services	Good
Gas	
Extraction	Good
Distribution	None
Supply	Good
Electricity	
Generation	Good
Transmission	None
Distribution	None
Supply	Good
Railways	
Tracks, stations and signalling	Very limited (alternative routes)
Services	Moderate (most profitable routes)
Water and sewerage	
Infrastructure	None (except at the borders of two service areas)
Supply	Moderate

Source: Baldwin and Cave (1999: 214)

2 Regarding the type and degree of competition introduced, differences among sectors are more pronounced. Output competition has been successfully introduced only in telecommunications and some electricity and gas services, while it has either not been achieved or has been prevented by the government itself in public transport, water and the rest of the electricity and gas markets. The main reasons for the failure to achieve competition are the poor potential for competition itself owing to conditions of natural monopoly (Table 3.1), the low market profitability of services and problems of monitoring quality.

Competitive franchising has only been formally introduced into public transport (as well as in the Post Office). In addition, in some electricity and gas sectors, the planned introduction of output competition has finally consolidated into what has been described as 'a form of quasi-franchise competition' (Helm and Jenkinson 1997: 3). Competitive tendering has been more extensively used in the water industry, where the scope for output competition is seriously limited. It has also been progressively applied to ancillary and support services in most of the public sector.

Finally, capital market competition has generally been prevented by the government through the use of golden shares. In the mid-1990s, however, these restricted shares expired in electricity and water, and a large number of takeovers took place, mainly by United States utilities and some by British companies operating different utility industries, bringing about 'multi-utility' companies. In general, the limited introduction of capital market competition from 1996 onwards seems, therefore, to move in the direction of re-concentration of business, which ultimately may jeopardize competition itself.

The costs of competition

One of the main pressures of re-concentration and vertical reintegration derives from contractual failures such as the hold-up problem and the issue of stranded assets. Long-term contracts constitute a useful mechanism for avoiding such failures. Contractual theory, however, suggests that policies to promote contestability and output competition can lead to stranded long-term contracts, especially in the presence of supply assistance policies to newcomers and tight price caps.

This is exactly what happened in both the gas and electricity sectors from the mid-1990s onwards. In the gas sector, for example, by March 1998 the more than 70 new gas suppliers had captured 70 per cent of the industrial and commercial market to which competition had initially been restricted. This was made possible by the stranded costs imposed on the incumbent by a large fall in the spot price of gas in the period leading up to liberalization, and by the unanticipated launching of output competition together with supply assistance policies. Similar problems have affected the United States and many European countries (Helm and Jenkinson 1997).

Not surprisingly, pressures to reintegrate vertically have mounted in the United Kingdom. In general, the regulator will have to choose between two undesirable options: exacerbated contractual failure (if it rejects reintegration in favour of competition) or deterred entry (i.e. increased risk of market failure) resulting from reintegration. It should be kept in mind that the first option entails significant risks of reduced efficiency: by discouraging long-term contracts, competition increases uncertainty and opens up the risk of under-investment. This is likely to result in higher required rates of return to investment, which may be translated into higher costs borne by consumers.

Competition has also contributed to other types of contracting and transaction costs. The most relevant of these are those derived from specifying, measuring and monitoring quality. Quality in public utilities has been reinforced by some alternative regulatory mechanisms (Rovizzi and Thompson 1992): publication of information on quality performance, adjustment of the price limits, customer compensation schemes and minimum quality standards. Such mechanisms have proved useful mainly because, in public utilities, reliable information is obtainable at a low cost and customers do not have difficulty interpreting the data appropriately. In some other public sector fields such as prison management, however, there is evidence that the existence of significant non-contractible aspects of quality has brought about quality-shading trends that may ultimately endanger both contracting and competition itself (Domberger and Jensen 1997).

Price regulation and cost-sharing practices

The British model initially advocated exclusive use of price cap regulation. Despite some desirable properties, the price cap system has shown some negative side-effects (Armstrong *et al.* 1994). This has been particularly so in the sectors most affected by market and contractual failures. Some of the more relevant problems have been the following:

- There is a strong case for supplementing price cap regulation with sometimes expensive quality controls because it introduces high incentives to reduce costs at the expense of quality.
- Investment incentives have been reduced by regulatory discretion, which may harm not only capital developments but also, and more importantly, long-term innovation.
- Initial price-setting practices allowed excess profits in some parts of an industry, while in others there was excessive cost bearing by incumbents' shareholders during later stages.

To avoid some of these problems, reviews became more frequent and were based on retrospective rate-of-return information. This resulted in price cap regulation that had some of the disadvantages of traditional rate of return regulation. In particular, cost-reduction incentives diminished, in the expectation that the regulators would respond by transferring accrued savings to consumers (what is known as the 'ratchet effect'), either in the form of lower prices – forced through tighter price caps – or increased taxes to the industry, as happened after the introduction of windfall taxes in 1997. Alternative solutions to these problems show similar disadvantages. The use of sliding scales or profit-sharing schemes, under discussion in the United Kingdom at the end of the 1990s (Baldwin and Cave 1999), implies that the responsibility for the excess costs and also for excess profits is shared between firm and regulator, which decreases the efficiency incentives put in place by competition.

Summarizing the evidence: lessons from British public utilities

First and foremost, the demands for regulation have not decreased with privatization of traditional public utilities. In fact, public intervention has probably increased. The critical stated objective of regulatory policy has generally not been achieved: regulation to deregulate (or competition as a substitute for regulation) only partly materialized in those utilities with higher competitive potential.[1]

Second, there is not sufficient evidence on the positive effects, or even the actual existence, of competition itself. Output, franchise and capital market competition did not openly start until 1995 and no conclusions can yet be drawn. In general, however, the available qualitative evidence points to significant difficulties encountered in those sectors subjected to greater market and contractual failures, such as railways, water and sewerage, and some subsectors within electricity and gas. In contrast, the experience with competitive

Figure 3.1 Distribution of savings from 203 studies of contracting-out

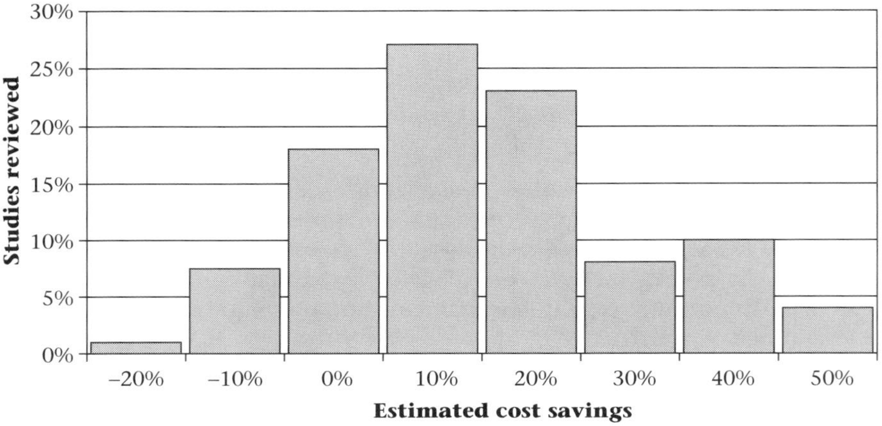

Source: Industry Commission (1996)

tendering has been much longer. A recent review of general contracting-out practices in the public sector worldwide offers fairly optimistic conclusions (Domberger and Jensen 1997). The most complete meta-analysis of international experience available to date, conducted by the Australian Government (Industry Commission 1996), shows considerable cost savings (see Figure 3.1). Most of these analyses, however, do not take account of quality. The few studies that tackle this critical issue (on cleaning services, for instance, see Domberger *et al.* 1995) did not find evidence of quality deterioration.

Third, the increased efficiency attributed to private ownership has proved to be an ideological belief rather than an empirical reality. For instance, Domberger *et al.* (1995) found that public providers winning competitive bids achieved similar savings to private ones. The authors conclude, accordingly, that 'the effect of ownership (private versus public) on both price and quality was negligible relative to that of competition' (p. 1469). More generally, total factor productivity seems to have decreased in most public utilities since privatization (Martin and Parker 1997), whereas labour productivity only increased in telecommunications (Baldwin and Cave 1999).

Fourth, the vagueness that characterized the design of competitive markets created important problems. This reflected a lack of anticipation by the regulator of some important constraints encountered by pro-competitive regulation. The following deserve mention.

1 Vertical and horizontal disintegration can impose significant unexpected costs (in particular, reduced complementarity and/or economies of scale and scope, stranded assets, hold-up and under-investment problems and lost opportunities for cross-subsidization across consumers).
2 The design and enforcement of regulation can be a costly exercise in and of itself, offsetting efficiency gains obtained through competition. As has been noted, 'regulation for competition has proved much more difficult than the regulation of monopoly' (Helm and Jenkinson 1997: 10).

3 Regulatory failures, such as ill-defined allocation of risks and costs, regulators' capture and regulatory discretion, can introduce additional uncertainty and distort the operation of competition.

Lessons for the health care sector

Comparing public utilities and health care

To make comparisons across sectors, it is necessary to determine the extent to which they share similar institutional, market and power structures. This is especially important in the case of regulation, which is targeted on institutional and organizational dynamics.

The main similarity between health services and public utilities concerns elements of natural monopoly and site specificity in infrastructure development. In health care, this problem is particularly pronounced for 'high-tech' hospital specialties, general hospitals in non-urban areas, emergency services, and pharmaceutical laboratories and wholesalers. Other health care services, however, such as primary and community care, general urban hospitals, pharmaceutical distribution and insurance, either do not require extensive capital investment or do not have important geographical elements, and there may thus be better prospects for competition. In addition, recent research has demonstrated that economies of scale in the operation of hospitals are not pervasive (Ferguson *et al.* 1997).

A second set of issues is somewhat similar across sectors, but the effects of these issues are much more pronounced in the case of health care. First, some public utilities have long been considered merit goods, owing to their impact on economic and social development (Baldwin and Cave 1999). This explains the significant amount of cross-subsidization across consumers and of access subsidies embodied in price structures, which might create considerable problems of selection ('cream-skimming') and missing markets once competition is introduced. These are much more of a problem in the case of health care, given the critical role that cross-subsidization plays to guarantee the sustainability of health care insurance itself, and the high political priority placed on equity and accessibility in this field. Second, complementarities and economies of scope are present to a significant extent in the provision of health care services. The joint operation of different clinical services within the same hospital facilities might benefit both quality and costs. There also are important efficiency incentives to be derived from the integrated operation of hospital, primary and community care services: under joint provision and/or management, prevention as well as gate-keeping will be taken seriously to reduce hospital costs. In addition, there is also some evidence of significant economies of experience in the provision of some complex treatments (Ferguson *et al.* 1997). These specifics make vertical and horizontal disintegration much more of a problem in health care than in the case of utilities.

Last, but not least, the health care sector presents some specific problems for competition that are not present in most public utilities. In particular, it suffers specific contractual failures related to information, which, in turn, are among the most important traditional causes of market failure.

First, asymmetric information problems are the rule. They appear mainly on two fronts: in insurance (creating problems of adverse selection and, ultimately, of missing markets) and in consumer purchasing (introducing the need for independent purchasers acting as agents of consumers, which, in turn, generates significant principal-agent problems). At the same time, insurance opens the way for moral hazard, as patients and doctors do not bear the full cost of their purchasing/providing decisions. Second, in health care, quality is multidimensional. Owing to problems of incomplete and asymmetric information, it is difficult to specify and evaluate in advance and costly to measure and monitor after the event. Especially relevant here is the fact that demand does not serve as an automatic mechanism to control quality, precisely because of the pronounced asymmetries of information that characterize doctor–patient relationships (Chalkey and Malcomson 1996). Third, there is a wide scope for undetectable selection ('cream-skimming') of patients, as the need for treatment is difficult to determine by purchasers and patients alike.

A final, institutional difference refers to the cornerstone of pro-competitive regulatory reforms in public utilities, namely transfer of the ownership of assets. Probably owing to the aforementioned specifics of health care, privatization has not been pursued in the health care sector. Instead, contracting has been selected as the core competitive strategy. This has important implications for the amount of state control retained: 'With contracting out, the client [i.e. the state] retains a fair level of control over the activities concerned, monitoring performance, imposing financial penalties, and replacing the contractor in cases of outright performance failure. This level of control is not afforded by privatization' (Domberger and Jensen 1997: 68).

Hospital care

In view of the specific constraints outlined above, prospects for either output competition or capital market competition in the hospital sector are not very good. As regards output competition, its applicability is mainly restricted to the case of elective services within urban general hospitals. And even in this case, it is likely that competition will be mainly on quality, leading to higher rather than lower prices. While this was the case in the United States prior to the introduction of managed care, there is some evidence that a similar process may be developing in the United Kingdom as a result of competition (Propper and Söderlund 1998).

The main alternative in health care, therefore, is contracting, in its two modalities. First, competitive tendering applied to inputs has already shown positive results. For example, in their study of domestic services in 3000 British hospitals, Domberger *et al.* (1987) found cost savings to be higher than 30 per cent. Nevertheless, a note of caution here derives from subsequent research on the same case study, which found that cost reduction was accomplished partly through further deterioration of the working conditions and wages of less-qualified personnel (Cousins 1988). Under a second modality, it has been suggested that both clinical services and hospital management could be successfully subjected to competitive bidding in cases where in-house teams prove incapable of increasing efficiency (Propper 1995; Ferguson *et al.* 1997). This is perhaps a sounder alternative than the one presently favoured by British National Health Service (NHS) regulators, which consists of forcing mergers between efficient hospitals and inefficient ones, by which the former manage the facilities of the latter. Franchise competition could also be fostered for the monopoly provision of integrated management of all health care services within a given territorial area – that is, for the functions currently performed by district health authorities (as are being piloted, for instance, in Catalonia).

The key issue, however, is the extent to which the potential beneficial effects of such competitive strategies will be overridden by contractual failures. Owing to the higher expected impact of selection and quality problems, experience from public utilities of access prices to the infrastructure network, *ex ante* service specification and other aspects of franchising are only partly applicable here. There is evidence that competitive tendering in water and franchising in railways have experienced problems of coordination, quality and selection (Cowan 1997; Gibb *et al.* 1998; Baldwin and Cave 1999), which may be considerably more damaging in the health care field. Starting in 1997, however, the emphasis placed on the development of evidence-based medicine, clinical management and audit, quality of service specifications and increased accountability of trusts for clinical quality (Robinson and Dixon 2000; Harrison 2001) may well reduce such contractual failures within the British NHS in the near future.

A third field from which lessons could be imported refers to price regulation. In fact, rate of return regulation, or cost of service regulation, is very similar to cost-based reimbursement traditionally applied to health services. It also mirrors NHS pricing rules for extra-contractual referrals and patients of general practitioner (GP) fundholders. For this reason, the introduction of price cap policies in the hospital sector has been advocated as an efficiency promoting strategy (Propper 1995; Ferguson *et al.* 1997). Nevertheless, there are reasons to believe that price-capping, as a purely prospective payment system, runs a serious risk of promoting 'cream-skimming' and quality-shading practices within the public sector (Newhouse 1996). For these reasons, after initial enthusiasm with prospective payment systems, current policies tend to favour mixed strategies. It is important to note here that price cap regulation with sliding schemes or profit-sharing arrangements is very similar to the use of supply cost-sharing mechanisms in financing health services (e.g. cost limits for individual patients in GP fundholding, cost-per-case complementary specifications in British hospital contracting, or additional payments for exceptionally expensive patients under Medicare).

An additional point is that the introduction of prospectivity in payment systems, together with other forms of pro-competitive regulation, have tended to increase provider concentration in both public utilities and health care in the United States (Arnould *et al.* 1997) and the United Kingdom (Ferguson *et al.* 1997; Cousins 1988). Such a development, which resulted from mergers, takeovers and pressure for vertical reintegration, may decrease the room for cost-reduction due to the increased market power of providers, and may ultimately endanger competition itself. The same is true with respect to long-term contracts (increasingly being used within the British NHS), which, as in public utilities, may nevertheless help prevent problems of stranded assets and hold-up related to infrastructure development.

In fact, under certain circumstances, provider concentration, like long-term contracts, may also be an efficient solution to the specific quality and access problems present in health care. Accordingly, a pertinent policy solution might be the one adopted by the Labour government from 1997 onwards, namely forcing purchaser concentration (to counterbalance the greater market power of providers) and promoting collaborative practices. In fact, there is reason to believe that higher purchaser concentration might achieve considerable cost savings (Propper *et al.* 1998) and that collaboration among providers and between purchasers and providers may reap significant benefits, which might complement those likely to be achieved through competition (Gibb *et al.* 1998; Goddard and Mannion 1998).

Primary and community care

In principle, the market for primary and community care is less plagued with market and contractual failures than the hospital sector. First, the capital investment required is low, making the issue of sunk costs less relevant. Second, this leads to a very low concentration of supply, and thus the problem of low market contestability does not apply. Third, the nature of services is such that information asymmetry is less consequential than in other health care services.

As recent experience in the United Kingdom suggests, however, there are significant problems for the market even in this field. For instance, there is evidence of collusive pricing practices in private medicine that emerged from the British Medical Association's guidelines. The problem required action by the Monopolies and Mergers Commission, which, in its first report on the issue in 1993, decided that a 'complex monopoly' does indeed exist in the market of private consultants (Smith 1993). On the other hand, choice of provider in community care (and, especially, in the home care sector) has been reported to be often curtailed by the scarcity of alternative providers at the local level (Mannion and Smith 1997). There has also been heightened concern about quality, as media reports have increasingly highlighted cases of poor standards and patient abuse (Robinson and Dixon 2000).

In addition, there are considerable entry restrictions in both the private and public sectors, stemming from professional accreditation practices (to guarantee minimum quality standards), and planning of the territorial distribution of GPs by the Medical Practices Committee. The latter aimed to guarantee adequate coverage in all areas, and operated through restricting entry in the most attractive practice areas. From the beginning of the 1990s, regulation of entry has become less restrictive and, as a result, NHS authorities are finding it difficult to attract sufficient GPs to traditionally underserved areas (Bartlett 1996).

The regulation of GP fundholding practices suggests that these concerns are being taken seriously in the United Kingdom. The sophisticated payment system put in place after the introduction of GP fundholding (Bloor *et al.* 1992;

Bartlett 1996) incorporates many of the lessons learned from price regulation in other sectors. In particular, cost-sharing practices (similar to price caps with sliding scales), in the form of stop-loss insurance to compensate for unusually expensive patients, seem to have been effective in preventing 'cream-skimming' incentives derived from pro-competitive policies (Glennerster *et al.* 1994).

Other problems have appeared, however, for which countervailing regulation was not so straightforward. First, there is evidence of price discrimination by hospitals to patients referred by GP fundholders, at the expense of higher prices applied to district health authority patients. This is consistent with evidence that GPs are more price-sensitive in their purchasing decisions than district health authorities (Propper *et al.* 1998). Second, and for similar reasons, there are also concerns that patients of GP fundholders obtain shorter waiting times and higher-quality services than non-fundholder patients. Third, the freedom conceded to GP fundholders to reinvest profits in the practice raised concerns about threats (and reported cases) of inefficient capital over-investment or support for commercial ventures related to health care; and, more generally, about 'the possibility that a profit orientation may undermine the trust relationship between doctor and patient' (Bartlett 1996: 17). The concerns and problems encountered by GP fundholding schemes explain the decision of the new Labour government to introduce reforms in primary care with the aim of eliminating the potential problems of fundholding while retaining its advantages.

Pharmaceuticals

In sharp contrast with changes in the regulatory environment of United Kingdom public utilities from rate of return regulation (RORR) to price cap regulation, for the last decade the British pharmaceutical industry has been kept within a RORR framework with only minor modifications. The profits of pharmaceutical firms are regulated through the Pharmaceutical Price Regulation Scheme (PPRS), a non-statutory scheme negotiated between the Department of Health and the Association of the British Pharmaceutical Industry that has been operating since 1957 (Robinson and Dixon 2000). Under PPRS, a firm's return on capital is calculated at the level of its total business with the NHS, by assessing profits minus allowable costs. The regulatory constraint is defined as the rate of return on the total NHS capital stock, with firm-specific target rates of return (Bloom and Van Reenen 1998). This target rate of return depends on the Department of Health's view of each company's degree of innovation and its commitment to the United Kingdom. If a firm exceeds the 25 per cent band of tolerance above the target, then it must cut drug prices or refund the surplus to the Department of Health.

Support to PPRS in the British pharmaceutical sector appears more related to industrial policy objectives than to pro-competitive or public health policy goals. In this sense, for example, the PPRS is very generous with research and development costs. The conclusions of a 1996 report to Parliament pointed out the main strengths and weaknesses of this regulatory framework (Robinson and Dixon 2000). The principal advantages of the PPRS most valued in the report are:

- the contribution to a strong industry capable of successful investment in research and development (promotion of the United Kingdom pharmaceutical industry);
- the provision of continuity and stability in the industry;
- encouragement of incentives to innovate; and
- the relatively low administration costs.

Nevertheless, some problems in the unchanged regulatory framework were identified in the report:

- a lack of transparency (high degree of discretion);
- a tendency to provide disincentives for efficiency, which negatively affects public cost-containment policies (by allowing excessively high prices); and
- the tendency of the system to act as a barrier to effective price competition in this market.

Conclusions

The institutional structure of the health care sector presents many of the classical difficulties that hinder the potential beneficial effects of pro-competitive policies. In this sense, it differs markedly from those public utilities that have more competitive potential. At the same time, however, the health care sector shares many of the market and contractual failures encountered in the public utilities field, which makes the comparison ultimately pertinent and allows some lessons to be applied across sectors.

These failures are considerably more acute in health care, which helps explain why the scope of pro-competitive policies has been much more restricted here. This might also explain an apparent paradox, namely that the regulation of health care markets is in some respects much more sophisticated than the regulatory policy for public utilities. The first important strength of health care regulation is that it has paid much more attention to quality, accessibility and equity, given their political importance in the health care field. In addition, micro-institutional aspects and contractual details have also been subject to considerable study and experimentation, which has not always been true in the field of public utilities. For this reason, further research on the extent to which lessons from health care might be usefully applied to the public utilities field looks promising, as the few attempts made in this direction exemplify (Else 1992).

Finally, it should be noted that, as natural monopoly problems may decrease due to technological innovation, this may also be the case for the specific market and contractual failures encountered in health care. In particular, some of the recent regulatory reforms applied in the United Kingdom, which are precisely targeted at reducing the negative effects of contractual failures on equity and quality through micro-institutional regulations and collaborative schemes, might also be usefully employed in the future to reap the benefits of competition without incurring its costs, at least in those health care sub-sectors (such as primary and community care) less prone to market failures. The transition stage, however, is likely to take longer in the health care field than in public utilities. In this respect, it should not be forgotten that the most successful regulatory experiences in public utilities proceeded cautiously and slowly.

Note

1 It is true that, in competitive sectors, the use of price caps has been reduced progress-ively (and from 1998 on, sharply). Nevertheless, the need to regulate other aspects such as market structure (e.g. takeovers) or quality has simultaneously increased.

References

Abbott, III, T.A. and Crew, M.A. (1995) Lessons from public utility regulation for economic regulation of health care markets: an overview, in *Health Care Policy and Regulation*. Dordrecht: Kluwer Academic.

Armstrong, M., Cowan, S. and Vickers, J. (1994) *Regulatory Reform: Economic Analysis and British Experience*. Cambridge, MA: MIT Press.

Arnould, R.J., DeBrock, L.M. and Radach, H.L. (1997) The nature and consequences of provider consolidation in the US, in B. Ferguson, T. Sheldon and J. Posnett (eds) *Concentration and Choice in Health Care*. London: Royal Society of Medicine Press.

Baldwin, R. and Cave, M. (1999) *Understanding Regulation: Theory, Strategy & Practice*. Oxford: Oxford University Press.

Bartlett, W. (1996) The regulation of general practice in the UK, *International Journal of Health Planning and Management*, 11: 3–18.

Bloom, N. and Van Reenen, J. (1998) Regulating drug prices: where do we go from here?, *Fiscal Studies*, 19: 321–42.

Bloor, K., Maynard, A. and Street, A. (1992) *How Much is a Doctor Worth?*, Discussion Paper No. 98. York: Centre for Health Economics, University of York.

Boscheck, R. (1994) Deregulating European electricity supply: issues and implications, *Long Range Planning*, 27: 111–23.

Burton, J. (1997) The competitive order or 'ordered competition'? The UK model of utility regulation in theory and practice, *Public Administration*, 75: 157–88.

Chalkey, M. and Malcomson, J.M. (1996) Contracts for the National Health Service, *Economic Journal*, 106: 1691–1701.

Colton, R., Frisof, K.B. and King, E.R. (1999) Lessons for the health care industry from America's experience with public utilities, *Journal of Public Health Policy*, 18: 389–99.

Cousins, C. (1988) The restructuring of welfare work: the introduction of general manage-ment and the contracting-out of ancillary services in the NHS, *Work, Employment and Society*, 2: 210–28.

Cowan, S. (1997) Competition in the water industry, *Oxford Review of Economic Policy*, 13: 83–92.

Domberger, S. and Jensen, P. (1997) Contracting-out by the public sector: theory, evid-ence, prospects, *Oxford Review of Economic Policy*, 13(4): 67–78.

Domberger, S., Meadowcroft, S. and Thomson, D. (1987) The impact of competitive tendering on the costs of hospital domestic services, *Fiscal Studies*, 8: 39–54.

Domberger, S., Hall, C. and Li, E. (1995) The determinants of price and quality in competitively tendered contracts, *Economic Journal*, 105: 1545–70.

Else, P.K. (1992) Criteria for local transport subsidies, *Transport Reviews*, 12: 291–309.

Ferguson, B., Sheldon, T. and Posnett, J. (1997) Introduction, in B. Ferguson, T. Sheldon and J. Posnett (eds) *Concentration and Choice in Health Care*. London: Royal Society of Medicine Press.

Gibb, R., Shaw, J. and Charlton, C. (1998) Competition, regulation and the privatization of British Rail, *Environment and Planning C: Government and Policy*, 16: 757–68.

Glennerster, H., Matsaganis, M. and Owens, P. (1994) *A Foothold for Footholding*. London: King's Fund.

Goddard, M. and Mannion, R. (1998) From competition to co-operation: New economic relationships in the National Health Service, *Health Economics*, 7: 105–19.

Goddard, M., Ferguson, B. and Posnett, J. (1997) Impact of the purchaser/provider relationship and implications for the regulatory framework, in B. Ferguson, T. Sheldon and J. Posnett (eds) *Concentration and Choice in Health Care*. London: Royal Society of Medicine Press.

Harrison, S. (2001) Structural interests in health care: 'reforming' the UK medical profession, in M. Bovens, P. T'Hart and G. Peters (eds) *Success and Failure in Government: A Comparative Analysis*. Aldershot: Edward Elgar.

Hart, O., Shleifer, A. and Vishny, R.W. (1997) The proper scope of government: theory and an application to prisons, *Quarterly Journal of Economics*, 112: 1127–61.

Helm, D. and Jenkinson, T. (1997) The assessment: introducing competition into regulated industries, *Oxford Review of Economic Policy*, 13(1): 1–14.

Industry Commission (1996) *Competitive Tendering and Contracting by Public Sector Agencies*, Report No. 48. Melbourne: Australian Government Publishing Service.

Manners, G. (1996) Gas market liberalization in Britain: some geographical observations, *Regional Studies*, 31: 295–309.

Mannion, R. and Smith, P. (1997) Trust and reputation in community care: theory and evidence, in P. Anand and A. McGuire (eds) *Changes in Health Care: Reflections on the NHS Internal Market*. London: Macmillan.

Martin, S. and Parker, D. (1997) *The Impact of Privatization: Ownership and Corporate Performance in the UK*. London: Routledge.

Newhouse, J.P. (1996) Reimbursing health plans and health providers: efficiency in production versus selection, *Journal of Economic Literature*, 34: 1236–63.

Propper, C. (1995) Regulatory reform in the NHS internal market, *Health Economics*, 4: 77–83.

Propper, C. and Söderlund, N. (1998) Competition in the NHS internal market: an overview of its effects on hospital prices and costs, *Health Economics*, 7: 187–97.

Propper, C., Wilson, D. and Söderlund, N. (1998) The effects of regulation and competition in the NHS internal market: the case of general practice fundholder prices, *Journal of Health Economics*, 17: 645–73.

Robinson, R. and Dixon, A. (2000) *Health Care Systems in Transition – United Kingdom*. Copenhagen: European Observatory on Health Care Systems.

Rovizzi, L. and Thompson, D. (1992) The regulation of product quality in the public utilities and the Citizen's Charter, *Fiscal Studies*, 13(3): 74–95.

Smith, R. (1993) Private medicine is a long way from being a perfect market, *British Medical Journal*, 307: 216–17.

Stern, J. and Davis, J.R. (1998) Economic reform of the electricity industries of Central and Eastern Europe, *Economics of Transition*, 6: 427–60.

chapter four

Accreditation and the regulation of quality in health services

Ellie Scrivens

The role of accreditation in the assessment of quality in health care

Accreditation is one process in a range of different approaches for checking and standardizing the quality of health care delivered by health service organizations (Scrivens 1996). The term is used here to describe the participation of a health care organization in a process of third-party assessment of health care systems and organizational structures, using written standards, which concentrates on assessing the organization of services and processes to enable the provision of high-quality performance. Until the 1980s, the term 'accreditation', when applied to health care organizations, was used to describe a voluntary, health service based activity that allowed all organizations, and particularly hospitals, to compare their organizational processes and procedures against accepted good practice. Frequently, the emphasis was on safety of procedures, the aim being to provide an environment in which clinical effectiveness could be maximized (Scrivens 1995). Traditionally, accreditation bodies have been self-funding and, in most cases, organizations seeking accreditation pay a fee (although, as will be shown later, all the parameters have been subject to modification). The end result of the accreditation process is the award of a grading or score denoting the degree of compliance with the standards. The grading is frequently characterized by a number of years before the next survey is required, the longer the period the better the degree of compliance (Scrivens 1995). Each accreditation system is controlled by an independent board, made up of representatives of health-related professional bodies. The board is responsible for the standards and for awarding the final grading (Hayes and Shaw 1995).

This chapter traces the origins and development of accreditation from its beginnings in the United States in the first half of the twentieth century to its adoption and adaptation in Canada and Australia in the 1950s and 1960s. Also addressed are the characteristics of accreditation systems and the growth in the popularity of accreditation in many countries in the 1990s. Curiously, although there has been growth in accreditation programmes in Europe, countries have found them hard to adopt and implement. The last section of the chapter addresses the relationship between accreditation and regulation.

The origins and development of accreditation in the United States, Canada and Australia

Accreditation first began in the United States as an initiative of the medical profession following a growing interest in the need to standardize the provision of health care (Roberts *et al.* 1987). In 1913, the American College of Surgeons was founded to promote the concept of hospital standardization. One of the main requirements for membership of the College was the production of satisfactory case records to demonstrate competence in surgery. This requirement revealed a lack of adequate record-keeping in most hospitals (Bogdanich 1988).

As a direct result, the College founded the hospital standardization programme in 1917. This laid down a number of principles that have formed the basis for accreditation ever since. There were written standards – five at the beginning. These covered the organization and qualifications of medical staff, what is now called 'clinical audit', the maintenance of adequate records and appropriate diagnostic technologies. Compliance with the standard was assessed by surveyors, who visited the hospital and examined hospital practices (Roberts *et al.* 1987).

By 1949, over half the hospitals in the United States were participating voluntarily in the programme. The manuals containing the standards had expanded to 118 pages, with a numerical method of evaluation known as the 'points rating system' reflecting the level of compliance with the standards that had been adopted. To cope with the expense of providing the accreditation service to an increasing number of hospitals, the American College of Surgeons came together with a number of related health service organizations to form the Joint Commission on the Accreditation of Hospitals (later Healthcare Organizations) (JCAHO). Medical membership dominated the Board and, although other professional and managerial groups subsequently joined, its clinical orientation is still apparent. During the following decades, the JCAHO extended its range to cover ambulatory care, long-term care, health care networks, behavioural care and mental health services. As the JCAHO reached out across the health care system, other accreditation bodies developed, covering a wide range of health services.

The Canadian Council on Health Services Accreditation (CCHSA) was established in 1958 following the introduction of the Canadian National Health

System. It followed the format of the JCAHO in all respects. Interest in hospital accreditation in Australia started as early as 1926 (Duckett 1983), although not until 1977 was a full accreditation system launched (in New South Wales). Accreditation subsequently spread to a number of states and has received support from medical professional organizations.

Accreditation, as a tool for evaluating health care organizations, has had to maintain its relevance to the health care systems it was designed to serve (Scrivens and Heidemann 1995). Consequently, the major accreditation systems have changed their emphasis, moving from an original focus on organizational structure to concerns about organizational performance. All the major accreditation systems have rewritten their standards to become what is termed patient- or client-centred, describing health care processes as they affect patients rather than simply reflecting the organizational structures (Heidemann 1995). In addition, they have all attempted to develop approaches for the identification and collection of performance indicators that can demonstrate health care performance. This latter development has proved to be extremely difficult for accreditation systems, as the systematic collection of large amounts of data to be produced voluntarily proved to be unpopular in health care communities, and the success of these initiatives has been limited (Schyve 1995).

Accreditation and licensing

The main purpose of accreditation is to focus health care organizations on improvement in performance. The emphasis of accreditation is on evaluating and supporting the participating organizations by looking at what the organization is doing right and how it can be improved. This contrasts with what is termed 'licensure', which is mandatory inspection undertaken by a government body (and usually funded by government money) to see whether an organization is doing something wrong or harmful. A key distinction is that accreditation standards are set at what are described as optimal achievable levels, providing a target to strive for. Licensing, in contrast, uses minimum standards that have to be passed to designate the organization fit to provide a service to the public (Scrivens 1995). The JCAHO and CCHSA argue that accreditation is intended to perform a very different function from government regulatory systems.

The original clear distinction between licensing and accreditation has become confused as accreditation systems, particularly in the United States, have had to fight for their existence in the health care marketplace. In the United States, the JCAHO purports to be a vehicle for promoting the dissemination of good practice, yet is used in many states as a tool of public regulation. The Health Care Financing Administration, which is a pure instrument of regulation arguably to protect the general public, uses JCAHO findings in some states as part of, or as a substitute for, its licensing process (Scrivens *et al.* 1995). Medicare and Medicaid reimbursements can be made on the outcome of a JCAHO report.

Figure 4.1 Internal and external review

The shape of accreditation

Central to accreditation systems are two features: the principle of external review and the use of standards (Scrivens 1996). External review requires an assessment by experts who, in the case of accreditation, are normally peers. This is in contrast to internal review systems, in which all reviews are conducted within and by the organization itself. Internal reviews can be conducted using professional judgement of organizational employees. This is a form of internal inspection in which existing practices and procedures are commented on and improvements suggested by staff from within the organization. Alternatively, internal review can use standards to assess organizational compliance but not employ external reviewers; the organization conducts a self-assessment and determines its own level of compliance.

In general, there are three types of external review: expert inspection, inspection using standards and accreditation. Expert inspection requires a senior health care professional to form a personal view of the quality of provision, based on personal experience, which results in a qualitative report (Figure 4.1). The second approach uses written statements or standards that describe expected good practice for, say, organizational processes and procedures, and against which the organization is assessed; the outcome is again a written qualitative report. The third approach, commonly referred to as accreditation, uses standards and expert judgement against those standards to assess the level of compliance, resulting in an overall grading or score (Scrivens 1995).

Approaches to accreditation can be placed in three categories: market-based, professionally self-regulated and government-owned. The original form of accreditation, as exemplified by the JCAHO in the United States, is a market-based system, competing in the market for quality assessment with other forms

Table 4.1 Dimensions in the construction of accreditation systems

Dimension	Original model adaptations
1 Levels of standards	optimum .... minimum
2 Geographical coverage	national .... local
3 Focus of standards	organizational .... process .... outcome
4 Pressure to participate	internal .... external
5 Number of agencies	one agency .... many agencies
6 Purposes of accreditation	self-development .... public reassurance
7 Participation	voluntary .... compulsory
8 Information	confidential .... public
9 Grading schema	pass/fail .... comparative assessment
10 Content	whole hospital .... single service
11 Surveyor employment status	part-time .... full-time

Source: Scrivens (1996)

of regulation and quality assurance processes. In many countries, the professional bodies review the facilities provided by hospitals and health care organizations to ensure that they are adequate for training purposes and that clinical procedures are carried out in an acceptable manner. This form of professional assessment frequently uses the judgement of peers rather than standards associated with accreditation, although standards-based systems are being developed by several professional organizations.

Government-owned accreditation is a relatively recent development and takes several forms. Although it is based on standards, there appears to be a natural tendency for governments to use accreditation to promote quality while transforming it into a kind of licensing activity rather than as a quality improvement activity on implementation. Government-based accreditation tends to be compulsory and, as such, the standards become perceived and indeed used as the minimum with which health care organizations must comply. Recent demands for open and transparent government have tended to require that the information collected by governments is placed in the public domain. Consequently, the original purpose of accreditation – to act as a confidential management tool to promote internal interest in quality – is diluted as health service performance is held to public scrutiny.

A number of dimensions characterize accreditation systems (Scrivens 1996), all of which are open to modification. Table 4.1 compares the dimensions as explained in the original model with adaptations that have occurred (Scrivens 1996). The original model of accreditation is based on the JCAHO, CCHSA and Australian Council on Healthcare Standards (ACHS). The adaptations have occurred in more recently developed accreditation systems. Although most accreditation systems subscribe to the principles of optimal achievable standards, it is possible to set the standards at a minimal level, particularly if they reflect legislative requirements.

Although accreditation systems tend to be discussed as national initiatives, it is possible to develop local variations. In the United Kingdom, for example, health authorities have developed local accreditation systems to assess the quality of general practices (Birch *et al.* 2000). Regional health bodies have developed their own accreditation systems. As demonstrated above, accreditation standards can be written to reflect very different aspects of health care provision, ranging from basic organizational features to standards written to reflect health care outcomes (Heidemann 1993). Participation in accreditation-type activities, although originally intended to be based on organizational self-development and therefore voluntary, can be changed through purchaser or governmental requirements to become compulsory and therefore to some extent regulatory. Compliance with accreditation standards can be perceived as offering public protection by ensuring that standards of health care are satisfactorily met. The difference hinges on the uses to which the outcomes of accreditation are put, and the extent of public access to the information.

Again the distinction that must be drawn is whether the interest in accreditation comes from pressures internal to the organization being accredited or from external sources such as a professional body or government. That is, the pressure to take part in such a system may come from within the organization, which makes participation voluntary, or may come from outside the organization, which makes participation compulsory and thereby changes the system from one of self-development to one of professional regulation. Where the demands for participation come from public agencies and bodies, the emphasis shifts from regulation of activities controlled by the profession to regulation controlled by government agencies; in this last case, participation is compulsory and accreditation has become a part of the public accountability process (Scrivens 1997).

The European experience of accreditation

Most health care systems within Europe have seen some experimentation with accreditation. In the United Kingdom, a charitable body, the King's Fund, piloted the CCHSA standards in a number of hospitals in 1980 (Maxwell *et al.* 1983). This proved to be of interest, and it was consequently decided to continue with the experiment of using standards to review National Health Service (NHS) hospitals. The CCHSA standards were replaced by the then current ACHS and over time developed into a tool for assessing NHS hospitals. This operated as a purely voluntary system, with hospitals paying for participation in the scheme, and the private sector became a significant customer for this service. The interest expressed by the private sector in accreditation-type activities in the United Kingdom can be attributed to its desire to break into the public sector funding. The lack of explicit means for demonstrating quality in the public sector forced the private sector hospitals to find a method for acquiring a mark that would demonstrate high quality and enable them to compete with public sector hospitals.

The King's Fund approach has been exported on an experimental basis to several countries. It has been used by groups of hospitals working together to establish some means of assessing the quality of hospital care. Finland, Portugal and Sweden have all seen some limited developments in the use of the King's Fund standards (Shaw 1998). In all these countries, however, although governments have been interested in the control of quality, none has chosen to use accreditation as a formal or mandated approach. The British Government has chosen intentionally to develop other methods for controlling quality, such as setting national targets for the performance of a limited number of aspects of hospital management, such as waiting times and the rights of patients to information. In addition, there is a government programme that essentially offers a prize for good practice to organizations that enter a national competition. More recently, the British Government introduced two national agencies to control aspects of quality in health service provision. These are the National Institute for Clinical Effectiveness, which will disseminate guidelines on good clinical practice, and the Commission for Health Improvement, which will inspect the systems of clinical management (known as clinical governance) in health care organizations (Department of Health 1998, 1999). The United Kingdom is not alone in having developed an array of government initiatives to promote the quality of health services. Sweden, for example, has experimented with a range of different approaches to quality management, including ISO 9000, the European Foundation for Quality Management model and King's Fund accreditation (Shaw 1998).

Pressure has been brought to bear in several countries, notably the Czech Republic, Germany, Hungary, Poland, Portugal, Spain and Switzerland, to introduce accreditation systems (Shaw 1998). The main pattern has been the development of health service interest, followed by a government review of the possibility of accreditation. In most cases, however, the interest in accreditation has been short-lived and governments have chosen to use other methods of improving quality. This pattern is found in many eastern European countries. Accreditation has been given serious consideration by governments, but most appear to have shied away from introducing or endorsing an accreditation programme.

The failure to introduce accreditation cannot be attributed to a single cause. In any country, several health service organizations may express a desire to introduce an accreditation system; this is then begun but fails to generate universal acceptance or government support. One contributing factor is probably the difficulty of establishing a complex assessment system within a limited time. The selection and writing of standards and the establishment of an accreditation process are time-consuming. The most common way to introduce an accreditation system into a country that has little or no previous experience is to approach an organization with expertise in developing accreditation, and also to translate existing standards into the language of the country (Bohigas and Asenjo 1995).

Several countries, particularly those in eastern Europe, chose to approach the international arm of the JCAHO. In Hungary, for example, a joint project on accreditation was launched. Five chapters of the 1996 JCAHO manual were translated into Hungarian and five hospitals entered the pilot study. After a 6 month preparation period, three JCAHO and eight Hungarian surveyors visited the hospitals to perform a mock survey. The participating hospitals were reported to have found the project to be useful and, as a result, decided to establish the Hungarian Hospital Accreditation Process (G. Simó, personal communication). In the next phase of implementation, three more hospitals were enrolled and two more chapters of the manual were translated. But the accreditation process did not receive government support and so did not progress. The USAID office was closed. Nevertheless, interest in accreditation continues and the Hungarian branch of the European Organization for Quality has formed a body to continue promoting the ideas behind improving quality in health care.

The Czech Republic has similar experience in terms of developing accreditation following mock accreditation projects. In 1998, a Joint Accreditation Committee was formed, with representatives of hospital associations and the Ministry of Health. Hospital accreditation is voluntary, but there are proposals to tie it to the main third-party payer (the General Health Insurance Office) and to make it mandatory (G. Simó, personal communication).

In Portugal, the interest in accreditation has continued in the form of a voluntary independent activity through the creation of a national organization to promote quality in health care (AQUAS), which has been working with the King's Fund. AQUAS is made up of various national professional organizations: the Ordem dos Medicos, the Ordem dos Farmaceuticos, the Associacão de Administradores Hospitales and the Associacão de Enfermerias (Shaw 1998). The JCAHO has also been active in Spain, translating its standards into Spanish for use in the Spanish Health Service. In addition, Spain has tried several times to organize a national or regional accreditation system. The only developed system, the hospital accreditation programme in Catalonia, has existed for 16 years. In this case, accreditation was used as a certification tool. The hospital accreditation programme in Catalonia was created by the Department of Health of Catalonia (Bohigas and Asenjo 1995). In contrast to Portugal, where the majority of hospitals are in government ownership, most hospitals in this region of Spain are private, non-profit organizations. All hospitals wishing to renew their contracts were requested by the Department of Health to become accredited; those that failed to meet the accreditation standards lost their contracts.

Increasing interest in accreditation has to be placed against a backdrop of growing concern in government about the quality of health care. Many European countries have passed legislation intended to focus attention on improving organizational and clinical quality (Shaw 1998). The precise demands placed on health service organizations by legislation vary, but they share a common requirement to demonstrate that quality is being pursued and achieved. This is documented in the research reports produced by the study of External Peer Review Groups, on which the following summary is based (Shaw 1998).

In 1993, Austria passed legislation requiring health care organizations to introduce a quality assurance system covering structure, process and outcome. Each hospital has to have a central quality assurance committee to promote, coordinate and support quality assurance projects and introduce necessary improvements. In 1987, Belgium passed legislation coordinating the legal responsibilities of hospitals. Hospitals are required to obtain licences for building, expansion and rebuilding and the use of medical technology, and are required to meet standards laid down by the National Board for Hospital Facilities. The standards describe the structure and operation of core services by hospitals and the organization of emergency medical care and the quality of medical services. In Germany, the Fifth Social Act passed in 1991 requires hospitals to implement quality assurance systems covering organization, performance and outcome. The individual *Länder* have responsibility for implementing these goals. Italy has legislation requiring that public organizations demonstrate conformity with minimum standards. Since 1997, every Italian administrative region has had to develop a version of the accreditation standards and assess compliance using surveys. The standards stipulate that health care organizations must have an office for quality improvement, which is responsible for policies and procedures, human resource management and training, information systems and clinical guidelines. The Netherlands has introduced two laws. The first, stemming from 1997, controls professional practice based on the principle of self-regulation by professional bodies, while the second requires health care organizations to have internal quality systems that address patients' views. In Greece, legislation on quality in health care is anticipated in the near future. France has introduced a national accreditation system and the United Kingdom has legislated for two national bodies, one of which will control the development of clinical guidelines while the other will inspect the quality of the management of clinical activities.

The list of legislative changes (Shaw 1998) demonstrates the increasing activity on the part of governments in quality assurance. Approaches range from self-regulation through professional bodies to government inspectorates. Equally, there is variation in the specificity of approaches: some are highly prescriptive, such as the French definition of an approach to accreditation, and some merely demonstrate a desire for government agencies to devise methods of assuring quality. Common to all the legislation is an inherent and growing concern to regulate the extent and the nature of quality assurance activities, and ultimately to deliver improved quality of health care.

Governments appear to be more likely to be concerned with minimum standards. Hungary and Italy, for example, have both passed legislation requiring the development of minimum standards. Hungary passed a 'minimum requirements act' in 1997 that is implemented by the regional offices of the Ministry of Health. Even though 35 per cent of Hungarian hospitals have failed to reach the minimum standards, none has been closed.

Italy has chosen to implement a system of 'authorization' that requires health organizations to achieve minimum standards. The standards are designed to ensure that public hospitals meet the minimum requirements; failure to do so will result in sanctions against the hospital, and all private health care organizations will have to comply to receive public money. There are minimum standards that have been approved by law. Each of the 20 administrative regions has responsibility for developing its own version of the standards, and all are trying to decide whether this should be monitored using an accreditation model. It is probable that the promotion of government-devised standards has discouraged the development of voluntary accreditation systems.

Only three European countries have introduced accreditation systems run by the national government: Belgium, France and Scotland. The Belgian system, introduced in 1987, is administered by local government. Participation is compulsory and proof of accreditation is required for contracting with, and reimbursement from, the national insurance system. The national standards are based on planning requirements, are structural in nature and local government can add standards to reflect local needs. This is in reality a form of inspection.

Surveys of compliance with the standards are undertaken by full-time civil servants, all hospitals being visited at least once every 5 years. Interestingly, this is probably closest to the model due to be adopted in the United Kingdom under the work of the newly created Commission for Health Improvement.

France adopted accreditation in the Ordinance of 24 April 1996, which requires that all health care organizations, public and private, should participate in an external procedure of evaluation called accreditation to ensure the continued improvement of quality and the safety of care. The accreditation process is managed by an external agency called the Agence Nationale d'Accréditation et d'Evaluation en Santé (ANAES), which has responsibility for developing the standards and designing and implementing the accreditation process. The accreditation process is directly designed to promote the safety and quality of care and to ensure greater standardization of hospital and health care organization (ANAES 1999).

Scotland has developed an approach that does not conform to the traditional model of organizational accreditation (Scottish Office 1998). Instead, the NHS in Scotland has chosen to develop an accreditation programme based on clinical priority areas such as cancer, coronary heart disease, stroke, diabetes and mental health. Each clinical area will give rise to an accreditation programme. To coordinate standards development and the accreditation programmes, Scotland has introduced a Clinical Standards Board.

Accreditation based on clinical service areas is becoming increasingly popular, with small clinically based accreditation programmes in many countries. These can be operated by professional bodies, as in the accreditation programmes of the Royal Colleges in the United Kingdom. Cancer services in particular have an affinity for accreditation approaches. Cancer is an area of clinical activity where variations in clinical practice and in outcomes are relatively easy to identify. Accreditation systems have been developed by several different bodies concerned with the delivery of cancer services. Examples include health service agencies such as the regional offices of the NHS in the United Kingdom or professional bodies as in Paris. There is also a growing awareness of the opportunity to establish international standards for the delivery of cancer services. The Federation of European Cancer Societies has launched a European accreditation programme for cancer services.

Belgium and France have chosen to use external review systems. Other countries have chosen instead to promote what is termed 'self-assessment'. This is based on agreed standards but, instead of external review, health care organizations are left to determine their own levels of compliance and to take action accordingly. Iceland, for example, has introduced the JCAHO standards but uses a self-assessment process. In many cases, health care systems have attempted to promote the search for quality rather than the assurance of quality. This has resulted in the increasing popularity of approaches such as ISO 9000 or the European Foundation for Quality Management model. The adoption of these approaches has been caused by individual health care organizations volunteering to participate rather than as a response to a central government mandate. As a consequence, across Europe, examples of all these approaches can be found in almost all countries. The Netherlands (which has a mixture of scientific peer review reflecting the self-regulation expected of professionals together with various other quality control initiatives) has found it necessary to try to coordinate all this disparate activity conducted in the name of quality. Thus the Foundation for the Harmonization of Accreditation in Health Care has been established to control and endorse a range of quality assurance activities across the health care system. In Spain, the European Foundation for Quality Management approach has been developed for use in some regions.

Approaches to monitoring quality

It can be seen that different countries have adopted different models for monitoring quality assurance processes, reflecting different funding and accountability structures. The result is a complex array of combinations of dimensions of accreditation and inspection: some are compulsory, others voluntary; some are based on written standards, others on the judgement of inspectors. In the United States, there is now a range of accreditation systems, which are permitted to substitute for state-controlled inspection systems in assessing whether an organization meets the standards for receiving Medicare and Medicaid funding. The voluntary accreditation system is allowed to act in a quasi-regulatory way, and acts as a form of certification as well as providing a graded assessment of conformance with standards. In Canada, which has a publicly funded health care system, the CCHSA is an independent body providing almost total national coverage for the monitoring of health care organizations (Heidemann 1995). In the United Kingdom, NHS regional offices are required to monitor the quality of cancer services. To achieve this, several regions have developed compulsory accreditation systems that are being used to determine the suitability of organizations to provide services. This is similar to the situation for publicly owned hospitals in Catalonia, in which accreditation is acting as a licensing system for publicly owned organizations.

Accreditation and regulation

The description of the developments in accreditation systems demonstrates that accreditation is continually developing to reflect the changing social, political and technological environments of each country and health service. The most radical change in the development of accreditation has been the move towards government promotion or ownership. This has stemmed from a growing interest by governments in improving the quality of health care, which has caused them to review the use of accreditation as a possible tool for that purpose.

Nevertheless, relatively few governments have decided that accreditation meets their needs for the control of health care quality. The reasons that most governments reject the idea of accreditation vary. Some have needed rapid solutions; the development of local accreditation standards is a costly and time-consuming process, and the needs of impoverished health care systems are for rapid means to establish good practices. Many of the mature accreditation systems have developed complex logics that underpin the writing of standards and require sophisticated management infrastructures. Taking current accreditation standards from systems in other countries, such as Canada or the United States, may not fulfil the requirements for minimal standards to perform the function of licensing. Also, accreditation standards and processes were originally designed for application by independent bodies. This defeats the purpose of government regulation. Accreditation by independent bodies demands either that the government accepts that provision will be questioned by a body over which it has no control, or that it establishes a complex and workable relationship with the accrediting body. In the case of France, ANAES has a quasi-independent relationship. In the United Kingdom, the new Commission for Health Improvement will have a similar quasi-independent status. The judgements made have to be in tune with government policy and the funding is from government, although the external body has to be seen to remain independent. These relationships are very difficult to manage from a governmental level. Brennan and Berwick (1995) refer to the difficulties associated with regulatory capture. The accrediting body becomes too close to the organizations it is surveying and is not as impartial as required. For governments this is a difficult issue; it is better to seek another mechanism that does not require such complex capabilities from the public administration system.

The operationalization of the regulatory framework tends to hinge on whether participation in the accreditation process remains voluntary or is made compulsory, whether there are standards and whether there is a scoring system that denotes a pass or a fail. Across Europe there are a range of different approaches. France, for example, has introduced a standards-based accreditation system, participation in which is compulsory but which offers a qualitative report rather than a rigid assessment. The United Kingdom will have a compulsory inspection system, which will probably operate without standards but through which qualitative reports will be provided. The other major factor influencing the operation of the review process is whether the findings of the review are to be placed in the public domain. For governments of countries where hospitals are felt to have social and community meaning, outright criticism of the quality of hospital care is difficult. Certainly comments on quality that suggest the need to close hospitals generate considerable local debate and intensify community interests to protect hospitals, which results in political pressure to increase funding to hospitals. This is undoubtedly the case where public hospitals are concerned. Where external review processes have been introduced, however, most governments are finding that it is necessary to make public the results of all reviews and inspections. This tends to result in reports on quality of services being open to public discussion and negotiation, rather than based on definitive quantitative algorithms. Thus regulation of quality has to incorporate discussion and negotiation with local communities.

If governments are to use a form of review that reveals failings of health care organizations, there is a need for mechanisms to act on the findings. This is particularly sensitive when hospitals are in public ownership. Frequently, the capacity of the health service is limited by the extent of public funding. For a government to produce information about failings that it cannot act on is, at best, to lose face and at worst to be considered incompetent. It is therefore possible to argue that accreditation, organized by independent bodies and established by the self-interest of the health care organizations, is preferable. Furthermore, self-regulating businesses are held to have a better understanding of their own processes and functions and can more easily identify and act on sources of problems. Based on a model presented by Braithwaite (1985), Brennan and Berwick (1995) argue that the debate about enforcement revolves around the distinction between deterrence and compliance. The deterrence model is based on a view that the regulation model must be rule-based, whereas the compliance model is based on persuasion and a desire to encourage the best behaviour.

Rule-based models require definitive prescription of processes and procedures. Nevertheless, there is a growing belief within health services that outcomes are of greater value than process in assessing quality. But this view questions the role and nature of regulation in the quality of health care. Can outcomes form the basis for the regulation of quality in health care? In 1979, McAuliffe made the following claim: 'No regulatory body can insist that patient outcomes be positive, nor do positive outcomes ensure that care was appropriate and skilful. The goal of quality assessment is not to produce health but to determine whether acceptable care was rendered' (McAuliffe 1979: 121). This statement assumes that the factors contributing to patient outcomes lie within the unforeseen response of an individual patient to treatment. All that could be expected was that patients were provided with the expected treatment, carried out in an expected manner. Two decades later, there is a greater belief that medicine can be the subject of systematic analysis leading to expected outcomes. Regulatory bodies are seeking measures of outcome to determine whether health care of an acceptable quality has been provided. But the diagnosis of the factors contributing to poor outcomes still requires process standards to impute where the health service system has failed.

Whether the focus is on outcome or process, the creation of standards requires a consensus across health care organizations. In countries such as Italy and Spain, and to some extent the United Kingdom, where the administration of health care is devolved to regional bodies or governments, there is tension between central government and regional control of quality. Where there is strong regional control of health service provision and performance, there is frequently pressure to ensure equity of provision and quality of care between the regions. This can lead to pressure, either from national governments or parts of the health service, to centralize the monitoring process. Nevertheless, the greater the autonomy given to the regions, the more likely it is that the regions will resist central control and institute their own forms of quality monitoring. In Italy and Spain, several regions have sought to develop quality assurance approaches. Independent national initiatives have failed to produce universal regional acceptance. Where the regions are not wholly autonomous, as in the United Kingdom, regional initiatives can still be found running alongside national governmental initiatives to promote quality of health care.

External review systems have been criticized by health care management experts as being punitive and demotivating to staff (Berwick 1989). However, as public concerns about safety and efficiency have demanded that health care systems demonstrate that they have quality monitoring systems in place, external review has become accepted as necessary. The crucial lesson learnt in recent times is that it is necessary to find a way of reviewing organizations and their performance against standards, while at the same time ensuring that staff are motivated to continually strive to achieve higher quality. The key is ensuring that the standards are written to reflect an appropriate level of performance, that the staff are encouraged not only to reach the standards but to find ways of surpassing them, and that the philosophy embedded in the conduct of accreditation continues to be one of support to achieve improvement rather than simply providing inspection. Brennan and Berwick (1995) claim that regulatory mechanisms were created to keep health care both honest and safe, but without change they may become serious impediments to the best efforts of health care to evolve and improve. 'They should attempt to cooperate with health care providers, to specify outcomes, and to cultivate innovation. They should adopt many of the modern methods of improving the quality of their work that providers are now adopting for theirs' (Brennan and Berwick 1995: 396). Regulation in the control of quality in health care cannot be based on coercion – it has to be based on persuasion and support to health care professionals.

References

Agence Nationale d'Accréditation et d'Evaluation en Santé (1999) *Préparer et Conduire votre Démarche d'Accréditation*. Paris: ANAES.

Berwick, D. (1989) Continuous improvement as an ideal in health care, *New England Journal of Medicine*, 320: 53–6.

Birch, K., Scrivens, E. and Field, S. (2000) *Quality in General Practice*. Oxford: Radcliffe Medical Press.

Bogdanich, W. (1988) Small comfort: prized by hospitals accreditation hides perils patients face, *Wall Street Journal*, No. 72.

Bohigas, L. and Asenjo, M.A. (1995) Hospital accreditation in Catalunya: an assessment of the performance in quality of hospitals, *International Journal of Health Planning and Management*, 10: 201–8.

Braithwaite, J. (1985) *To Punish or Persuade*. Albany, NY: State University of New York Press.

Brennan, T.A. and Berwick, D.M. (1995) *New Rules*. San Francisco, CA: Jossey-Bass.

Department of Health (1998) *The First Class Service*, London: Department of Health.

Department of Health (1999) *Clinical Governance*. London: Department of Health.

Duckett, S. (1983) Assuring hospital standards: the introduction of hospital accreditation in Australia, *Australian Journal of Public Health*, 42: 385–402.

Hayes, J. and Shaw, C. (1995) Implementing accreditation systems, *International Journal of Quality in Health Care*, 7: 165–72.

Heidemann, E. (1993) *The Contemporary Use of Standards in Health Care*, WHO/SHS/DHS/93.2. Geneva: World Health Organization.

Heidemann, E. (1995) Client centred accreditation, *International Journal of Health Planning and Management*, 10: 209–22.

Maxwell, R., Day, M., Hardie, R., Lawrence, H., Rendall, M. and Walton, N. (1983) Seeking quality, *Lancet*, 1: 45–8.

McAuliffe, W. (1979) Measuring the quality of medical care, *Milbank Memorial Fund Quarterly*, 57: 118–52.

Roberts, J.S., Coale, J.G. and Redman, R.R. (1987) A history of the Joint Commission on Accreditation of Hospitals, *Journal of the American Medical Association*, 258: 209–22.

Schyve, P. (1995) Models for relating performance measurement and accreditation, *International Journal of Health Planning and Management*, 10: 231–43.

Scottish Office (1998) *Acute Services – Review Report*. Edinburgh: Scottish Office.

Scrivens, E. (1995) *Accreditation: Protecting the Professional or the Consumer?* Buckingham: Open University Press.

Scrivens, E. (1996) A taxonomy of accreditation systems, *Journal of Social Policy and Administration*, 20: 114–24.

Scrivens, E. (1997) Assessing the value of accreditation systems, *European Journal of Public Health*, 7: 4–8.

Scrivens, E. and Heidemann, E. (1995) Editorial, *International Journal of Health Planning and Management*, 10: 1–5.

Scrivens, E., Klein, R. and Steiner, A. (1995) Accreditation: what can we learn from the Anglophone model?, *Health Policy*, 34: 193–204.

Shaw, C. (1998) *External Peer Review in Europe*. London: CASPE.

chapter five

Corruption as a challenge to effective regulation in the health sector

Tim Ensor and Antonio Duran-Moreno

Introduction

Corruption has been defined by the World Bank (1997: 8) as the 'abuse of public office for private gain'. We will adapt this definition to recognize that much corruption takes place at the nexus of state, private and quasi-private activity. The chapter focuses on the use of power and influence by a practitioner, official or organization for self-enrichment that conflicts with the official public role. It examines both individual corruption, where state officials act in a quasi-private role to use their influence and public resources to obtain unofficial benefits, and organizations that operate in a coordinated way to exploit their position.

Opportunity to act in an exploitative manner occurs in a number of ways. One example is the availability of payments that can be obtained from those requiring a commodity or service that significantly exceeds the official price demanded of the consumer. Such payments may occur when government controls the availability of a product and minimizes the market. Command economies that seek to control the supply of commodities are seen by some as ideal breeding grounds for such corrupt practices (Lui 1996).

Although corrupt activity can result from government control, regulation as such is not necessarily wrong. Governments may intervene for good microeconomic reasons when a market mechanism fails to maximize welfare. In the health sector, the principal–agent relationship generates considerable potential for supplier-induced demand. If governments do not control this practice, it can lead to escalating costs and a misallocation of resources to treatments that are profitable but not necessarily effective.

Institutional arrangements can also provide opportunities for corruption (Mauro 1998). In the health sector, hospitals frequently behave like local monopolies.

This power, combined with the fact that costs to patients are subsidized, provides an opportunity for providers to exploit their position and extract extra payments. A further issue is the ability of medical practitioners to generate demand themselves, arising from unequal information on illness and treatment options. This provides an opportunity for obtaining payments above what would be obtained with full information.

Mauro (1998) has suggested that the opportunity for obtaining bribes is likely to lead to excess expenditure on investment as opposed to recurrent spending. The reason is that large bribes are likely to be obtained from companies seeking contracts for large capital projects or pharmaceutical supplies. In contrast, bribes from spending more money on items such as staffing or hospital food could be harder to coordinate.

The level of accountability is important in moderating the amount of corruption. If decisions by officials are openly known and subject to close public accountability, then although opportunity for rents may exist, the ability to benefit from them may be low. On the other hand, individual corrupt activity is more likely where administrative corruption is endemic, as the pressure to accept bribes is much greater (Advig 1991; World Bank 1997). System administrators may, for example, tolerate the taking of bribes by practitioners provided that they themselves are permitted to take bribes from supply companies.

Types of health sector corruption

The number of groups involved in the health care system and the numerous interactions between them provide various opportunities for corrupt practices (Figure 5.1). Corruption can be classified into four main types – bribes, theft, bureaucratic corruption and misinformation. Each is motivated by potential gain from exploiting one's position in the system – either direct financial gain through individual or institutional financial transactions or, more generally, through an increase in power and influence. The first three draw on the definitions described in the World Bank report on corruption (World Bank 1997).

Bribes

Bribery involves payments made to (state) officials to secure services that should be made without payment, to ensure higher quality services, or to circumvent a queue or tender process. Bribes may be paid for essentially two purposes: to secure or guarantee a service that the official should provide but withholds in whole or in part (demand side), or to secure preferential access to contracts (supply side).

Demand-side bribes

Many of the unofficial payments by patients to doctors and other medical staff can be classified as demand-side bribes. Bribes may be used to ensure adequate service quality or to obtain quicker access to services. In each case, the practitioner

Figure 5.1 Health service actor relationships and types of corruption

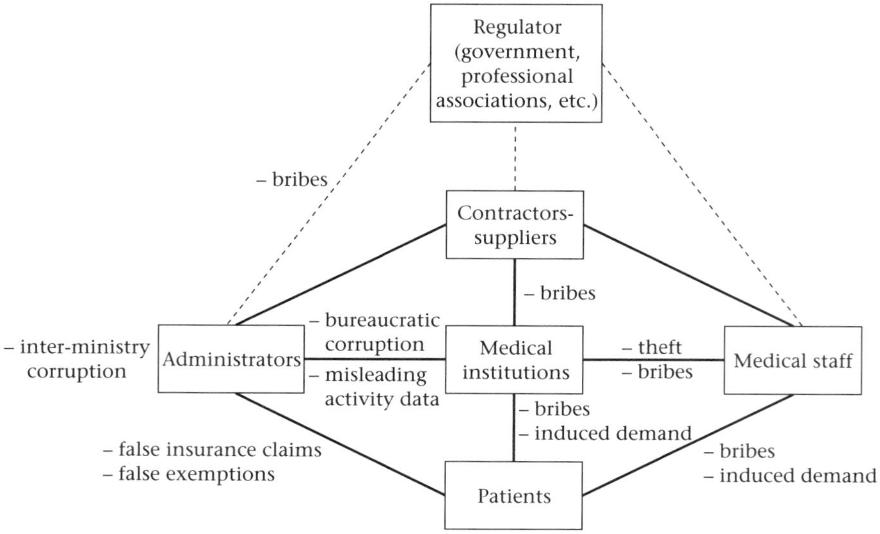

is abusing a position of power when there is a limited supply of the service and where a significant subsidy is publicly provided. Some patients need medical care quickly and are willing to pay considerable sums to secure treatment. This provides the necessary opportunity in terms of expected (financial) benefit.

Several types of payment may appear to be bribes but have a rather different purpose. For example, a patient may pay for drugs or other supplies because the facility does not have sufficient funds to pay for them. The payments may be made directly to staff, or a patient or relative may buy the supplies from a retailer. Essentially, the payment arises because of a gap between the state commitment to finance health care and actual available resources. Payments might be regarded as a product of the state's inability to provide what was promised, but they cannot be regarded as corruption. The alternative to this type of contribution is that patients do not receive effective treatment due to a lack of supplies. This may contribute to delays in treatment or, in the case of Bulgarian hospitals at the end of 1996, to large numbers of patients being sent home because of a lack of resources. An exception to this is where staff intentionally withhold available supplies from a patient because they know a patient will pay for them. The payment itself, while notionally for supplies, actually goes to staff.

A second, more contentious example is when a facility has insufficient funds to pay the staff their full wages. This is similar to a lack of medical supplies, but in this case a patient's payment goes to the staff. We might even extend this definition to include failure not just to pay official wages but an inability to pay the worker's target wage.

A related issue is whether physicians can legitimately accept gifts from patients without reciprocal favours. Even if payment is not made until after treatment, there is an implication that an explicit or implicit agreement to the payment is made prior to treatment (Lyckholm 1998). The issue is made more complex by the fact that a patient could use the gift to guarantee good service next time. It should be noted that in the countries of the Commonwealth of Independent States (CIS), bribes are often called 'gratitude payments', even though they are expected by staff and determine the service provided.

Supply-side bribes

Supply-side bribes arise when an official, or group of officials, has some discretion over who should supply services. Companies or individuals who wish to supply a particular service give bribes to those in the position to agree to the contracts. Endemic corruption within different organizations may lead to tacit 'contracts' or understandings between organizations.

'Kick-backs', whereby medical professionals accept monetary or non-monetary payments for buying and prescribing certain drugs or referring their patients to certain private services, are a well-known form of bribe. Group practices providing services for populations of between 5000 and 10,000 can have substantial public budgets to purchase medical supplies and services. Pharmaceutical companies are widely believed to influence drug purchase decisions through free samples and invitations to conferences in exotic places.

Another example is fee-splitting, whereby a specialist shares a fee with the referring physician. The considerable autonomy of the medical profession over prescribing and referral means that the potential for such behaviour is considerable. In 1998, for example, a group of Italian general practitioners (GPs) were suspended for accepting bribes to send their patients to a particular private centre for radiological examinations (Turone 1998).

Theft

The theft of state assets by officials charged with their stewardship is a second common type of corruption. In the health sector, there are several ways this might occur.

Pilfering of supplies

Petty pilfering of supplies is common in many state and private organizations. In the United Kingdom, it is estimated that pilfering, for example of bandages, medication and stationery, adds up to more than £15 million annually (*BBC Online* 1998a). In an Andalusian hospital in Spain, it was estimated that pilfering of food supplies led to per capita catering costs that were higher than those of a good restaurant (Hospital Universitario Virgen del Rocío 1994).

Public subsidy for private services

Staff in public medical institutions have the opportunity to deliver private care using public resources. This includes the use of equipment, supplies and, perhaps most importantly, time. Sometimes known as creeping privatization or privatization from within, the practice is common in transition economies (Ensor 1997) but is also prevalent in established market economies. Services offered to patients may include simple additions to the treatment already provided as part of the official state package of care. Alternatively, a doctor may provide treatment entirely on a private basis during the time he should be spending on public duties and/or using public supplies and equipment.

Another possibility is for a public doctor who also has a private practice to spend less time than contracted for in public facilities to extend the amount of time in private practice. It is almost commonplace in the United Kingdom to suggest that consultants spend time in private clinics when they should be attending to their public duties. Some hospitals have gone so far as to hire private investigators to follow consultants in an effort to estimate the extent to which this occurs (Rogers and Lightfoot 1995). Similar concerns can be heard in other countries, particularly in southern but also in eastern Europe.

The presence of creeping privatization and private practice impinging on public duties may be seen to be different sides of the same coin. In countries where non-staff inputs are relatively expensive, and regulation of behaviour in the public facility is weak, the first pattern of practice is likely to be favoured. Where the cost of non-staff inputs is trivial compared to staff costs, and there is strong control over the public facility, then the latter practice may be favoured.

Large-scale theft of public money

It is often argued that changing the method of allocating funding from one that is dependent on input normatives and tight control of budget line items to one that is output- or outcome-oriented can increase efficiency. This shift, however, may place an unprecedented amount of financial power in the hands of health service managers. Suddenly, hospital directors control entire hospital budgets rather than having most spending predetermined by the size of the institution. Insurance fund directors have control of large amounts that would previously have been channelled through the tax collection authorities. Not surprisingly, these and other 'reforms' increase the scope for corruption, particularly in societies in recession.

A number of examples of insurance fund fraud have come to light in transition economies. In one country in central Asia, a head of a regional private insurance fund was convicted of embezzling the funds of the company. Later, the same person was appointed head of the regional public fund! In Estonia, there were several insurance fund scandals in 1994 involving the directors of the newly created county funds, who made use of the fund reserves for their own private purposes. In the Russian Federation, the head of the Perm *oblast* health insurance fund was dismissed and later prosecuted for fraud. Although the actual charges were of personal fraud, allegations suggested misuse of insurance revenues for the benefit of fund officials amounting to more than 130 million (old) roubles (Tchugaev 1996).

Bureaucratic and political corruption

State officials and politicians may make policy decisions for financial reasons or to further their own careers. They may, for example, approve the building of a hospital, or stop its closure, to increase the chance of being elected to parliament or some other representative body. Whether this behaviour is punished or even considered as corruption probably depends on the nature of the transaction. If a politician works to keep an inefficient or unneeded hospital open for political gain, he is likely to be applauded by the local community. On the other hand, where state assets are disposed of to gain favour – which might be classified as a form of theft – then corruption is more likely to be identified. The motivation behind such actions is often ambiguous, making regulation difficult.

Abuse of state resources ultimately led to the resignation of the Luxembourg health minister in January 1998 (Ramsey 1998). The Ministry was accused of paying more than US$1.66 million over 6 years to private organizations, including construction companies, to garner influence with industry.

The misallocation of money in the health sector is often covered up by complex rules on the allocation of finances. In Italy, there are reports of contracts obtained under fraudulent circumstances to build hospitals that are still incomplete 10 years later (*The Economist* 1998). In the former Yugoslav Republic of Macedonia, the health minister was ousted after corruption charges, including claims that he had obtained generic drugs through fictitious companies and that humanitarian aid for Albania was diverted to his country and sold at western prices. There is an implication that he benefited directly from this corruption (*Nova Makedonija* 1996).

Misinformation for private gain

The misuse of information for private gain has a number of forms.

Abuse of the principal–agent relationship

The health care market is dominated by a principal–agent relationship where a patient trusts an agent (often but not always a doctor) to make an informed choice about the best treatment. The agent does not have full information but has more information than the patient or is in a better position to make use of it. Corrupt activity might be defined as the agent deliberately misusing and misleading the patient for his own private gain. This may be in the form of misleading a patient into agreeing to inappropriate or ineffective treatment (supplier-induced demand) or into obtaining less than the appropriate level of treatment (supplier-reduced demand).

One of the dangers of provider payment reform in transition economies is that it may introduce incentives for inducing demand without installing systems for monitoring and control. A good example is the introduction of diagnostic-related groups (DRGs), which (even in the United States with its relatively sophisticated systems of control) led to reported instances of

DRG creep, such as reclassifying patients into more lucrative categories (Culyer and Posnett 1990). This raises questions about the introduction of similar systems in transition countries, where management control systems are far less developed.

Collusive fraud

Another type of information problem is where the patient and the practitioner collude with each other to deceive some other agent, often the state. In Kazakhstan, for example, it is reported that doctors regularly provide false health reports, in return for payment, so that patients can obtain driving licences. Similar behaviour may exempt people from serving in the armed forces or secure sick leave from work. Certain doctors may build up a reputation for providing such 'services'. Indeed, it has been argued that, in some countries, a system of GPs funded by capitation would lead to competition for patients on the basis of doctors who offer the most certificates!

A further form of fraud through misinformation is where practitioners forge medical consent forms for patient participation in medical trials to boost income. In 1996, an English GP was struck off for forging 12 consent forms (Dyer 1996).

Prescription fraud

The position of GPs provides opportunities for prescription fraud. General practitioners, operating in collaboration with pharmacists, may issue bogus prescriptions. In Spain, GPs and pharmacists colluded in prescribing a non-existent and expensive drug that had been placed on the prescribing list by mistake. When the patient went to pick up the drug from the pharmacy, he was given a cheap drug with a similar name (Bosch 1998). In the United Kingdom, it is estimated that prescription fraud resulting from forged prescriptions by pharmacists, together with patients falsely claiming exemptions, costs around £30 million annually (Warden 1996). Similar stories are told in Spain (*El País* 1999). In the Russian Federation, prescription fraud has become a massive problem, partly because the system of exemptions is largely not computerized. In Germany, certain sickness funds are suspected of granting illegal exemptions to strengthen their market position (Flintrop 2000).

False insurance claims

Patients may also be involved in health service corruption through false claims on insurance premium forms. Since such declarations mostly refer to risk-rated systems, this is mainly a problem that relates to voluntary private insurance. The state equivalent of this phenomenon is where people avoid paying or pay a reduced contribution for state insurance. Self-employed people may make false declarations of income for tax purposes. People who are employed may cover up the fact to qualify for state assistance. This type of corruption begins to blur with wider issues of tax and social security fraud and will not be pursued further here.

Impact of corruption

The possible impact of corrupt activity can be divided into three areas: the health care system and health, entrepreneurial activity and the macro-economy.

Impact on the health care system and health

Contributions to the cost of care made by patients may have the potential to maintain the health system. All the other types of unofficial activity are likely to damage the ability of the health care system to deliver good quality and effective care to those most able to benefit. Some, such as pilfering and unnecessary prescriptions, simply divert public money into private hands without any gain for patients. Where commodities such as drugs are sold on to other consumers, the end users will often be those who can pay the highest price rather than those with the greatest need. Bribes may permit some patients to obtain treatment more quickly or to a better standard, but to the detriment of others. The system perverts the principle of allocation according to need to one of allocation according to income.

Misallocation of public money for political purposes is theft on a grander scale, often for non-financial but nevertheless self-enriching reasons. Again, resources are diverted away from health care. Unnecessary induced demand implies expenditure on services that are not clinically effective, appropriate or cost-effective. In addition, those most in need are likely to suffer. In fact, there is growing evidence that high levels of corruption make people poor, increase inequalities and reduce health status.

The overall impact on the health sector is hard to quantify in any country. Reports from Moscow have suggested that up to 30 per cent of the (federal) budget is not accounted for. In the United Kingdom, estimates of £115 million are given for prescription crime alone, a substantial figure but small (about 0.2 per cent) in comparison to the overall budget (Department of Health 1998; *BBC Online* 1999).

Impact on entrepreneurial activity

The presence of a substantial quasi-private system operating within the public sector is arguably detrimental to the development of a strong private sector. It may often be more profitable to provide private services using the convenience of public facilities, supplies and public time and also a ready supply of patients, rather than go to the expense of establishing a private clinic and mechanism for recruiting patients.

A key policy question is whether doctors should be permitted to work both in the public and private sectors. While this question has some meaning in the wealthier European countries, in the poorer ones the real question is what type of private practice should be encouraged – quasi-private or fully private? This is an extremely complex issue. Prohibiting fully private out-of-hours practice may help to ensure that public physicians do not attend private clinics when they should be doing their public practice. It also reduces the possibility that physicians will refer patients to their own private practice or increase public waiting times to encourage greater use of the private sector. At the same time, it is likely to increase the chance that they will carry out unofficial private activities during state hours.

As with other forms of corruption, it is important to consider whether the activity arises mainly because wages are low or because of inadequate regulation. In the former case, quasi-unofficial and private practice can be viewed as just two of a number of 'coping' strategies for providing a target income. If all opportunities are closed to staff through greater enforced penalties, then they may leave the sector altogether. Where corruption takes place mainly because regulation is lax or corruption is endemic, the policy responses need to be rather different. The challenge is to develop a regulatory framework that isolates instances of such corruption.

Impact on the macro-economy and international status

Much of the recent literature on corruption (World Bank 1997; Mauro 1998) argues that corruption significantly reduces economic growth and private-sector investment. As in other sectors, corruption in the health sector has spill-over effects on the macro-economy. Resources might be wasted, as with unfinished hospitals, or lost to the domestic economy, as with the loss of contracts for prescriptions to international business. Productivity could also suffer as a result of treatment taking longer than necessary because of the need to pay a bribe before treatment commences.

Assessing the level of corruption

There is no objective measure of health service corruption that can be consistently applied across the region. Even a simple count of the number of reports on corruption in each country is prone to error and systematic bias. High numbers are likely to reflect the relative openness of reporting, or the level of public antipathy towards the practice, as much as the overall level of corruption.

Evidence of unofficial payments in the health sector

There is a small but growing body of evidence on the prevalence of unofficial payments for health care in the transitional countries of the WHO European Region. For example, the informal cost of an operation per patient in Bulgaria amounted to more than 80 per cent of average monthly income (Delcheva *et al.* 1997). A recent study in Poland found that 46 per cent of patients paid for services that were officially free (Chawla *et al.* 1998). In Kazakhstan, estimates suggest that patients contribute around 30–35 per cent of state spending in unofficial payments (Ensor and Savelyeva 1998; Sari and Langenbrunner 1998). Since the estimates were derived from both patient and household surveys, it is likely that they underestimate the amount given directly to staff. Patients are often reluctant to reveal amounts given to staff, particularly during a short, impersonal and quantitative interview.

In an unpublished survey conducted in Bulgaria in 1994, almost 43 per cent of 1000 respondents reported having paid cash for officially free services in a state medical facility in the preceding 2 years. Nearly two-thirds of respondents were in favour of introducing official user fees (Delcheva *et al.* 1999). In 1999, in another survey conducted by the same team with 412 respondents, the proportion of those who had paid a doctor or dentist had risen to 51 per cent; of these, 77 per cent said they were 'not satisfied' with the public service.

Ladbury (1997), employing in-depth focus group techniques, found that, in one poor rural area of Turkmenistan, patients make a range of substantial non-monetary gifts to practitioners. Doctors make treatment conditional on payment and tailor their demands to a patient's income. Estimates suggest that the payments, when valued in money terms, collectively contribute more than 13 per cent to actual expenditure on health care.

Several studies point to a semi-structured system that rewards most levels of staff at different stages of the care process. In Kazakhstan, specialist hospitals have developed a sophisticated system of referring patients from one professional to another, with payments made at each stage in order to receive care (Thompson and Rittmann 1997). A 1998 report in the Albanian *Klan* magazine suggested that workers ranging from porters and cleaners to doctors all receive payments, the highest being for those carrying out specialist procedures such as heart surgery. The same magazine found typical payments for routine surgery in the range US$15–100, compared to the average monthly salary of a university professor of US$135.

Most of these studies, however, have not attempted to gauge the importance of wages in relation to payment. Physicians in OECD countries generally receive incomes 2.5–4 times the national average wage. Since physicians in eastern Europe receive a wage that does not normally exceed the national wage, it could be argued that unofficial payments that are less than double wages should not be considered rent-seeking behaviour. Arguably, this could be considered part of the survival strategy of workers and is, at worst, an example of what has been described as 'petty' corruption (Pope 1995).

Classifying countries by corruption level

From a theoretical perspective, countries might be divided into three categories: where corruption is endemic, where there are corruption epidemics and where corruption is limited to isolated instances. Subdividing further, the types of corruption might be divided into grand and petty corruption (Table 5.1). Grand corruption is where either large financial transactions are involved or where the activity leads to large-scale distortion of policies or power relationships. Petty corruption is where the corrupt activity does not lead to large

Table 5.1 Levels of corruption in society

	Endemic	*Epidemic*	*Isolated*
Grand corruption	Widespread bureaucratic corruption	Widespread prescription fraud	Isolated instances of any of the corruption types
Petty corruption	Small and routine payments to doctors – also cultural corruption	Petty theft	
Misconduct/survival strategies	Cost contributions for medical supplies	Promoting better access	

distortions. In practice, the division may take the form of a spectrum, but the basic distinction between grand and petty corruption still holds.

Both petty and grand corruption need to be distinguished from misconduct, which is based on personal or community survival strategies. This distinction does not have as much to do with the size of the transaction (some survival strategies may necessitate substantial payments) as with the reason for the activity. While both grand and petty corruption principally distort the optimum (community) allocation of resources for personal gain, in the case of survival strategies mutual benefit is produced through resource reallocation. Although the boundary may not always be very clear, this fundamental distinction would appear to hold in a wide variety of cases.

The strategies for dealing with countries that fall into different cells are likely to vary. In countries where there are isolated instances of even major corruption, the approach may be to deal with institutions or individuals on a case-by-case basis while improving the general regulatory framework as a result of case experience. In countries where corruption is endemic, an individual approach is unlikely to get to the heart of the fundamental problem. In these countries, it becomes much more important to develop transparent mechanisms for reporting and separate regulatory institutions. Apart from these extremes there may also be countries where, although corruption cannot be considered an accepted part of daily life, levels are high. This could be categorized as epidemic corruption. An example is prescription fraud and the petty theft of supplies from health facilities.

While there are no health corruption indexes, there are general corruption measures that, while being prone to error, can give a general picture of practice across Europe. One measure is the annual survey-based *Corruption Perspectives Index* published by Transparency International (1999), which attempts to measure business perceptions of corruption. Another measure is to use the black market factors included in the *Index of Economic Freedom*, published regularly by the Heritage Foundation (O'Driscoll *et al.* 2000). The index itself includes many factors reflecting overall levels of 'freedom'. While there is a strong ideological dimension to the index, there are six indicators of black market activity that appear to be reasonably free of bias (smuggling, piracy of intellectual property, agricultural, manufacturing, transportation, and labour and services supplied on the black market).

Although the positions vary for some countries, the two indices are quite similar for most. Countries can be divided into three or four distinct groups. Those with relatively low black market and corrupt activity include most of north-western Europe, while those with a moderate level include the southern part of western Europe and one or two 'western-leaning' central or eastern European countries such as Hungary. Much of eastern Europe falls into the next category, along with the more developed CIS countries. Finally, the less developed CIS countries fall into the high-corruption group, along with several of the poorer eastern European countries.

Assuming that health sector corruption mirrors general corruption, these measures give some indication of the extent to which corruption is embedded in society. Where corruption is strongly embedded, it is likely that levels of all types of corrupt activity will be high and the health sector will also be affected.

Approaches to policy

Regulating corrupt activity within the health sector is a complex and difficult task. In developing a strategy, several important conceptual and practical issues should be addressed. The first and most important of these is to determine the underlying reason for corruption. For example, do unofficial payments ensure survival of the system (by cost contributing) or do they reduce its impact through efficiency and equity loss (by bribery)? Policy decisions must be made as appropriate responses to the source of corruption or the underlying problem will not be addressed.

Second, it is imperative to distinguish between societies where corruption is an endemic and cross-sector problem and others where epidemics or isolated instances of corruption are the norm. In the former case, it is unlikely that specific attempts to eliminate instances of health service corruption can fully succeed, since the root cause is institutionalized within structures that cross sectoral boundaries.

Cost contributions

When payments are made to close the gap between the state promise to finance health care and the actual funding available, this helps the systems to survive. There are equity implications, however, since the poor may be discouraged from accessing facilities as a result. On the other hand, informal cross-subsidy and price discrimination may mean that lower payments are sought from this group.

Imposing harsh regulation in this case could simply have the effect of making it unprofitable for staff to remain in the state health care sector. They may leave for the private health care sector or for other employment opportunities. Since better doctors have greater potential to earn income in other occupations, it is likely that such a policy would reduce the quantity and quality of medical practitioners. A necessary, but not sufficient, condition for reducing corruption might be to ensure that civil servants, including medical staff, receive a salary that is comparable with that which they would receive in a similar job (and with job security) in the private sector (Pope 1995).

Reducing cost contributions in a meaningful way requires a reduction in the size of the gap. This can be done either by reducing the scope of the service guaranteed or by *increasing the funding available*. Most transitional countries have attempted to do the latter by introducing compulsory health insurance. Many have found that the extra resources provided are quite small and are outweighed by practical problems of coordinating multiple funding sources and developing a meaningful purchasing capacity. *Reducing the state guarantee* is being examined by several countries. Georgia, which has suffered the largest decline in revenue of all the CIS countries, has already introduced quite substantial reductions in the scope of state-financed care. In other CIS countries, changes have been less pronounced (Ensor and Thompson 1998). The Russian Government is currently engaged in an ongoing review of the benefits package, and changes to increase the efficiency and reduce the scope of financed services are under consideration (Feeley *et al.* 1999).

There is a danger with the restriction of guarantees approach – particularly where it leads to differential access, for example by providing some services for low-income groups but not others – that one type of unofficial payment will be substituted for another. Rather than cost contributions, people may pay instead for the right to obtain discretionary free services. There is some evidence in the former Yugoslav Republic of Macedonia, for example, that differential exemptions led to the extraction of bribes from people in return for certificates of exemption (Duran *et al.* 1995).

A complementary approach is to *formalize patient contributions* to care. This is certainly attractive to some as a way of making unofficial contributions to care more explicit, as a survey in Bulgaria showed (Delcheva *et al.* 1999). There are dangers with such a policy. One is that unofficial payments are often charged in a way that permits subsidy from rich to poor. This may be more difficult to do within a formalized system. Another is that patients may actually prefer paying unofficially, since they are then sure that they can get a particular doctor. Paying a charge to the hospital or clinic puts them back in the lottery of obtaining a good or poor quality practitioner. It is likely, therefore, that a such a policy could only work if choice over the medical practitioner is maintained.

Another issue is that, while formalization of payments may reduce contributions, it does not solve the problem of extracting rents from patients. It may, however, make it easier to distinguish between the two types of 'bribe' and therefore easier for policy-makers to penalize continuing offenders. The focus should be on the incidence of major corruption. All too often the reverse is the case: it is often easier to make an example of one or two minor cases while leaving the endemic corruption in place.

Demand-side bribes

In contrast to cost contributions, regulation through penalties for demanding additional payments will not deter doctors from the sector. To separate those taking cost contributions from those taking rent payments, it will be important to raise the average incomes of practitioners. Simply paying practitioners in different ways – incentive payments based on fee for service, for example – is unlikely to be effective unless the practitioner can achieve his or her target income.

In terms of current regulation, there are few accounts of people who have actually been prosecuted for accepting unofficial payments. Indeed, there is anecdotal evidence from some countries that, even if professionals are held to account and prosecuted, the case often fails because key members of the legal system are paid off. However, a number of cases of health professionals who have been prosecuted for receiving unofficial payments have been reported. On 11 January 1999, the Bulgarian newspaper *Standard* reported on a doctor who was arrested for taking a bribe of more than US$1100. Only a few days later, on 24 January, the same newspaper wrote that a doctor unofficially took more than US$230 (Davidov, personal communication 1999). Given that a state doctor's salary is less than US$100 per month, such payments probably convert into annual sums that exceed the benchmark of 2.5–4 times the national average income suggested earlier.

Corruption, particularly endemic corruption, may be a symptom of deeper problems that cannot simply be dealt with through the creation of new agencies, greater penalties, internal regulating mechanisms or better pay for health staff. A country that does not have a clear system of property rights, an independent legal system and an accountable public sector may produce more corruption opportunities than countries that do have these institutions.

Creating accountable systems

Simple and accountable systems

A principal enemy of good regulation is the use of payment systems that are either overly complex or management systems that are not sophisticated enough. In the United Kingdom, an example would be the complex reimbursement regulations that are used for NHS contractors. Simpler and more transparent procedures, it is argued, could reduce the scope of confusion and possibility of fraud (*BBC Online* 1998b). In Moscow, the immense workload imposed by monitoring a vast number of prescription exemption claims, together with the lack of a computerized information system, has led to substantial fraud.

Many countries, particularly those in eastern Europe, are reforming their provider reimbursement systems. Often reforms have dismantled, or have suggested dismantling, centrally planned normative systems in favour of local control of budgets or cost-per-activity systems. Although there is no direct and automatic link between the payment system and the level of corruption, both changes have potential problems. In the latter case, the systems have tended to lead to an increase in the supply of services (Von Bredow 1995; Ensor 1997). If the additional services are inappropriate, however, and are thus added solely to receive additional payment (as seems to be the case in many transition economies), this itself could be described as a type of corruption.

In the case of a global budgeting system, the main concern is that spending responsibility is allocated to providers without establishing an adequate system for accountability. While eastern European systems are quite good at regulating expenditure when money is centrally allocated, systems for auditing decentralized systems based on modern income and expenditure accounting are not yet in place. Another concern is that, when a system involving weighted capitation is used, the subsystems required to construct weights are not transparent and are open to abuse.

Separation of sector functions

Health sector financing and organization are dominated by three resource factors: sources of overall financing, allocation of funding and use of resources to provide service. Ensuring that these three functions, and the flows between them, are transparent is an important part of any anti-corruption strategy. When the rules and flows are not clear, there is much more potential for corruption.

One way of improving transparency is to encourage an organizational separation between these functions. The insurance fund–provider split developing in much of eastern Europe is one example of such a separation. The aim is to make the financial allocation on the one hand, and the outcome of funding on the other, more transparent and open to evaluation.

In eastern Europe, a key problem has been ensuring that agencies, such as insurance funds and health administrations, are really independent of other organizations involved in finance, and at the same time are accountable to a regulatory agency. In practice, new organizations such as insurance funds have often remained inextricably linked to administrative agencies. It would also be a mistake to imagine that such institutions can overcome the strong culture of endemic corruption existing in such countries simply by being new and (ostensibly) independent.

Developing regulatory strategies

Several strategies can reduce the prevalence of corrupt activity. For regulation to be effective, patients' rights must be clear, channels for complaints must be simple and well defined, regulatory agencies must be strong and trusted by the public, and ways of combating corruption must be as public and transparent as possible.

Regulatory agencies

A question of major importance is the development of agencies charged with auditing public-sector institutions. In the Russian Federation, for example, the federal budget payment monitoring organization monitors the spending of the state budget. It is appointed by the legislature (Duma) to which it reports. Reports suggest that, while it has often revealed instances of public-sector corruption, action is rarely taken against the perpetrators. It has also been implicated itself in some corruption scandals. Development of a truly effective system of auditing and accountability that not only reveals corruption but acts on the findings remains one of the greatest challenges and stumbling blocks to reform in European transitional economies.

Transparency International (Pope 1995) has recommended a number of principles that should apply to the development of an ombudsman or regulatory agency. Members should be well paid and appointed for a limited period of time in an open and accountable way. Lay membership in the agency ensures that proceedings are less likely to be governed by the interests of the profession and that the agency will respond in an impartial manner. Meetings of the agency should be open where possible. The agency should have the legal power to require that departments provide the information necessary to prosecute individuals found to have abused their position.

Transparent processes

An important part of anti-corruption strategies is to make all processes more explicit and transparent. Publishing information on public perceptions of corruption about particular government departments or medical institutions could be used as a measure of public service quality. Surveys of patients as to whether they have to make payments at specific facilities could also be useful.

A further possibility is that, within existing institutions, workers who are dedicated to reducing corruption should form anti-corruption groups. These are partly self-help, self-support groups to help workers maintain their anti-corruption stance. They function to inform the public that bribes are not required for this group of workers. For example, doctors dedicated to not accepting unofficial payments could publicize the fact through their membership of such a group. Publicizing membership of these groups alongside surveys of patient payments would provide useful information for patients when choosing health facilities.

The effectiveness of information disclosure depends on several factors. One is whether patients have a choice over which facility to attend. Another is whether consumers view unofficial payments as an unambiguously negative aspect of the system.

Rights and compensation

Ensuring that the rights of patients are clear, realistic and enforceable is key. Coalition 2000 (1999), a non-governmental group of civil society organizations in Bulgaria backed by the President and committed to reducing the prevalence of corruption, has suggested that the system for making complaints and taking these through the courts should be simplified and made less costly. Although out-of-court settlements can be easier for patients wishing to settle quickly, the danger is that these are preferred by those accused of corruption because they minimize publicity. A straightforward complaints procedure where less serious offences are dealt with by an independent ombudsman is preferred.

Many constitutions in former communist countries of Europe create high expectations of what is guaranteed by the state. This has contributed to the gap between what is promised and what is provided and has led to unofficial cost contributions by patients. In Kazakhstan, for example, regional insurance fund heads often complain that they spend a considerable amount of their time in court defending the fund against accusations of negligence, which arise mostly from a lack of funding. It is important that patients' rights are realistic or it will be impossible to distinguish between genuine instances of corruption and those created by artificially high expectations.

Given that it may be difficult to assign responsibility to one individual, legislation may be required that makes the head of an organization or department legally responsible for the actions of that body. This would circumvent a common problem in the Russian Federation, for example, where lack of individual responsibility means that no-one is properly held accountable.

Market incentives

Baldwin and Cave (1999) suggested that market incentives might be used to provide more effective regulation of an industry. These could be applied to address health sector corruption. One way of doing this is to embody good practice in an enforceable and revocable contract with providers. A method considered, but not used, in Romania was to give senior specialists a 5 year contract that would pay them 2–3 times their current salary for good practice. The contract would contain a clause that revoked the contract if unofficial payments were accepted. Regulation through peer pressure can be exploited, since those who do not receive such a contract (and thus who receive a much lower official salary) have an incentive to report the holder for taking payments. One problem with the latter mechanism is that this is only successful if workers do not collude to play the system. Contract holders might agree, for example, to pay part of the additional salary to non-holders in return for not informing on their unofficial activities. The advantage of incentives is that, unlike specific regulatory procedures, they are introduced for everyone, and do not require individual instances of delinquent behaviour to be isolated.

International cooperation

For countries where corruption is endemic, a great deal could be done to begin to reduce it. Yet it is not possible to do this alone. Increasingly, independent groups such as Transparency International, and bilateral and multilateral institutions such as the World Bank and OECD, are recognizing the need for international cooperation. One such measure is for established industrialized countries to make it a criminal offence for their citizens to bribe foreign officials. A multilateral convention to this effect was recently signed by 34 countries, although most have yet to ratify the document (*The Economist* 1999).

It is highly desirable that an international capability is developed that looks specifically at corruption in the health sector and that takes account of the specific features of these markets.

References

Advig, J.C. (1991) The economics of corruption: a survey, *Studi Economici*, 43: 57–94.

Baldwin, R. and Cave, M. (1999) *Understanding Regulation: Theory, Strategy and Practice.* Oxford: Oxford University Press.

BBC Online (1998a) NHS fraud-buster appointed, *BBC Online*, 28 May.

BBC Online (1998b) NHS fraud soars. Quotation by Stephen Thorton, Chief Executive of the NHS Confederation, *BBC Online*, 9 December.

BBC Online (1999) Porter clears her name in appeal, *BBC Online*, 30 April.

Bosch, X. (1998) Spanish doctors on trial for drug fraud, *British Medical Journal*, 317: 1616.

Chawla, M., Berman, P. and Kawiorska, D. (1998) Financing health services in Poland: new evidence on private expenditures, *Health Economics*, 7: 337–46.

Coalition 2000 (1999) *Clean Future*. Sofia. http://www.online.bg/coalition2000/ (accessed 12 June 2001).

Culyer, A.J. and Posnett, J. (1990) Hospital behaviour and competition, in A.J. Culyer, A.K. Maynard and J.W. Posnett (eds) *Competition in Health Care*. Basingstoke: Macmillan.

Delcheva, E., Balabanova, D. and McKee, M. (1997) Under-the-counter payments for health care: evidence from Bulgaria, *Health Policy*, 42: 89–100.

Delcheva, E., Balabanova, D. and McKee, M. (1999) *Unofficial Fees in Bulgaria*. London: London School of Hygiene & Tropical Medicine.

Department of Health (1998) *Countering Fraud in the NHS*. London: Department of Health.

Duran, A., Hoare, G. and Baris, E. (1995) *Health Care Reform in Macedonia*. Copenhagen: WHO Regional Office for Europe.

Dyer, O. (1996) GP struck off for fraud in drugs trials, *British Medical Journal*, 312: 798.

El País (1999) Juicio en Barcelona por un fraude médico [Trial in Barcelona for medical fraud], *El País*, 4 March.

Ensor, T. (1997) What role for state health care in Asian transition economies?, *Health Economics*, 6: 445–54.

Ensor, T. and Savelyeva, L. (1998) Informal payments for health care in the former Soviet Union: some evidence from Kazakhstan and an emerging research agenda, *Health Policy and Planning*, 13: 41–9.

Ensor, T. and Thompson, R. (1998) Health insurance as a catalyst to change in former communist countries?, *Health Policy*, 43: 203–18.

Feeley, F.G., Sheiman, I.M. and Shishkin, S.V. (1999) *Health Sector Informal Payments in Russia*. Moscow: Institute for the Economy in Transition.

Flintrop, J. (2000) Werbemaßnahmen auf Kosten der Vertragsärzte?, *Deutsches Ärzteblatt*, 97B: 1334

Hospital Universitario Virgen del Rocío (1994) *Informe sobre las Cocinas Centralizadas del HU Virgen del Rocío* [*Report on the Centralized Kitchens of the University Hospital Virgen del Rocío*]. Seville: Hospital Universitario Virgen del Rocío.

Ladbury, S. (1997) *Turkmenistan Health Project Social Assessment Study*. Ashgabat: World Bank/Government of Turkmenistan.

Lui, F. (1996) Three aspects of corruption, *Contemporary Economic Policy*, 14: 26–9.

Lyckholm, L.J. (1998) Should physicians accept gifts from patients? *Journal of the American Medical Association*, 280: 1944–6.

Mauro, P. (1998) Corruption: causes, consequences, and agenda for further research, *Finance and Development*, 35: 11–14.

Nova Makedonija (1996) Health ministry corruption, *Nova Makedonija*, 27 February.

O'Driscoll, G.P., Holmes, K.R. and Kirkpatrick, M. (2000) *2000 Index of Economic Freedom*. Washington, DC: The Heritage Foundation/Wall Street Journal [summary available at http://www.heritage.org/index/execsum.html].

Pope, J. (ed.) (1995) *National Integrity Systems –The TI Source Book*. Berlin: Transparency International.

Ramsey, S. (1998) Corruption proves end of Luxembourg health minister, again, *Lancet*, 351: 349.

Rogers, L. and Lightfoot, L. (1995) NHS hires private detectives to spy on doctors, *The Sunday Times*, 15 January.

Sari, N. and Langenbrunner, J. (1998) *Out-of-Pocket Payments in Health Care: Evidence from Kazakhstan*. Washington, DC: World Bank.

Tchugaev, S. (1996) Chevrolet, for health and wealth, *Izvestia*, 16 July.

The Economist (1998) Laughter through Italian tears, *The Economist*, 5 December.

The Economist (1999) A global war against bribery, *The Economist*, 16 January.

Thompson, R. and Rittmann, J. (1997) A review of specialty provision: urology services, in R. Thompson, T. Ensor and J. Rittmann (eds) *Health Care Reform in Kazakhstan*, Compendium of papers prepared for the World Bank Health Reform Technical Assistance Project, 1995–96. York: Centre for Health Economics.

Transparency International (1999) *The Corruption Perceptions Index*. http://www.transparency.org/documents/cpi/index.html (accessed 12 June 2001).

Turone, F. (1998) Italian GPs suspended for accepting bribes, *British Medical Journal*, 316: 1264.

Von Bredow, L. (1995) The reform of health care in the Czech Republic, *Eurohealth*, 1(2): 22–5.

Warden, J. (1996) Fraud squad gets to work on prescriptions, *British Medical Journal*, 312: 730.

World Bank (1997) *Helping Countries Combat Corruption: The Role of the World Bank*. Washington, DC: World Bank.

Where entrepreneurialism
is growing

chapter six

Regulating entrepreneurial behaviour in hospitals: theory and practice

Reinhard Busse, Tom van der Grinten and Per-Gunnar Svensson

Getting the best of both worlds

In an entrepreneur's ideal world, one could decide to set up a hospital, determine how to run it and be responsible for all losses and profits. Such an unstructured and unsupervised environment would provide entrepreneurs with a wide variety of opportunities, some of which might be seen as desirable. Hospitals might invest quickly in new technologies or provide services that previously required hospital treatment on an outpatient basis. But such an environment would also pose serious problems in societies that had social objectives they sought to achieve, such as equity, social cohesion and protecting the health of the population. It is also inconsistent with the needs of public and statutory third-party payers seeking sustainable health care expenditure.

If a fully entrepreneurial landscape for hospitals is at the same time non-social, a fully anti-entrepreneurial environment would be one in which the national government decides the position and size of hospitals according to a public plan. Planning authorities would determine the range of services offered, and services would be delivered free to all citizens at the point of service; hence no prices would need to be set. Hospitals in both cases are not regulated in a specific sense. In the first case, there are no regulations to restrict the entrepreneurial behaviour of the hospital owners or managers, other than the general rules of competitive behaviour. In the latter case, the hospital is subject to public-sector 'command-and-control' without any discretionary power. In practice, most hospital environments fall somewhere between these two extremes and require substantial regulation to enhance, steer, support and restrict entrepreneurial behaviour within them.

After presenting a typology of hospitals, we outline how hospitals in various European countries currently fall between the two unregulated extremes described above. We analyse recent reforms in the hospital sector that seek to enhance hospital autonomy, and examine which areas of entrepreneurial behaviour should be regulated to achieve societal goals such as equitable access or the protection of the public's health. The essentials of support to entrepreneurial behaviour at the level of the hospital are then presented and are followed by brief conclusions.

Types of hospital in European countries

Typology of public hospitals

The OECD classifies hospitals into three groups: public, private not-for-profit and private for-profit. On closer examination, this classification is not sufficient for the current purpose, since 'public' covers a wide spectrum from 'command-and-control' to institutions with a great deal of independence. In the terminology of a recent World Bank study, they extend from 'budgetary' through 'autonomized' to 'corporatized' organizations (Harding and Preker 2000).

Budgetary organizations

A 'budgetary' hospital is an integral part of the public health service. The managers of such a hospital are essentially administrators. The health service's hierarchy of officials and rules controls all strategic issues and determines most day-to-day decisions related to the production and delivery of services (staff mix and levels, services offered, technology used, accounting and financial management methods, salaries, and so on). The term 'budgetary' refers to the fact that revenues are determined through a line-item budget, which is commonly set in relation to historical norms. If the allocated budget produces any 'excess revenues', it must either be returned or spent as directed. Any 'excess losses' are also covered by the public purse.

Autonomized organizations

'Autonomization' of such hospitals is a reform that focuses on transforming administrators into managers by shifting much of the day-to-day control of decision-making from the hierarchy to management. Accountability arrangements still generally come from hierarchical supervision, but objectives are now more clearly specified.

Implementation of autonomization in the health sector has led to a wide variety of arrangements. The amount of actual autonomy given to management has varied considerably. In some cases, the organization has been legally established as a new form of government agency, serving to define the new governance arrangements, secure the changes made and persuade management that the changes are irreversible. These performance requirements have sometimes been recorded in a framework agreement or 'performance contract'. Financial autonomy is also increased, usually by moving from a line-item to a global budget, whereby savings in one service or budget area can be shifted to another. Additionally, the global budget may be adjusted by case-mix or activity and the hospital may be allowed to generate additional revenue (such as through private patients) or retain a portion of any budgetary surplus from one year to the next.

Corporatized organizations

If autonomy is taken a step further to 'corporatization', provisions for managerial autonomy are even stronger, giving managers virtually complete control over all inputs and issues related to the production of services. The hospital is legally established as an independent entity and hence the transfer of control is hard to reverse. The independent status includes a budget constraint or financial 'bottom-line' – which makes the organization fully accountable for its financial performance – with liquidation at least theoretically being the final solution in case of insolvency.

Market-derived incentives are based on a combination of an increased portion of revenue coming through contracts (rather than budget allocation) and more possibilities for keeping extra revenue. The independently managed hospital is thus often more a residual claimant than is the autonomized one, in that it can retain excess revenues, but is also responsible for losses. In an independently managed hospital, directors and board members usually have absolute responsibility for the performance of the hospital and are fully accountable to the (governmental) owner. In this case, the governmental owner does not behave very differently from private not-for-profit owners.

Public and private not-for-profit hospitals

While in the countries in north-western Europe with a Beveridge-type health system (Ireland, the United Kingdom and the Scandinavian countries) hospitals are almost entirely public (with more than 90 per cent of beds being public),[1] the actual division across the spectrum described above is less clear and is constantly changing. The same applies to the public hospitals in the national health service (NHS) type of system in Italy, Portugal and Spain, where the public share of hospital beds is 78, 77 and 69 per cent, respectively, but with large variation between regions. In Spain, public hospitals fall into two categories of roughly equal size: those owned by local governments and those owned by the institutions managing health services (such as INSALUD). The former have much in common with public hospitals in Bismarckian countries, since they need a contract with INSALUD or the equivalent regional authority, while the latter have much in common with British hospitals before the purchaser–provider split. In the countries of central and eastern Europe (CEE), as well as in those of the Commonwealth of Independent States (CIS), most hospitals are public, usually owned by local and less frequently by national governments (Jakab *et al.* 2001).

In the 'classical' social health insurance (SHI) countries there are two different patterns, both of which differentiate them from Beveridge-type countries: the mix between public and non-public hospitals and the status of public hospitals *vis-à-vis* third-party payers. Hospitals in Austria, Belgium and Germany are mainly public (with some 69, 60 and 55 per cent of beds, respectively) with not-for-profit hospitals in second place (about 26, 40 and 38 per cent of beds, respectively). France also has mainly public hospital beds (65 per cent) but private for-profit hospitals take second place (20 per cent) and not-for-profits third (15 per cent). Hospitals in Luxembourg are equally divided between public and private not-for-profit; only in the Netherlands are all hospitals (except the university hospitals) legally private not-for-profit entities. One needs to be careful with labels, however, as similar legal entities are categorized in one country as 'public' and in another as 'private not-for-profit'.

'Public' hospitals in these countries (as well as in CEE countries that introduced SHI systems in the 1990s) are never typical 'command-and-control' institutions. Due to the natural purchaser–provider split, every hospital has a certain degree of managerial independence, since it has to sign contracts with the health insurance funds. This situation may even be fixed by law; for example, the hospital law in the German *Land* of North Rhine-Westphalia demands that public hospitals be 'independent and economically operating units' (Pugner 2000).

Every public hospital in SHI countries is thus, at least to a certain extent, an 'autonomous' and often 'corporatized' actor in health care.[2] A second characteristic that differentiates public hospitals in Bismarckian countries is that the (local or regional) public owners are not the same as the (regional or national) public regulators in governments or governmental agencies.[3]

The situation is also different for private not-for-profit hospitals in SHI countries. In contrast to Beveridge systems, where such hospitals typically are less controlled through the governmental hierarchy than public hospitals, not-for-profit hospitals in Bismarckian countries are usually subject to the same amount of regulation as public hospitals concerning capacity planning, resource allocation and reimbursement, quality assurance, etc. Differences exist only in ownership and in regulations concerning governance and management issues.

Private for-profit hospitals

Besides public and private not-for-profit hospitals, most European countries have a private for-profit hospital segment. This varies in size, but is particularly relevant in the south-western European countries of France (20 per cent of all beds), Spain (18 per cent), Portugal (10 per cent) and Italy. This segment, however, usually has two very different sub-segments: those hospitals that are contracted by health authorities or health insurance funds to provide publicly financed health care services (in Italy, this is the case for almost 80 per cent of private beds; Marinoni and Macchi 1999) and those that deliver services for private payers only. The first group is usually subject to regulation similar to that of other hospitals, while the latter is closer to the initially described entrepreneur's ideal world. In fact, many of the attributes of the latter type of private hospital result from not having a contractual relationship with health authorities or sickness funds – that is, from being exempted from most regulations that ensure equal distribution, access and financial sustainability.

The changing landscape: transforming hospitals into more autonomous actors

A major focus of government activity towards hospitals in the 1990s was the attempt to make them and to encourage them to become more entrepreneurial.

Beveridge countries

The English White Paper *Working for Patients* stated that making hospitals self-managed and permitting them to compete to attract patients would improve efficiency, quality and the responsiveness of services (Secretaries of State for Health 1989). A similar reasoning is heard in other countries following the British reforms, most notably in Sweden, Italy, Spain and, more recently, in Portugal.

The 1991 British reforms that transformed hospitals from 'directly managed units' of the health authorities into trusts have various facets that should be clearly differentiated: the introduction of a purchaser–provider split, the development of contractual arrangements between the two sides, and increasing latitude in decision-making and financial autonomy for the hospitals regarding salaries and staff mix.

Most Beveridge-type countries have given attention to only one or two of these issues. Only in some parts of Spain and in Sweden (especially in Stockholm and Bohus) were all components pursued simultaneously. Spain has recently seen a considerable variety of new forms of hospital autonomy, as various regions have created different versions (Martin Martin 1999). In 1990, Catalonia was the first region to formalize a purchaser–provider split and invented 'consortia' as a legal form, both allowing minority private participation as well as contracting out management or other functions to the private sector. Consortia are governed by a mixture of public and private law, the best known example being the Consortium of the Hospitals of Barcelona. Andalucia established the status of an 'entity of public law' for the new Costa del Sol Hospital in 1992. The hospital is governed by private law but is owned by the regional government. Galicia was the first to give its new Hospital Verin the status of a 'foundation', while others invented 'mercantile societies' in which the regional government is the shareholder. The Basque Country transformed its whole regional health service into a 'public entity under private law'; that is, individual hospitals form only part of the corporatized unit. The central government, which still controls health services in ten regions through INSALUD, followed the Galician example and transformed two new hospitals into foundations. Owing to labour contracts, however, the transformation of existing hospitals proved to be difficult. Late in 1998, a new variant – 'public health care foundation' – was therefore created to enable the transfer of personnel. Nevertheless, the use of this instrument is hindered by the fact that health care powers have to be devolved to the ten INSALUD regions, which have their own views on hospital management.

One clear lesson from the Spanish experience is that national governments can pursue *either* a programme of hospital autonomy *or* a programme of devolving powers to regions. Sweden faced this decision earlier and decided to opt for devolution, albeit under a tight national regimen of cost control (Diderichsen 1995). The widely differing routes towards hospital management included selling the operating activities of the public St Görans hospital in Stockholm to Bure AB, a private for-profit company, for some 210 million kronor in December 1999. This privatization had been facilitated by the hospital's transformation in 1993 into a limited company under the full ownership of the county council. As a privately operated hospital, St Görans has to contract with public purchasers – the first 3-year contract was part of the takeover agreement (K. Essinger, personal communication). That privatization could happen against the will of the national government demonstrates that every step towards corporatization has to be carefully considered, as it might have unforeseen consequences.

Finland is an example of a purchaser–provider in which several municipalities form a hospital district, which in turn operates the public hospital for the municipal owners. Contractual arrangements concentrate on the issue of dividing costs among the owners. Italy, on the other hand, places more emphasis on hospital autonomy with approximately 100 major hospitals transferred into trusts. Only in Lombardy was there a more systematic split between local health authorities and 27 hospital trusts. Contractual relationships between local health authorities and hospitals are weak, as regional health services have to reimburse hospitals directly. In the absence of a checks-and-balance system through contracts, the main outcome of reform was greater opportunity for opportunistic entrepreneurial behaviour by hospitals (L. Brusati and G. Fattore, personal communication). In another example, Portugal initially placed more emphasis on autonomy, by allowing public hospitals to be put under the control of private-sector management and releasing them from public employment regulations (Dixon and Reis 1999). Since 1997, this has been complemented by the gradual introduction of contracting agencies and a purchaser–provider split.

Other reforms also incorporate elements of these issues. In Denmark, the creation of Copenhagen Hospital Corporation in 1995 as an independent authority represents a purchaser–provider split, but not between a purchaser and an individual hospital but rather between a group of hospitals and a regional public purchaser (Ministry of Health 1999).

The United Kingdom experience has recently been evaluated in terms of efficiency, equity, quality, choice and responsiveness, and accountability (Hamblin 1998; Mays *et al.* 2000). Two observations apply. First, even for the comparatively well-researched United Kingdom, the quality and quantity of evidence on trusts is relatively low compared with that on other reforms such as fundholding. Second, the two issues (split and autonomy) are not considered separately and, therefore, conclusions cannot necessarily be extrapolated to countries with only one component. Using this framework of evaluation, conclusions about the United Kingdom reforms can be summarized as follows.

Efficiency

There is only limited evidence that trust status made British hospitals more efficient than they would otherwise have been. Bartlett and Le Grand (1992; 1994a,b) found some evidence that trusts have lower unit costs than directly managed units, but noted that first-wave hospitals appeared to be a self-selected group that had lower than average costs before becoming trusts. This view was challenged by Söderlund et al. (1997: 1128), who argued that when variation in case mix is included in the analysis, 'costs decreased significantly with the change from directly managed to trust status'. They conceded that it was possible that hospitals were intentionally less productive before becoming trusts, so that large gains could be shown on changing status. Since higher management costs could wipe out efficiency gains, two more recent studies on the relationship between management costs and hospital performance in the United Kingdom are particularly relevant. Söderlund (1999) found that higher spending on top-level management was associated with poorer productivity, and that total administrative inputs had a weaker though still negative association with productivity. Productivity could not be corrected for quality, however, so it might be possible that quality improvements reduced or even reversed the observed productivity losses. Street et al. (1999) found no general relationship between management costs and three dimensions of hospital performance (achievements of financial targets, meeting waiting time standards and costs) but suggested that performance reaches an optimum when management expenditure is around 5–6 per cent of hospital income.

For Sweden, a longitudinal analysis covering the years 1989–95 came to the conclusion that those counties that had introduced purchaser–provider splits with contracts, and a subsequent shift from input-oriented budgets to output-based allocations, demonstrated an increased technical efficiency resulting in potential savings of 9.7 per cent (Gerdtham et al. 1999).

In Spain, while economic studies analysing hospital efficiency and productivity are plentiful – among them cross-sectional studies concluding that public hospitals are either less efficient than private ones or that there is no significant difference (Puig-Junoy and Dalmau Matarrodona 2000) – specific evaluations of transformed hospitals are rare. Ventura and González (1999) come to the conclusion that the introduction of contracts between INSALUD and its own hospitals has reduced hospital inefficiencies. Similarly, a study comparing the one hospital performing as a public enterprise in Andalusia with 18 otherwise comparable hospitals came to the conclusion that it is the most efficient in the group of 19 hospitals (Casado and Rico 2000). A caveat is warranted, however, since the public enterprise hospital was not completely comparable, owing to its new buildings, new technology and younger staff.

Equity

Ensuring equity was not a major objective for trusts in the United Kingdom. There is some evidence that trusts gave preferential treatment to patients of general practitioner fundholders (Mays et al. 2000).

Quality

As no studies with a control group or a before-and-after design exist, the impact on the quality of services is difficult to judge. There are some concerns that different trusts in the United Kingdom had conflicting incentives that threatened the continuity of care. The positive example often cited is the reduction in waiting times but, as Hamblin (1998: 111) pointed out, 'any success of the waiting time initiative may be just that, the success of a specific policy with specific funding, rather than a product of the internal market'. If the latter had been the case, trusts should have reduced their waiting times more quickly than directly managed units. Smee (1995) noted, however, that the percentage of patients waiting for over a year fell between 1991 and 1993 at trusts and directly managed units alike. Similarly, the total numbers waiting increased at both trusts and directly managed units.

Choice, responsiveness and accountability

There is no evidence that trusts in the United Kingdom increased patient choice, and there are several convincing arguments why it was impossible for them to do so. One is the requirement placed on trusts to produce a 'business case' for all innovations; that is, to put efficiency over patient choice (Hamblin 1998). Another is the general purchaser-led decision-making in the NHS. Other countries that introduced more patient-led decision-making such as Italy and Sweden had different experiences (see below). It is therefore important to realize that autonomy *per se* does not improve choice and responsiveness. The same is true for accountability: although the United Kingdom hospitals trusts gained their own boards of directors, there is no evidence that trusts became more accountable to their local populations (Hamblin 1998).

Bismarckian countries

In Bismarckian countries, reforms often sought to increase the latitude and financial autonomy of decision-makers. The Netherlands, for example, transformed its remaining public hospitals into independent not-for-profit entities under private law during the 1990s. In Germany, the privatization of acute care hospitals has led to an increase in the share of private for-profit beds under contract with the sickness funds, from 3.7 per cent in 1990 to 6.8 per cent in 1998 (Busse 2000). At least as important, however, is the trend in contracting out the management of public hospitals to private companies. For example, the Sana Kliniken-Gesellschaft (owned by 33 private health insurance companies) manages 25 small- to large-size hospitals, among them two large teaching hospitals in Stuttgart.

In 1992, Germany abolished the full-cost cover principle for hospitals that had tied total reimbursement to total costs, and excluded both deficits and profits (Busse and Schwartz 1997). While this made hospitals (or hospital owners) residual claimants, one can argue that the decision-making latitude of hospitals was actually reduced. Previously, they could negotiate staffing inputs (and therefore costs) with the sickness funds, while both the fixed budgets from

1993 to 1996 and the prospective case and procedure fees since 1996 were regulated by the Federal Ministry of Health. The standardization of hospital reimbursement will be complete when the new system based on diagnostic-related groups (DRGs) takes effect from 2003 (Busse 2000).

In SHI countries, the introduction of volume- or case-mix-adjusted budgets or prospective performance-related reimbursements such as diagnostic-related groups does not generate increased autonomy for hospitals, as negotiated per diem rates have left more rights of decision-making to hospitals. Other components also make the direction of reform less uniform than in Beveridge countries. Since 1997, France has effectively united sickness funds as purchasers of hospital care within new regional hospital agencies, which act as contractors of hospital care (Mosse 1998). Similarly, Austria has sent a mixed message to its hospitals: DRG-type reimbursement with retained surplus is coupled with the introduction of regional authorities as purchasers of hospital care.

CEE and CIS countries

Hospitals in the CEE and CIS countries have been confronted with a variety of rapidly changing conditions. Two are especially relevant: the split between payers and hospitals and the growing autonomy of the hospitals themselves. By changing their financing systems to SHI, most countries have also separated payers from providers. This separation, however, requires a degree of autonomy for hospitals that is not always the case, such as in many Russian regions. In most countries, hospitals no longer function as direct budgetary units of the core public sector bureaucracy (Jakab *et al.* 2001). Nevertheless, the current organizational structure of the hospitals cannot (yet) be clearly labelled, as there is no consistency in their features within and across countries. In some other countries, such as Kyrgyzstan, many hospitals have remained real budgetary units.

General trends

Table 6.1 summarizes the major trends and outcomes of hospital reforms in European countries.

A final caveat about autonomized and corporatized hospitals should be mentioned here. If publicly owned health providers become more subject to market mechanisms, then the extension of the market to public services may become required under the provisions of the World Trade Organization (Price *et al.* 1999) and the European Union's Single Market (Belcher 1999). Paton *et al.* (2000) point out that, while some market-oriented regulation is needed, it should take into account the special nature of the health sector by allowing continued preferential treatment for rural areas, sharing expensive equipment between institutions, and so on. In the absence of such a strategy, the only option to exempt health care from the full force of Single Market legislation may be to make all providers (and third-party payers) part of government administration. Countries with SHI systems would clearly find this difficult if

Table 6.1 Major trends and outcomes of hospital reform in Europe

System	Purchaser–hospital split	Relationship between purchaser and hospital	Latitude for decision-making by hospital regarding services, staffing, etc.	Financial autonomy of hospital	Closeness to regulator ('regulator–hospital split')
Beveridge countries	Traditionally non-existent; fully introduced in Finland, Italy, Portugal and United Kingdom, and to a lesser extent in Denmark, Spain and Sweden	Traditionally part of the same hierarchy; contractual arrangements introduced as a result of purchaser–hospital split (notable exception: Italy)	Slightly to considerably increasing, e.g. in United Kingdom and some hospitals in Italy, Spain and Sweden	Moderately to considerably increasing, e.g. in United Kingdom and some hospitals in Italy, Portugal, Spain and Sweden	Increasing closeness in United Kingdom; other countries decreasing (Italy, Portugal, Spain) or continuously distant (Finland, Sweden)
Bismarckian countries in western Europe	Traditionally existing	Traditionally collective contracts between sickness funds as purchasers and hospitals; in Austria and France, increasing government involvement through regional purchasing agencies	Usually limited; no uniform direction of reform	Existing and arguably increasing through prospective forms of reimbursement, at least if they allow retention of profits	Generally distant; increasing closeness in Austria and France
CEE countries (except Albania)	In 1990, non-existent; during 1990s, introduced by changing to SHI	Traditionally part of the same hierarchy; contracts introduced as result of SHI	Generally low (high in certain Estonian hospitals)	Introduced but varying in extent	Not yet generally distant, as certain hospitals remain in national ownership
CIS countries	Varying widely from non-existent (e.g. Kyrgyzstan) to complete split (e.g. Georgia)	Depending on the existence of a split, often still part of the same hierarchy	Varying, but usually low	Varying, often low (but high, for example, in Georgia)	Often still high, although hospitals have often been passed to regional or local government

not impossible (Raad voor de Volksgezondheid & Zorg 2000). NHS-type countries, which have moved from direct command-and-control arrangements to giving hospitals more autonomy, may also be reluctant to take such a decision.

What areas of entrepreneurial behaviour need to be regulated?

Greater latitude for decision-making and financial autonomy for hospitals is only one side of the coin. The other is to guide such opportunities through regulations that steer hospital care towards fulfilling societal objectives such as equality in access and service quality, protection of the public's health (which also includes that of hospital employees) and sustainability of funding.

Enabling hospital care

All European countries seek to provide their citizens with access to high-quality hospital care. The first step is ensuring that the right physical structures are in the right place (McKee and Healy 2001). If the government is providing the hospital infrastructure through public hospitals, no regulation is necessary. In such countries, private hospitals may exist but are not taken into account in the planning process.

Countries that rely on a mix of public, not-for-profit and for-profit providers, however, proceed differently to ensure equal access to hospital care. Two main regulatory strategies can be differentiated: an *ex ante* approach through which the establishment of future hospital capacity is regulated, and an *ex post* approach through which existing capacity is (or is not) incorporated into a plan.

The *ex post* approach is used in Switzerland, where the health insurance law demands that private hospitals be 'appropriately' taken into account when the lists of hospitals are drafted by the cantons. Listed hospitals, regardless of their ownership, then qualify for reimbursement of services under the compulsory health insurance as well as for public subventions. The canton's decision on inclusion or exclusion can be challenged by submission to the federal government (Minder *et al.* 2000).

The *ex ante* approach is employed in Germany and the Netherlands. In the Netherlands, the Hospital Facilities Act of 1971 regulates the establishment of new hospital capacity. For this purpose, the country is divided into 27 planning regions, hospital plans being based on bed need standards prepared by the respective provincial government. Hospitals may not be constructed or renovated without successfully completing a declaration and licensure process. This is a four-step process including declaration of need, estimation of the area required and approval of the building plan, and issuance of the actual licence. Boot (1997: 175–6) concluded ambiguously 'that planning under the Hospital Facilities Act works well' but 'a better model may be needed'. He proposed that future regulation should be less detailed and leave more leeway to the individual hospitals.

In Germany, the approach to hospital plans varies between the various *Länder*. In Bavaria, the conservative government calls for 'mutual cooperation and division of tasks' (Bayerisches Staatsministerium 1992: 5). In Hesse, however, the then red–green government was of the opinion that 'further regulation is necessary' (Hessisches Ministerium 1993: 22). Bennema-Broos *et al.* (2001) demonstrate that the latter approach led to a more equal distribution of hospital beds in the state than the former. Nevertheless, lower costs per bed-day (7–8 per cent) and per case (4–5 per cent) in Bavaria (Statistisches Bundesamt 2000) could point to a possible trade-off between equity and efficiency.

Regarding payment for capital investment, the difference between the Netherlands and Germany is that the former demands the inclusion of depreciation costs in hospital budgets (which are paid to the hospitals in the form of per diem fees), while the latter covers them directly if an investment reflects the hospital plan – independently of ownership. In this respect, Belgium occupies an intermediate approach: 60 per cent of capital investment is directly covered by the regions and 40 per cent by the federal government via per diem fees (Kerr and Siebrand 1999).

The SHI countries that rely on regulation appear to be as successful in guaranteeing an equal distribution of hospital beds as NHS-type systems with direct public provision. In 1990, the coefficient of variation for regional numbers of hospital beds was below the average of 16.2 in all the SHI countries studied: Belgium 12.3, Germany 12.6, France 13.2, Austria 15.0 and the Netherlands 15.6. Within NHS-type systems, however, equitable distribution varied greatly: Finland 11.0, Sweden 13.1, Norway 13.3, Denmark 17.2, England 18.8 and Scotland 23.8. The least equitable distribution (29.1) was observed for Switzerland, which was also one of only two countries that had not improved in this respect since 1970 (Westert and Groenewegen 1999).

It is unclear whether arrangements such as the private finance initiative in the United Kingdom will lead to a more unequal distribution of hospital beds, as the additional charges and interest costs involved force hospitals to build fewer beds than deemed necessary by the government. In the case of the first 11 hospitals financed under the scheme, the resulting reduction amounted to 31 per cent (Pollock *et al.* 1999). A similar capital funding arrangement exists in the Spanish region of Valencia, where a private hospital was given a monopoly ('concession') to provide publicly financed health services in its catchment area.

Specifying and rewarding hospital services

Once hospitals are established, key policy issues include access, what types of service they should or may offer, whether they have to meet a minimum standard of quality and how they should be reimbursed.

Access

There are three major issues regarding access: (1) Does a hospital have an obligation to treat any patient requiring care, regardless of insurance status or potential profitability? (2) Is a hospital required to have an emergency department? (3) Are there physicians available at all times? Regulatory standards are typically imposed by government to ensure positive answers.

The issue of patient choice has also received attention. In the United Kingdom, neither a purchaser–provider split nor hospital autonomization led directly to increased choice. Once again, increased regulation does not automatically mean fewer entrepreneurial opportunities for hospitals, as the case of Sweden demonstrates. During the early 1990s, Sweden's county councils took steps to enhance patient choice and create incentives for public hospitals to improve their services. County councils revised their budgeting arrangements so that 'money follows the patient' rather than being allocated in advance to the hospital (Anell 1995; Rehnberg 1997; Harrison and Calltorp 2000). These reforms aimed to provide patients with prompt care and ensure their choice of provider instead of this being determined by residence. This was a similar move to that in Denmark in 1993 (Ministry of Health 1999) and in Norway through the 1999 Act on Patients' Rights. Together with other concurrent developments, such as the separation of purchasing from provision, this pro-choice regulation also laid the grounds for limited competition between hospitals that centred on access to care and, to a lesser extent, on perceived quality.

As a result, 2–5 per cent of total health care resources shifted to different providers compared to the previous allocation system (Rehnberg 1997). At the same time that it sought to generate demand-led pressures for improving services, the government also made a traditional move that created direct incentives for improving service quality. To guarantee prompt treatment for procedures having long waiting times, the government granted extra funding to hospitals but made these grants contingent on treating patients within 3 months of diagnosis (Hanning 1996). Similar steps were taken in Denmark, Finland and the United Kingdom (see above). These 'waiting time guarantees' are a separate regulatory instrument, and diminishing (visible) waiting lists are thus most likely not to be the direct effect of hospital autonomization.

In Sweden, patient choice and hospital competition appear to have led to substantial changes in the behaviour of hospital administrators and medical staff. For the first time in their history, these providers sought to compete with one another to provide prompt access to elective surgery. Although service quality improved, the market mechanisms had no noticeable negative affect on existing clinical quality (Harrison 1999). Not surprisingly, total utilization (and therefore expenditure) went up, creating the need for new budgetary regulations. This trade-off between choice and cost containment is also underlined through the Italian experience. In an environment with free patient choice and a DRG-based payment system, autonomized hospitals rapidly showed increased numbers of cases and thereby higher expenditure, forcing the government to cut DRG fees by 20 per cent.

Types of service

Should hospitals be allowed to offer whatever services they want or is regulation necessary? An often cited example of regulation that seemingly restricts entrepreneurial opportunities and innovation is the strict separation between ambulatory care and hospital care in Germany. From 1993, hospitals were allowed to offer ambulatory surgery and ambulatory care of inpatients for a few days before and after inpatient treatment. The incentives for these services were initially weak, however, since remuneration was included in the hospital budgets (Busse 2000). Obviously, giving legal monopolies to a group of providers (in this case the office-based physicians) may be to the detriment of potential efficiency gains. If, however, hospitals were allowed to compete fully with office-based physicians, then conditions such as reimbursement should be equal. This would necessitate the abolition of public subsidies for capital investments, which, in turn, could lead to a less equitable distribution of necessary technology.

Reimbursement

While financing hospitals through line-item budgets does not stimulate entrepreneurial behaviour, all other forms of financing (e.g. by individual procedure, bed-day, case or global budget) possess incentives to increase or reduce the number of cases, the length of stay, the number of procedure per case, and so on (Wiley 1998; Langenbrunner and Wiley 2001). The question is: Should payment be uniform via regulation or should hospitals be allowed to be paid differently, depending on their negotiations with the respective purchaser(s) or third-party payer(s)? While there are good reasons to regulate certain aspects of individual payment systems, there appears to be no compelling evidence for demanding an equal payment system for all hospitals. Transparency, lower transaction costs and ease of administration could be arguments for regulating reimbursement, but only if policy-makers rank these objectives as highly as ensuring equal access or high quality. Whether a particular payment system induces the desired entrepreneurial behaviour – or the opposite – often depends on local circumstances.

Protecting hospital employees

Another set of regulations concerns the protection of hospital employees. These regulations are usually not specifically directed at hospitals but rather towards employers in general. In some cases, hospitals have argued successfully that their specific requirements will not allow their inclusion in directives regulating all employers. The best known example is the Working Time Directive (93/104/EC). The 1998 proposal by the European Commission to include junior doctors met resistance from Ireland and the United Kingdom, where comparatively low levels of staffing among doctors are compensated for by long working hours. These countries pressed successfully for long transition periods before agreeing to the amendment (Belcher 1999).

Steering the business behaviour of hospitals

Once hospitals become established as an autonomized, corporatized or other kind of public enterprise that at least partially operates under private law, national regulators have to determine the appropriate financial restrictions and obligations to place on these actors. These include whether they can: roll over operating surpluses to the next budget year; borrow money from banks; sell their own assets; engage in activities outside the core business of providing care to patients; take over other hospitals; or merge with nursing homes or ambulance services.

The United Kingdom NHS has addressed some of these questions in guidance that regulates mergers, the exit of providers, conduct concerning pricing and costing, and collusive behaviour (Goddard *et al.* 1997). Difficulties of detection are acknowledged, especially as providers may engage in tacit rather than overt collusion. The penalties for collusion are cancellation of the contracts and 'management action' (NHS Executive 1994).

The guidance did not, however, prevent a substantial number of takeovers and mergers between trusts. In England, 54 trusts merged into 27 on 1 April 1999 alone (Robinson and Dixon 1999). One of the largest factors behind these mergers was the regulator and the government themselves (Dobson 1998).

Supporting entrepreneurial behaviour at hospital level

One important manifestation of entrepreneurial behaviour in European hospitals is *social entrepreneurship*. This variant mobilizes the entrepreneurial spirit for the public good – in this case, health care. The result is the application of elements of entrepreneurship in fields previously dominated by bureaucratic or professional medical principles. The aim is to achieve public goals with the aid of private-sector principles, including an orientation towards opportunity-seeking, a focus on innovation, the taking of commercial risks and an acceptance of responsibility in terms of the success or failure of business management. In this regard, social entrepreneurs do not differ from private entrepreneurs. Rather, differences emerge with respect to the specific goals and the context within which these tasks are realized.

To perform the function of social entrepreneur properly, four important preconditions must ideally be satisfied: trust, transparency and public accountability, supervision and entrepreneurial skills (Raad voor de Volksgezondheid & Zorg 1996, 1997; Thalhuber 1999; De Waal 2000).

Trust

Trust is a vital precondition for entrepreneurship, as organizations are more innovative and function more effectively on the basis of trust and confidence than on the basis of suspicion. This calls for a good deal of latitude in the legislation and, where possible, abandonment of a system of 'prior consent' for all kinds of decisions that have to be taken at the level of the individual hospital. This needs to be replaced by a clear division of tasks between the government and the hospital, as part of which the rules of the game are laid down in advance while performance is audited retrospectively.

Transparency and public accountability

It must also be possible for the confidence to be substantiated. Hospitals need to operate on an open basis and actively provide information to the various stakeholders outside the organization, especially to the government and third-party payers. They are the first to whom the social entrepreneurs are required to render account for the way in which they achieve public goals with public and private resources (Van der Linden and Meijs 1998). Social entrepreneurship in health care thus requires a clear, strong and independent system of accountability and control on the basis of which adjustments can be made.

Supervision

The third pillar is supervision. Regulations are required to establish the rules of the game in advance and auditing in retrospect. In the case of supervision, the social legitimization of entrepreneurial behaviour must be added. Put differently, the procedures, structure and organization of regulation need to ensure that the conduct of social entrepreneurs measures up to the applicable rules and generally accepted values and norms in the health care system (Commissie Health Care Governance 1999).

Entrepreneurial skills

Entrepreneurship is also characterized by personal qualities such as initiative, creativity, motivation, perseverance, enthusiasm, competitiveness, inventiveness and willingness to assume risks (Drucker 1986). In the case of the social entrepreneur, the same qualities come into play, but several others are added relating to 'political' skills in respect of stakeholder, network and media management (Drucker 1992; Osborne and Gaebler 1992) and the skills needed to run a professional organization. This calls for investments in training programmes aimed at social entrepreneurship and at attracting, supporting and keeping talented social entrepreneurs. Analyses of social entrepreneurship have to date paid little attention to the incentives for entrepreneurial behaviour. The right balance between financial and psychological rewards could eliminate the need for excessive bureaucracy.

   These conditions for social entrepreneurship are directly affected by regulation – either hindered or supported. The support of entrepreneurial behaviour is not necessarily identical with its stimulation *per se*, as regulation may also restrict entrepreneurial behaviour from heading in an undesirable direction.

Conclusion and discussion

Europe's hospital landscape is changing rapidly. While previously public hospitals under command-and-control management were the norm in Beveridge-type systems, hospitals are now usually separated from purchasers, and often this split is accompanied by managerial autonomy for the hospitals. In the CEE countries, the introduction of SHI systems also separated hospitals from the (newly established) payers, but autonomy has been slow to follow. The fewest changes have occurred in western European SHI systems with traditional hospital–payer splits and a public–private mix of hospitals.

The transformation of hospitals from institutions under 'command-and-control' financed by line-item budgets into autonomous, corporate and sometimes private entities requires regulation that was previously not necessary. In this respect, what is often viewed as 'deregulation' (i.e. giving more independence to hospitals) actually increases both the scope of regulation and the demands on regulators. An important conclusion is that increased regulation does not automatically mean less entrepreneurial opportunities for hospitals.

While many countries are following the route to autonomy, the empirical evidence to support this move in terms of efficiency, equity, quality, choice, responsiveness and accountability is not clear-cut. Most studies have focused on efficiency and the results ranged from beneficial (in Sweden) to probably beneficial (in the United Kingdom). These efficiency gains might be partly offset by higher management costs, however. In terms of quality, the often cited example of reduced waiting lists is probably more directly due to specific regulations focusing on this issue.

Notes

1 Although a variety of sources was used for calculating the percentages, the *Health Care Systems in Transition* profiles (HiTs), if they existed for the countries in question, served as the primary source.
2 The term 'corporatized' in this sense should not be confused with 'corporatism', which, in the context of SHI systems, refers to self-regulation by corporatist institutions such as hospital associations, with powers delegated to them by law.
3 This is also the case in decentralized Beveridge-type systems, such as those in the Scandinavian countries. In the United Kingdom, however, the transformation of hospitals into trusts has led to the opposite.

References

Anell, A. (1995) Implementing planned markets in health services: the Swedish case, in R.B. Saltman and C. von Otter (eds) *Implementing Planned Markets in Healthcare*. Buckingham: Open University Press.
Bartlett, W. and Le Grand, J. (1992) *The Impact of the NHS Reforms on Hospital Costs*. Bristol: School for Advanced Urban Studies, University of Bristol.
Bartlett, W. and Le Grand, J. (1994a) *Costs and Trusts*, Studies in Decentralisation and Quasi-Markets No. 18. Bristol: School for Advanced Urban Studies, University of Bristol.
Bartlett, W. and Le Grand, J. (1994b) The performance of trusts, in R. Robinson and J. Le Grand (eds) *Evaluating the NHS Reforms*. London: King's Fund.
Bayerisches Staatsministerium für Arbeit, Familie und Sozialordnung (1992) *Krankenhausplan des Freistaates Bayern*, Stand 1.1.1992 (17 Fortschreibung). Munich: Bayerisches Staatsministerium für Arbeit, Familie und Sozialordnung.

Belcher, P. (1999) *The Role of the European Union in Healthcare.* Zoetermeer: Raad voor de Volksgezondheid en Zorg.

Bennema-Broos, M., Groenewegen, P.P. and Westert, G.P. (2001) Social-democratic government and spatial distribution of health care facilities: the case of hospital beds in Germany, *European Journal of Public Health*, 11(2): 160–5.

Boot, J.M. (1997) Hospital planning, in A.J.P. Schrijvers (ed.) *Health and Health Care in the Netherlands.* Maarsen: Elsevier/De Tijdstroom.

Busse, R. (2000) *Health Care Systems in Transition: Germany.* Copenhagen: European Observatory on Health Care Systems.

Busse, R. and Schwartz, F.W. (1997) Financing reforms in the German hospital sector – from full cost cover principle to prospective case fees, *Medical Care*, 35(10): OS40–9.

Casado, D. and Rico, A. (2000) Nuevas formas de organización gestión en sanidad, in G. Lopez-Casasnovas (ed.) *La evaluación de las políticas de servicios sanitarios en el Estado de las Autonomías. Análisis comparativo de las Comunidades Autónomas del Andalucía, Cataluña y el País Vasco.* Bilbao: Fundación BBV e Institut d'Estudis Autonomics.

Commissie Health Care Governance (1999) *Health Care Governance: Aanbevelingen voor Goed Bestuur, Goed Toezicht en Adequate Verantwoording.* Soesterberg : C-3 Consultancy.

De Waal, S.P.M. (2000) *Nieuwe strategieen voor het publieke domein: Maatschappelijk ondernemen in de praktijk* [*New Strategies for the Public Domain: Social Entrepreneurship in Practice*]. Alphen a/d Rijn: Samsom.

Diderichsen, F. (1995) Market reform in health care and sustainability of the welfare state: lessons from Sweden, *Health Policy*, 32: 141–53.

Dixon, A. and Reis, V. (1999) *Health Care Systems in Transition: Portugal.* Copenhagen: European Observatory on Health Care Systems.

Dobson, R. (1998) Hospital trusts in Wales halved, *British Medical Journal*, 316: 1040.

Drucker, P.F. (1986) *Innovation and Entrepreneurship.* New York: Harper & Row.

Drucker, P.F. (1992) *Managing the Non-Profit Organisations.* Guildford: Butterworth-Heinemann.

Gerdtham, U.G., Lothgren, M., Tambour, M. and Rehnberg, C. (1999) Internal markets and health care efficiency: a multiple-output stochastic frontier analysis, *Health Economics*, 8: 151–64.

Goddard, M., Ferguson, B. and Posnett, J. (1997) Impact of the purchaser–provider relationship and implications for the regulatory framework, in B. Ferguson, T. Sheldon and J. Posnett (eds) *Concentration and Choice in Healthcare.* London: FT Healthcare.

Hamblin, R. (1998) Trusts, in J. Le Grand, N. Mays and J-A. Mulligan (eds) *Learning from the NHS Internal Market.* London: King's Fund.

Hanning, M. (1996) Maximum waiting time guarantee – an attempt to reduce waiting lists in Sweden. *Health Policy*, 36: 17–35.

Harding, A. and Preker, A.S. (2000) Organizational reform in the hospital sector: a conceptual framework, in A.S. Preker and A. Harding (eds) *Innovations in Health Care Reform: The Corporatization of Public Hospitals.* Baltimore, MD: Johns Hopkins University Press.

Harrison, M.I. (1999) Health professionals and the right to health care, in A. den Exter and H. Hermans (eds) *The Right to Health Care in Several European Countries.* The Hague: Kluwer Law International.

Harrison, M.I. and Calltorp, J. (2000) The reorientation of market-oriented reforms in Swedish healthcare, *Health Policy*, 50: 219–40.

Hessisches Ministerium für Jugend, Familie und Gesundheit (1993) *Krankenhausplan des Landes Hessen* (3. Fortschreibung allgemeiner Teil). Wiesbaden: Hessisches Ministerium für Jugend, Familie und Gesundheit.

Jakab, M., Preker, A. and Harding, A. (2002) Linking organizational structure to the external environment: experiences from hospital reform in transition economies, in M. McKee and J. Healy (eds) *Hospitals in a Changing Europe*. Buckingham: Open University Press.

Kerr, E. and Siebrand, V. (1999) *Health Care Systems in Transition: Luxembourg*. Copenhagen: European Observatory on Health Care Systems.

Langenbrunner, J. and Wiley, M. (2002) Hospital payment mechanisms: theory and practice in transition countries, in M. McKee and J. Healy (eds) *Hospitals in a Changing Europe*. Buckingham: Open University Press.

Marinoni, A. and Macchi, C. (1999) Public health policies in Italy, in W. Holland and E. Mossialos (eds) *Public Health Policies in the European Union*. Aldershot: Ashgate.

Martin Martin, J.J. (1999) Tema 6: 'Innovaciones y reformas organizativas en el Sistema Nacional de Salud español', in *Curso Experto Universitario en Gestión de Unidades Clinicasm*, Vol. 4. Madrid: UNED-ENS.

Mays, N., Mulligan, J-A. and Goodwin, N. (2000) The British quasi-market in health care: a balance sheet of the evidence, *Journal of Health Services Research and Policy*, 5: 49–58.

McKee, M. and Healy, J. (2002) Improving performance within the hospital, in M. McKee and J. Healy (eds) *Hospitals in a Changing Europe*. Buckingham: Open University Press.

Minder, A., Schoenholzer, H. and Amiet, M. (2000) *Health Care Systems in Transition: Switzerland*. Copenhagen: European Observatory on Health Care Systems.

Ministry of Health (1999) *The Danish Health Care Sector*. Copenhagen: Ministry of Health.

Mosse, P. (1998) Implementing health care reforms in Europe: policies, actors and institutions, *Japanese Journal of Health Economics and Policy*, 5: 5–30.

NHS Executive (1994) *The Operation of the NHS Internal Market: Local Freedoms, National Responsibilities*, HSG(94)55. London: HMSO.

Osborne, D. and Gaebler, T.A. (1992) *Reinventing Government: How the Entrepreneurial Spirit is Transforming the Public Government*. Reading, MA: Addisson-Wesley.

Paton, C., Bellanger, M., Berman, P.C., Busse, R. and Hunter, D.J. (2000) *Scientific Evaluation of the Effects of the Introduction of Market Forces into Health Systems: Final Report*. Dublin: European Health Management Association.

Pollock, A.M., Dunnigan, M.G., Gaffney, D., Price, D. and Shaoul, J. (1999) The private finance initiative: planning the 'new' NHS: downsizing for the 21st century, *British Medical Journal*, 319: 179–84.

Price, D., Pollock, A.M. and Shaoul, J. (1999) How the World Trade Organization is shaping domestic policies in health care, *Lancet*, 354: 1889–92.

Pugner, K. (2000) Hospital governance in England and Germany in the 1990s. Unpublished PhD thesis, London School of Economics and Political Science.

Puig-Junoy, J. and Dalmau Matarrodona, E. (2000) ¿Qué sabemos acerca de la eficiencia de las organizaciones sanitarias en España? Una revision de la literature económica [What do we know about the efficiency of Spanish health care organisations? A review of the economic literature], in Asociación de Economia de la Salud (ed.) *Avances en la Gestión Sanitaria: Implicaciones para la Politica, las Organizationes Sanitarias y la Práctica Clinica*. Barcelona: Asociación de Economía de la Salud.

Raad voor de Volksgezondheid & Zorg [Dutch Council for Health and Social Services] (1996) *Het Ziekenhuis als Maatschappelijke Onderneming* [*The Hospital as a Social Enterprise*]. Zoetermeer: Raad voor de Volksgezondheid & Zorg.

Raad voor de Volksgezondheid & Zorg [Dutch Council for Health and Social Services] (1997) *Verzekeraars op de Zorgmarkt* [*Insurers at the Health Care Market*]. Zoetermeer: Raad voor de Volksgezondheid & Zorg.

Raad voor de Volksgezondheid & Zorg [Dutch Council for Health and Social Services] (2000) *Europa en de Gezondheidszorg* [*Europe and Health Care*]. Zoetermeer: Raad voor de Volksgezondheid & Zorg.

Rehnberg, C. (1997) Sweden, in C. Ham (ed.) *Health Care Reform: Learning from International Experience*. Buckingham: Open University Press.

Robinson, R. and Dixon, A. (1999) *Health Care Systems in Transition: United Kingdom*. Copenhagen: European Observatory on Health Care Systems.

Secretaries of State for Health (1989) *Working for Patients*, Cm.55. London: HMSO.

Smee, C. (1995) Self-governing trusts and GP fundholders: the British experience, in R.B. Saltman and C. von Otter (eds) *Implementing Planned Markets in Healthcare*. Buckingham: Open University Press.

Söderlund, N. (1999) Do managers pay their way? The impact of management input on hospital productivity in the NHS internal market, *Journal of Health Services Research and Policy*, 4: 6–15.

Söderlund, N., Csba, I., Gray, A., Milne, R. and Raftery, J. (1997) Impact of NHS reforms on English hospital productivity: an analysis of the first three years, *British Medical Journal*, 315: 1126–9.

Statistisches Bundesamt (2000) *Gesundheitswesen – Reihe 6.3: Kostennachweise der Krankenhäuser 1998*. Stuttgart: Metzler Poeschel.

Street, A., Carr-Hill, R. and Posnett, J. (1999) Is hospital performance related to expenditure on management?, *Journal of Health Services Research and Policy*, 4: 6–15.

Thalhuber, J. (1999) *The Definition of a Social Entrepreneur*. Minneapolis, MN: National Center for Social Entrepreneurs.

van der Linden, J.C. and Meijs, L.C.P.M. (1998) *Public Accountability in Nonprofit Organisations*, Working Paper, Management Report Series. Rotterdam: School of Management, Erasmus University.

Ventura, J. and González, E. (1999) Análisis de la eficiencia técnica hospitalaria del Insalud G.D. en Castilla y León, *Revista de Investigación Económica y Social de Castilla y León*, 1 : 39–50.

Westert, G.P. and Groenewegen, P.P. (1999) Regional disparities in health care supply in eleven European countries: does politics matter?, *Health Policy*, 47: 169–82.

Wiley, M.M. (1998) Financing operating costs for acute hospital services, in R.B. Saltman, J. Figueras and C. Sakellarides (eds) *Critical Challenges for Health Care Reform in Europe*. Buckingham: Open University Press.

chapter seven

Entrepreneurial behaviour in pharmaceutical markets and the effects of regulation

Elias Mossialos and Monique Mrazek

Introduction

This chapter focuses on the effects of regulation on entrepreneurial behaviour in the market for pharmaceuticals. The pharmaceutical market is characterized by both private- and public-sector entrepreneurial behaviour. Entrepreneurs in both sectors are identified by the presence of some common attributes that underlie their behaviour: opportunism, innovativeness, risk-taking, ability to think strategically, and being imaginative and proactive (Ennew *et al.* 1998). These entrepreneurs are motivated to seek opportunities that maximize their profits or utility. Although these characteristics may not seem consistent with public-sector values, particularly those related to health care, private-sector concepts of entrepreneurial behaviour are not uncommon in pharmaceutical markets.

Entrepreneurs in the market for pharmaceuticals include drug manufacturers, wholesalers, physicians, pharmacists, health care payers and other health care providers. These actors organize, manage and assume the risks of researching, developing, manufacturing, supplying and delivering pharmaceutical products to patients. They have adapted to changing market conditions by taking advantage of opportunities that maximize their own profits or utility. In so doing, however, entrepreneurs may simultaneously generate negative outcomes for other actors in this market. For example, the development of a new pharmaceutical product can yield valuable results both in terms of profits for the innovating firm and years of life gained by patients. Because the firm has opportunistic motives, however, the products it manufactures may not be as safe or efficacious as claimed. Similarly, giving physicians or pharmacists financial incentives to consider costs when prescribing or dispensing may yield positive outcomes for health care payers by controlling pharmaceutical expenditure, but it may simultaneously yield negative outcomes for patients who may receive fewer or less effective medicines. Consequently, to minimize the negative effects of opportunistic behaviour, entrepreneurs in the pharmaceutical market are regulated.

In practice, few markets are as heavily regulated as the pharmaceutical market. Regulators face a difficult set of contrasting objectives that need to be balanced. First, regulators are concerned with securing health policy objectives: protecting public health; guaranteeing patient access to safe, efficacious and cost-effective medicines; and ensuring that reimbursement agencies stay, as far as possible, within limited budgets. At the same time, regulators seek to balance against these health policy objectives quite different objectives of industrial policy that support the development of innovation in the pharmaceutical sector. As a result, a variety of regulations and incentives are used in different countries in an attempt to balance effective and efficient allocation of pharmaceutical resources against the need not to restrain innovation.

In this chapter, we analyse the impact of these different regulatory actions on entrepreneurial behaviour in the supply and demand of pharmaceutical products. We discuss some examples of entrepreneurial behaviour in pharmaceutical markets and examine the effect of regulation on entrepreneurial behaviour in this market. Finally, we look at the impact of health care reforms and changes to entrepreneurial behaviour in drug markets and draw some conclusions.

Sources of entrepreneurial behaviour in pharmaceutical markets

Entrepreneurial behaviour in pharmaceutical markets is predominantly associated with the behaviour of the pharmaceutical industry itself. The bottom line for the pharmaceutical industry is that, for any investment it makes – in research and development or the manufacture or marketing of a new compound – the outcome must be profitable. The industry as a whole is highly profitable. Compared to other industries, between 1960 and 1991 the United States pharmaceutical industry ranked either first or second in terms of median after-tax profit returns on stockholders' equity of the Fortune 500 companies (Scherer 1996).

Through constant attention to innovation, risk-taking and a proactive response to changing market demands, the pharmaceutical industry has been very successful in maintaining this high level of profitability. In 1997, 20 of the leading pharmaceutical companies spent between US$781 million and US$1892 million on research and development, or 11–21 per cent of their pharmaceutical sales (Centre for Medicines Research 1999). It is estimated that bringing a new chemical entity to market costs over US$500 million and takes between 7 and 10 years (Centre for Medicines Research 1999).

Although the process of drug discovery is certainly expensive, risky and time-consuming, the profit-maximizing objectives of manufacturers nevertheless lead one to ask whether the better-than-average profits enjoyed by the pharmaceutical industry are justifiable (Maynard 1993). The number of new chemical entities introduced on the world market has steadily decreased, from 100 in 1963 to 37 in 1998 (Centre for Medicines Research 1999). In addition, there is the question of whether opportunistic behaviour of the pharmaceutical industry leads to appropriate allocation of research and development spending to areas of unmet health need. The imbalance in the allocation of research and development resources is exemplified by the fact that, between 1976 and 1990, cardiovascular and anti-infective drugs accounted for nearly half (47 per cent) of all approvals of new chemical entities in the United States (Kaitin *et al.* 1993).

The strategies used by pharmaceutical companies to sustain profitability are as much a response to pressure to reduce research and development costs as they are a response to pressure for local responsiveness to regulation. Governments impose regulations that affect competition in drug markets, such as tariffs, as well as local rules for market approval and content requirements. Such regulations may require firms to invest in local operations so that products meet local requirements. At the same time, however, such regulations allow firms to participate in a protected market, facilitating their market penetration. Regulatory barriers between countries have encouraged firms to engage in mergers and acquisitions, as well as direct foreign investment, to gain a presence in a given market.

Profit maximization is certainly an important factor in determining not only the behaviour of the pharmaceutical industry, but also of other 'firms' participating in the pharmaceutical market: pharmacies, wholesalers, parallel importers and pharmaceutical benefit management organizations. These actors have all used entrepreneurial strategies to adapt to changing market conditions. For example, the branching and chaining of pharmacies has become a common strategy, where this is permitted, to take advantage of economies of scale and reduce expenditures through bulk purchasing and the spreading of fixed costs. Consolidation among wholesalers in key markets, such as Australia, Germany, Italy, Japan and the United States, has been a common response to market demands for economic and strategic reasons (IFPW 2001). Moreover, the Single Market of the European Union (EU) has resulted in an increased number of companies engaging in the importation and parallel distribution of licensed pharmaceuticals from countries with low drug prices to those with higher prices. In each of these examples, entrepreneurs acted strategically and proactively in response to changing market conditions to increase profits.

Pharmacy benefit managers in the United States provide another example of strategic, profit-maximizing entrepreneurial behaviour. Pharmacy benefit managers emerged simultaneously with managed care to handle the purchasing and distribution of prescription drugs for health maintenance organizations, other managed-care organizations and third-party payers. Pharmacy benefit managers tend to centralize prescribing and dispensing through the adoption of a formulary that allows for greater control over costs. Pharmacists and physicians are given incentives to prescribe and dispense from the narrower product range of the formulary. For every prescribed drug that pharmacists are able to switch, they receive a higher margin. Physicians are also instructed to prescribe the cheapest alternative from the list of drugs covered by a particular plan. Pharmacy benefit managers also sign contracts with manufacturers in exchange for rebates for inclusion of their products on a formulary.

Although this strategy has undoubtedly been profitable for pharmacy benefit managers (as well as health maintenance organizations, other third-party payers, pharmacists and physicians), whether the promotion of cheaper alternatives, and in particular generics, has been equally beneficial for patients is not so clear. In 1989, the US Attorney's office in Baltimore uncovered several cases of bribery and fraud in the generic drug approval process of the Food and Drug Administration that called into question product safety and efficacy. Certainly, this opportunistic behaviour on the part of some drug manufacturers had significant opportunity costs for patients.

Finally, health care payers can also be considered entrepreneurs in the pharmaceutical market. Health care payers have the responsibility to seek new methods to enhance the quality of life of their patient population by bringing together unique combinations of resources to capitalize on value-creation opportunities. In private health care plans, there is a clear objective to maximize profits. For public health plans, the objectives can be quite diverse: effectiveness, efficiency, equity and responsiveness to name but a few. In some cases, those responsible for the management and use of pharmaceuticals in the health care sector have acted entrepreneurially to find new solutions to improve efficiency in the use of resources. For example, some health care payers introduced financial incentives to influence prescribing behaviour through drugs budgets. These financial incentives in themselves initiated entrepreneurial behaviour among budget-holding physicians. Nevertheless, as mentioned earlier, health care payers have also been responsible for instituting regulatory mechanisms that have negatively affected entrepreneurs in this market.

Effect of regulation on entrepreneurial behaviour

Intervention in the pharmaceutical market through regulation and incentives has been necessary because opportunistic behaviour by entrepreneurs in the pharmaceutical market has either had a negative influence on patients or has made the securing of an efficient allocation of health care resources very difficult. Put more formally, regulatory intervention in pharmaceutical markets is necessary because of market failure in both supply and demand.

On the demand side, consumers are often unable to fully evaluate information on pharmaceuticals because of its complex technical nature. This has led to the unique system of the physician prescribing and the pharmacist dispensing. Demand can, therefore, be described as four-tiered: the physician prescribes, the pharmacist dispenses, the patient consumes and, in most cases, an unrelated insurer pays. As a result, the demand – prescribing, dispensing and consumption – of prescription medicines is inefficient. Some economists believe that one of the major factors leading to upward pressure on public pharmaceutical expenditure is the phenomenon of 'moral hazard'. This phenomenon arises when patients are not required to pay the costs of the medical treatment they receive, so that neither they nor their physicians have any incentive to economize (i.e. neither the physician nor the patient has any incentive to be price-sensitive).

The supply side of the pharmaceutical market is equally imperfect as a result of barriers to entry. Several sources of entry barrier can be identified in the pharmaceutical sector: patents, the process and length of regulatory approval, product differentiation and brand loyalty. The effect of these imperfections, combined with those on the demand side, has generated a substantial portion of regulatory intervention in the market for pharmaceuticals.

In this section, we briefly examine regulations that have broadly affected entrepreneurial behaviour in this market: patents, consumer protection regulation and product licensing, patent extensions and drug price competition regulation. This is followed by examples of regulation that has targeted specific entrepreneurs in the pharmaceutical market and their behaviour.

It is important first to mention briefly who regulates pharmaceuticals. The multifaceted objectives of regulators in the pharmaceutical market demand the involvement of various levels of governments, ministries and agencies to regulate this market. Issues such as patents are often resolved at the supranational level through agencies such as the World Trade Organization, which is responsible for securing international patent rights, or the European Commission, which has introduced supplementary protection certificates extending the life of patents. Market authorization, once a wholly nationalized procedure, is becoming the responsibility of a cross-national EU licensing agency, the European Medicines Evaluation Agency (EMEA). By contrast, pricing and reimbursement, as well as incentives for research and development, are generally nationalized, reflecting the different objectives of different countries. Regulation of pharmaceutical markets at the national level most often involves not only the ministry of health but also the ministries of trade and finance.

Patent regulation

Because of patents, regulatory intervention in pharmaceutical markets affects both the timing and rate of imitation of drug products. Patents grant exclusive rights over innovative pharmaceuticals, creating a monopoly and a significant barrier to entry into the market. The purpose of the patent system is to reward the innovative producers of new products with profits, thus providing an incentive for undertaking further research and development. Patents protect the property rights of a manufacturer from unauthorized use of the invention for a limited period of time. The pharmaceutical sector, more than any other industrial sector, regards patents as essential in protecting technological innovation (Wyatt *et al.* 1985; Howells and Neary 1995). Nevertheless, the costs associated with patent applications can be considerable. In addition, the length of the application review process can be an impediment to the commercialization of pharmaceutical products.

For many years, the duration of a patent varied from country to country. In most industrialized countries, the period of protection provided by a patent from the date when the patent is filed ranged from 15 to 20 years. This variation in the length of patent protection, as well as the fact that intellectual property rights were often left unprotected in developing countries, led to the Uruguay Round of multilateral trade negotiations in 1993, whereby GATT signatories agreed to provide substantial patent protection for drugs and other products (Correa 2000). The resulting Trade Related Issues in Intellectual Rights Protection (TRIPs) Agreement has provided for a patent period of 20 years from the date of filing.

The value of patent protection to society is that it provides incentives for innovators to conduct research and development that may yield products to improve the quality or quantity of our lives. Once a drug is developed, the marginal cost of provision is almost zero, leading to the problem of 'free-riding'. As people begin imitating and marketing similar products, the profits from the original product shrink. The imitative process may evolve so rapidly that the discounted sum of the profits is less than the value of the innovator's initial investment in research and development (Scherer 1996). However, patents also delay access to medicines for patients in developing countries who, in many cases, cannot afford to purchase medicines that are still under patent.

It is important to note here that it has been much debated as to whether or not patents do create a truly monopolistic situation for pharmaceuticals. Although patents (as well as licensing and cross-licensing agreements prevalent among patent holders) do limit competition, they do not completely stifle competition among patented drugs. Within therapeutic categories, there are often products that are close substitutes (commonly known as 'me-too' products) that differ only in pharmacological properties (e.g. side-effect profiles) or a number of product attributes (e.g. dosage or mode of delivery). Consequently, there is often competition between the brand leaders and the 'me-toos'. For example, when the third product to use the same mechanism to block the body's ability to make cholesterol (HMG-CoA reductase inhibitor) was launched on to the American market, the initial price was 50 per cent of that of the two earlier products (Bosanquet and Zammit-Lucia 1995). Although none of these products is a perfect substitute for the others, their mode of action and clinical outcomes were similar enough for them to be viewed as competitors.

Consumer protection regulation and product licensing

Consumer protection regulation and product licensing are intended to prevent opportunistic behaviour because of asymmetric information that may compromise patient safety in the consumption of medicines. Regulators also intervene in the market to protect consumers by requiring that new pharmaceutical products meet licensing requirements before they receive market authorization. Principal–agent relationships develop in the market for pharmaceuticals; first, there is an agency relationship between the patient and both the physician who prescribes and the pharmacist who dispenses; second, there is an agency relationship between the manufacturers and the demanders – physicians, pharmacists and patients. Because of the complex technical nature of pharmaceutical products, it is not possible for physicians, pharmacists and patients to adequately appraise the claims manufacturers make about the safety and efficacy of a given product. As a result, a product licence must be granted to ensure that patients are given safe and efficacious medicines.

In the 1960s, stringent product licensing requirements became the norm for market approval in many countries. Until the thalidomide tragedy, prescription medicines were put on the market at the discretion of the manufacturer and did not require a special licence. The 1968 Medicines Act in the United Kingdom, and similar legislation in other countries, was introduced to ensure that only safe and efficacious drugs were marketed.

Gaining a product licence is intensive in both time and resources. Market approval requirements entail reviews of clinical information in support of product safety, efficacy and quality. Manufacturers need to prove that the new product has some therapeutic benefit for a given set of conditions and that it is safe for human use at specific dosages to be determined. This is done through extensive pre-clinical and clinical trials where the above qualitative attributes are tested on groups of patients. The process of clinical investigation can take up to 10 years, and would potentially yield access to a specific market. If the manufacturer is to gain access to several markets, it needs to conduct part of the clinical trials locally so that a more representative patient sample is constructed and, often, because local regulatory bodies require companies to do so.

Producing results suitable for regulatory approval is not always guaranteed, and continuation from one phase of trials to another is conditional on meeting standards satisfactorily at each stage. Raising capital to perform clinical trials on a promising molecule is particularly difficult, especially in the biotechnology sector that is dominated by small- and medium-sized enterprises. Often smaller firms form strategic alliances with larger pharmaceutical companies, or rely on shareholders to fund development (Kanavos 1998).

After having conducted clinical trials, the manufacturer submits a dossier (a New Drug Application or NDA) to the regulatory authorities, which aims at registering the substance as a medicine for human use. The manufacturer must also specify exactly what clinical conditions the substance will be used for and at what dosages. The regulator reviews all the evidence from the clinical trials and, if the evidence on safety, efficacy and quality is sufficient, approves the medicine for the specified clinical conditions. Once the review has been completed, the drug is registered and licensed for sale.

Clinical trials and the fulfilling of other requirements in obtaining a product licence increase the length of time it takes to get a product to market, thus eroding the effective life of a patent and reducing revenues. Some regulatory agencies are more efficient in reviewing a medicine than others, thereby shortening the total period of approval (Randy Stround Consulting 1995). Moreover, a parallel review process or 'fast track' was introduced by the US Food and Drug Administration to allow more rapid access to medicines for the treatment of certain conditions, such as AIDS, once drug safety had been established in the first phase of clinical trials. To compensate for this loss of patent life, patent extension terms have been adopted, such as the Supplementary Protection Certificate in the EU in 1994. The extension of the patent term has implications for post-patent competition, as discussed below.

There have been attempts to harmonize the authorization process at supranational and international levels to minimize the repetition of the approval process in different countries. Such attempts include the establishment of the EMEA in 1995 as part of the harmonization of different national drug approval procedures. At the international level, the International Conferences on Harmonization has tried to bring together the regulatory authorities of the EU, the United States and Japan to promote harmonization of technical requirements.

After pharmaceuticals are approved and marketed, different regulatory mechanisms are used to ensure that manufacturers adhere to the terms and conditions of approval described in the product licensing application, and that the product is subsequently manufactured in a consistent and controlled manner. Regulations for good manufacturing practices set out the minimum current manufacturing methods to be used in the manufacturing, processing, packing and storage of finished pharmaceuticals. The regulations generally also set out requirements for facilities, or the controls to be used in the manufacturing of pharmaceuticals. Good regulation of manufacturing practice aims to ensure that the manufacturing of a pharmaceutical meets the characteristics of identity, strength, quality and purity that the manufacturer purports the product to possess. These regulations are enforced through periodic unannounced inspections of drug production and control facilities. Even before market approval, regulators may inspect and audit development facilities, planned production facilities and clinical trial facilities. Regulators also gather information from a variety of surveillance systems to assist them in identifying a manufacturing or control problem.

Deregulation of generic markets and the creation of a competitive environment

In an effort to increase competition in the post-patent period, the United States took a unique approach and to some extent 'deregulated' the post-patent market. While it was not a complete deregulation, barriers to entry were lowered as part of the Drug Price Competition and Patent Term Restoration Act (DPC & PTR Act) of 1994. This Act, which is better known as the Waxman-Hatch Act, decreased the requirements for generic equivalents of an original branded drug seeking market approval. To further speed up generic entry following patent expiration, the Act also allowed a generics firm to collect data for regulatory purposes and to conduct bioequivalency tests up to 6 months before the expiration of the patent. Stockpiling, which is essential for entry immediately after patent expiry, was not allowed under this provision.

The effect of the DPC & PTR Act was such that it reduced the time between patent expiration of a brand-name drug and the arrival of generic copies on the market from more than 3 years to less than 3 months (Congressional Budget Office 1998). Consequently, the number of generic drugs on the market increased, as did the number of drugs that experienced generic competition (Caves *et al.* 1991). Between 1984 and 1987, there were on average five new generics introduced in the first year post-patent, with three additional entrants in each of the following 3 years (Frank and Salkever 1997). As the number of entrants increased, the price of generics decreased. The price of generics was found to be between 50 and 60 per cent of the price of the original brands within 3 years of entry (Caves *et al.* 1991; Grabowski and Vernon 1992, 1996;

Frank and Salkever 1997). Discounting to gain market share was also found to be greater when there were two or more generic manufacturers producing the same equivalent drug (Congressional Budget Office 1998). It is estimated that generics gained a 10 per cent increase in market share for every 6 per cent reduction in price (Grabowski and Vernon 1992). This evidence suggests that the DPC & PTR Act contributed to facilitating the availability of lower-price generic drug substitutes to consumers after patent expiration. Other regulations and incentives affecting the prescribing, dispensing and consumption of generic medicines, particularly those associated with managed care, were also responsible for the increased competition in off-patent drug markets in the United States.

Despite incentives created through initiatives such as the DPC & PTR Act, barriers to entry may still remain because of certain strategies employed by the owners of the original brand to delay the impact of patent expiration. These strategies include developing a branded generic, securing raw materials and increasing the standards of technical specification. The original producer may also continue to enjoy the benefits of multiple patents, such that after the expiration of the main patent the secondary patents will continue to ensure some protection of market share, for certain formulations, where generic entry is not possible.

Regulatory reforms and entrepreneurial behaviour

Most OECD countries, economies in transition and upper- to middle-income economies have implemented, or are in the process of implementing, profound reforms in their health care systems that are intended, in particular, to contain costs and increase efficiency (OECD 1992, 1994; Saltman *et al.* 1998). Reforms have been directed towards cost-effective resource allocation, with a trend towards introducing budgets for overall health spending and for individual providers. In addition, several policies to contain pharmaceutical expenditure were introduced that had a direct effect on the behaviour of different entrepreneurial actors in the market. Some of these initiatives are examined in this section: direct price regulation of manufacturers and distributors, profit regulation of manufacturers, reference pricing, and prescribing budgets for doctors.

Direct and indirect drug price regulation

Deciding what is an appropriate or reasonable price for a product is a particular problem in pharmaceutical markets because, as mentioned previously, market failure prevents the determination of an efficient price. Consequently, health care payers have relied on various forms of direct and indirect price regulation to keep drug prices 'reasonable' and ensure pharmaceutical expenditures stay in check. Direct price regulation takes on various forms that are too numerous to cover here. Instead, this section focuses on two forms of direct price regulation: the setting of a maximum reimbursement price or reference price, and the setting of drug prices according to cost-effectiveness criteria. In addition, we consider here an alternative to direct price regulation, that of indirect price controls or profit regulation.

Reference pricing

The purpose of reference pricing or fixed reimbursement levels is to limit the rise in pharmaceutical expenditure by setting a limit on the price that health care payers will fully reimburse. The reimbursement price is set by reference to the price of other drugs in a given category. Different mechanisms are used to calculate the reference price: it may be based on the average price of drugs in a category, on the price of the cheapest drug, or on the price of the cheapest generic drug plus an additional sum. The patient must pay the difference between the price of the prescribed drug and the reference price if the former is priced higher. A common reimbursement price for products that are close equivalents creates an incentive for physicians and patients to consider cost when making choices. In this way, reference pricing was expected to bring the prices of all products in the same reference price category down to the same level.

Reference pricing has gained acceptance as a policy tool because it can be effective in eliminating price gaps between therapeutically similar products and for improving the transparency of the market (Giuliani *et al.* 1998). The scheme has been applied in several countries (Germany, New Zealand, Sweden and the Canadian province of British Columbia) with some differences in terms of how reference prices are calculated or how reference categories are defined. In general, reference pricing applies only to those products that are interchangeable because they have similar mechanisms of therapeutic action or produce similar clinical outcomes. Classifying products by comparable therapeutic effects, however, is often controversial and administratively difficult (Rigter 1994). Although new products for which there are no clear substitutes are most often excluded from reference pricing schemes, the price of these new medicines can be expected to converge to the reference price of competitor products. In addition, the price of some products such as generic equivalents, originally priced below the reference price, were found to rise to the reference price in some countries (Zweifel and Crivelli 1996).

Cost-effectiveness pricing

Economic criteria are used in some countries, and frequently discussed in others, to justify drug prices at reimbursement (Drummond *et al.* 1997; Siegel *et al.* 1997; Freemantle 1999). In 1993, Australia became the first country to require applicants for reimbursement to state what price they feel the product should have, and to make economic calculations accordingly to justify this price. Since then Canada, in 1995, and Finland, in 1999, have introduced similar requirements for manufacturers to submit pharmacoeconomic studies when seeking eligibility for reimbursement for new products. Other countries, such as the Netherlands, Portugal and the United Kingdom, have introduced guidelines for pharmacoeconomic studies that allow the government to demand economic evidence for reimbursement decisions.

The aim of cost-effectiveness pricing is to establish a fair reimbursement price for medicines according to value-for-money criteria. This method of pricing is based on utilitarian principles that are intended to lead to greater efficiency in the utilization of health care resources. A premium price for a drug decided on by the manufacturer would be justified through cost-effectiveness on the grounds that it could provide substantial cost savings (Reekie and Buxton 1994). It is argued that firms may choose to forego the development of some drugs if the expected cost-effectiveness ratio of the standard in the future is so low that the product in development cannot be introduced profitably (Abbott 1995).

The application of cost-effectiveness pricing is not without problems. The dimensions of the cost-effectiveness analysis are sensitive to change. For example, if actual practice differs from the assumptions made in a hypothetical model, a given product may not achieve anticipated levels of cost-effectiveness in practice. This sensitivity to assumptions makes comparisons of the cost-effectiveness ratio between models difficult. The standardization of methods in economic evaluation through the use of guidelines is one means of ensuring the compatibility of results, and whether differences between studies are due to real factors or methodological differences. Nevertheless, even where guidelines for pharmacoeconomic studies have been applied, such as in Australia, significant problems were identified between studies (Hill *et al.* 2000).

Economic evaluations impose practical problems for the pharmaceutical industry, both in funding the studies and in the need to modify clinical trials to facilitate the collection of economic data (Drummond 1994). It is often difficult to locate the robust data required for the evaluations and to evaluate changes in cost-effectiveness over time. Applying study results from one setting to another or from one country to another may introduce biases.

Linked to the idea of cost-effective drug utilization has been the increased used of restricted reimbursement lists. Restricted lists can be either positive – listing all products reimbursable under a given system – or negative – listing all products that are to be excluded from reimbursement. Positive lists are useful for reducing variations in prescribing between medical practices and for promoting the use of generics, whereas negative lists prevent specific drugs from gaining widespread use. Restricted lists can also be a non-transparent means of price fixing, encouraging companies to agree to price reductions to avoid having their products removed from positive lists or added to negative lists. In terms of their effect on demand, restricted lists limit the range of drugs available, thus affecting prescribing freedom.

Profit regulation

Profit controls or rate-of-return regulation (RORR) is an indirect means of controlling drug prices that takes into account a manufacturer's contribution to drug development and the economy. This mechanism of control aims to ensure that a firm is not making excessive profits, particularly on those products still under patent. At present, this regulatory mechanism is unique to the United Kingdom through the Pharmaceutical Price Regulation Scheme (PPRS).

The PPRS attempts to balance the securing of 'reasonably' priced medicines for the National Health Service (NHS) against ensuring that a strong, efficient and profitable pharmaceutical industry in the United Kingdom is capable of sustained research and development.

Although the general PPRS agreement is negotiated between the Department of Health and the Association of British Pharmaceutical Industry, profit targets are negotiated between the Department and companies on an individual basis. The target profits are set according to the overall return achieved by all sectors of British industry, and are currently set at 17–21 per cent. A margin of tolerance of 25 per cent is set either side of this target. The pharmaceutical company is free to set the prices of its products as long as the return is within the margin set by the Department of Health. If the profit exceeds the margin, then the company may repay the excess above the 25 per cent margin or reduce the price of some of its products to ensure that profits do not exceed the target level in the coming year. Should profits fall below the target, then the company may be eligible for a price increase.

The strengths and weaknesses of the PPRS have been well documented elsewhere (Maynard and Bloor 1997; Mossialos 1997; Slater 1997). The scheme helps to maintain an operational relationship between government and industry (in contrast to the situation in other European countries), ensuring that no sudden policy changes occur and thereby offering a stable and predictable regulatory environment to the companies considering investment. Moreover, its non-statutory nature provides the regulator with various options, flexibly tailored to the needs of each individual company. Its administrative simplicity is reflected in the limited number of personnel employed to operate the regime and the minimal compliance costs, as auditing is based on published statutory accounts. Finally, and most crucially, the PPRS is thought to have encouraged innovation by allowing levels of expenditure on research and development above the worldwide average to be included in the calculated costs, and granting free pricing rights to innovative products – that is, new active substances not previously on the British market.

The limitations of the PPRS are common to other RORR-type regulatory schemes. RORR-type regulation provides little incentive for operational efficiency, to the extent that increased costs can be recovered through increased prices being allowed. Moreover, and to the extent that returns are calculated as a percentage allowance on the capital invested, the company might end up over-investing in capital equipment or artificially inflating the asset base (Baldwin 1995). This is similar to the Averch-Johnson-Wellisz effect associated with rate-of-return regulation of public utilities (Mossialos 1997). Rate-of-return regulation may also give firms incentives to shift production costs from an unregulated to a regulated division if they operate in several markets – for example, a firm manufacturing both patented medicines regulated under the PPRS and generic medicines that fall under an alternative scheme. Finally, as target profits are negotiated and the process may not be transparent, there is the potential for regulatory capture. The determination of the 'proper or fair' rate of return essentially requires great insight into the industry in question, major information collection exercises and, inevitably (in relation to enforcement), negotiations.

Price regulation of drug distribution

Regulation and health system reforms have also affected entrepreneurial behaviour in drug distribution. Drugs are normally distributed from the manufacturer either directly to the hospital and retail pharmacies or via a wholesaler. In some countries, the distribution chain is left unregulated, whereas in others it is regulated either in whole or in part. Regulation of the distribution chain affects not only the end price of the products but also incentives for entrepreneurial behaviour.

In Germany, the pharmaceutical supply chain – manufacturer, wholesaler and pharmacist – is heavily regulated. Both the wholesaler's and the pharmacist's margins are fixed. Although the pharmacist's margins are digressive, varying inversely as a percentage of product price, more income is generated in absolute terms for dispensing higher-priced products. As there is limited potential for wholesalers to grant discounts, the German generics market is not price-competitive. German generics manufacturers must compete for market share by promoting their products under their own brand name. The effect of this heavy regulation of the supply chain is a high price and one of the lowest percentage ratios earned by manufacturers in Europe (Selke and Schröder 1997).

By contrast, retail margins in both the United Kingdom and the United States are regulated to some extent from the top but remain unregulated from the bottom. In the United Kingdom, the drug tariff scheme sets the maximum reimbursement prices for unbranded generic medicines. Similarly, maximum allowable cost prices have been widely applied and set maximum reimbursement prices for generic medicines. In both countries, discounting occurs below these reimbursement limits. Discounting is motivated by the profit incentives of pharmacists, who receive larger margins for less expensive medicines. This practice of discounting has in part led to cheaper generics as a percentage of total prescription costs in both the United Kingdom and the United States as compared to Germany (Mrazek and Mossialos, 2000).

Prescribing budgets for physicians

The regulation of prescribing can be classified as being one of two types: financial incentives and non-financial inducements. Financial incentive regulation has taken the form of cash-limited prescribing budgets, which either extract a monetary penalty from physicians exceeding their budgets or reward physicians who stay within the budget by allowing them to retain some portion of the savings.

Two prescribing budget schemes were introduced in the United Kingdom as part of the 1990 NHS reforms: the Indicative Prescribing Scheme (IPS) and general practitioner (GP) fundholding. The IPS was applied to all non-fundholding GPs, who were encouraged to keep their prescribing expenditures within non-cash-limited 'target' budgets that reflected existing prescribing costs as well as demographic, social and epidemiological factors. Indicative budgets were monitored monthly and, if the GP exceeded the budget by a certain amount, a warning was issued by the Regional Medical Officer. Although penalties for over-prescribing GPs have been in place since 1974, they have rarely been applied. As no penalties were used against GPs who exceeded their budgets, the indicative budgets served as an indicator of expected performance rather than as a strictly controlled cash limit.

By contrast, cash-limited prescribing budgets were set individually for each GP fundholder; 55 per cent of GPs were part of the fundholding scheme when it ended in 1998 (Robinson and Dixon 1999). General practitioners who stayed within their budgets were rewarded by being able to transfer any savings to another area of their practice budget or to use them to improve their practice facilities. These financial incentives led fundholders to incur smaller increases in prescribing costs than non-fundholders (Bradlow and Coulter 1993). These relative cost savings were due to a lower average cost per item prescribed rather than the prescribing of fewer items (Harris and Scrivener 1996), achieved through higher levels of generic prescribing (Gosden and Torgerson 1997). The effect of NHS policies promoting generic prescribing and dispensing has meant that, between 1989 and 1997, generic prescribing increased by 12 per cent while generic dispensing increased by 18 per cent (Department of Health 1998). For these reasons, GP fundholders have come to be known as entrepreneurs (Bain 1993; Ennew *et al.* 1998).

Prescribing budgets have also been introduced in Germany. Unlike the individual budgets in the United Kingdom, in 1993 cash-limited budgets in Germany were set collectively for all GPs in a district. A collective penalty was applied to any overspending of the budgets as a way of controlling rising drug expenditures. In the first year after their introduction, there was a 30 per cent fall in the number of prescriptions written as well as a decrease in the value of prescriptions, largely associated with an increase in generic prescribing (Busse and Howorth 1999). Thus prescribing budgets in Germany had the same initial effect on generic prescribing as they did in the United Kingdom.

Despite the limited success of cash-limited prescribing budgets, there are several caveats. The search for cheaper therapies may not necessarily be more cost-effective. In addition, prescribing economies are short- rather than long-term. There may also be a perverse incentive to refer more patients to hospital, thus shifting costs away from the physician's budget but increasing overall health care costs. Moreover, there may be problems of 'cream-skimming' associated with costly referrals to hospital (Goodwin 1998).

To ensure physicians do not engage in opportunistic behaviour that is detrimental to patients, several initiatives are commonly used to monitor prescribing behaviour. Prescribing data are monitored for changes in the number and type of prescriptions written. Prescribing data are used to provide physicians with reliable, regular and prompt information on their current prescribing to improve cost awareness, leading to more effective and economical prescribing. The usefulness of prescribing data in initiating change is limited to the range, quality, reliability and comparability of data, while the effectiveness of this strategy in improving prescribing depends on the willingness of physicians to consider costs when prescribing. Although physicians have been found not to be adverse to considering costs (Denig and Haaijer-Ruskamp 1995; Ryan *et al.* 1996), other criteria such as personal experience have been found to be valued more than cost (Denig and Haaijer-Ruskamp 1995).

Prescribing guidelines are used to reduce inappropriate variations in pre-scribing between physicians and to ensure that prescribing is cost-effective. Periodic prescribing audits can be carried out to evaluate the quality of drug prescribing on a continual basis against quality indicators. Prescribing patterns found not to be consistent with predetermined standards of clinical guidelines can then be targets for educational interventions. The monitoring of physi-cian behaviour is important for ensuring that opportunistic behaviour by physicians does not have negative consequences for patients.

Conclusions

While entrepreneurial behaviour in pharmaceutical markets can help to improve efficiency, it can also introduce the need for regulation to prevent negative opportunistic behaviour. Both public- and private-sector entrepreneurs involved in the market for pharmaceuticals are motivated by opportunities to maximize profits and their utility. Entrepreneurial behaviour in pharmaceutical markets has been beneficial yet negatively opportunistic. Regulatory interventions such as patents, deregulation of the post-patent pharmaceutical market, reim-bursement decisions based on cost-effectiveness, and schemes such as the Pharmaceutical Price Regulation Scheme in the United Kingdom have attempted to promote entrepreneurial behaviour in pharmaceutical markets.

At the same time, regulation has attempted to mitigate the negative effects of opportunistic entrepreneurial behaviour, both on patients and in preventing efficient resource allocation. Consumer protection regulation, product licensing and the monitoring of prescribing and dispensing are examples of regulation that has been used to ensure safety, efficacy and quality in pharmaceutical utilization. Direct and indirect price regulation of the supply chain from manu-facturer through to wholesaler and pharmacist, as well as budgets for doctors, are a few examples of where regulation has been used in an effort to improve efficiency in resource allocation. These methods, however, are not without limitations. In fact, evidence suggests that a less regulated supply chain may lead to more market-driven outcomes. Nevertheless, these outcomes are not necessarily more cost-effective, as opportunistic entrepreneurial behaviour may lead to less efficient outcomes where patients are concerned. Regulators need to keep these conflicting considerations in mind when designing policies in the pharmaceutical market.

References

Abbott, T.A. (1995) Price regulation in the pharmaceutical industry: prescription or placebo?, *Journal of Health Economics*, 14: 551–65.

Bain, J. (1993) Budget holding: Here to stay?, *British Medical Journal*, 306: 1185–8.

Baldwin, R. (1995) *Regulation in Question: The Growing Agenda*. London: London School of Economics.

Bosanquet, N. and Zammit-Lucia, J. (1995) The effect of competition on drug prices, *PharmacoEconomics*, 8: 473–8.

Bradlow, J. and Coulter, A. (1993) Effect of fundholding and indicative prescribing schemes on general practitioners' prescribing costs, *British Medical Journal*, 307: 1186–9.

Busse, R. and Howorth, C. (1999) Cost containment in Germany: twenty years experience, in E. Mossialos and J. Le Grand (eds) *Health Care and Cost Containment in the European Union*. Aldershot: Ashgate.

Caves, R.E., Whinston, M.E. and Hurwitz, M.A. (1991) *Patent Expiration, Entry and Competition in the US Pharmaceutical Industry: An Exploratory Analysis*, Brookings Papers on Economic Activity: Microeconomics. Washington, DC: Brookings Institute.

Centre for Medicines Research (1999) *The Pharmaceutical R&D Compendium: CMR International/Scrip's Complete Guide to Trends in R&D*, Vol. 1. London: CMR International and PJB Publications.

Congressional Budget Office (1998) *How Increased Competition from Generic Drugs has Affected Prices and Returns in the Pharmaceutical Industry*. Washington, DC: Congressional Budget Office.

Correa, C.M. (2000) *Integrating Public Health Concerns into Patent Legislation in Developing Countries*. Geneva: South Centre.

Denig, P. and Haaijer-Ruskamp, F.M. (1995) Do physicians take cost into account when making prescribing decisions?, *PharmacoEconomics*, 8: 282–90.

Department of Health (1998) Statistics of prescriptions dispensed in the community: England 1987 to 1997, *Statistical Bulletin*, 24 July.

Drummond, M.F. (1994) The emerging government requirement for economic evaluation of pharmaceuticals, *PharmacoEconomics*, 6 (suppl. 1): 42–50.

Drummond, M.F., Jonsson, B., Rutten, F. *et al.* (1997) The role of economic evaluation in the pricing and reimbursement of medicines, *Health Policy*, 40: 139–43.

Ennew, C., Feighan, T. and Whynes, D. (1998) Entrepreneurial activity in the public sector: evidence for UK primary care, in P. Taylor-Gooby (ed.) *Choice and Public Policy: The Limits to Welfare Markets*. London: Macmillan.

Frank, R.G. and Salkever, D.S. (1997) Generic entry and the pricing of pharmaceuticals, *Journal of Economics and Management Strategy*, 6: 75–90.

Freemantle, N. (1999) Does the UK National Health Service need a fourth hurdle for pharmaceutical reimbursement to encourage the more efficient prescribing of pharmaceuticals?, *Health Policy*, 46: 255–65.

Giuliani, G., Selke, G. and Garattini, L. (1998) The German experience in reference pricing, *Health Policy*, 44: 73–85.

Goodwin, N. (1998) GP fundholding, in J. Le Grands, N. Mays and J. Mulligan (eds) *Learning from the NHS Internal Market: A Review of the Evidence*. London: King's Fund.

Gosden, T. and Torgerson, D.J. (1997) The effect of fundholding on prescribing and referral costs: a review of the evidence, *Health Policy*, 40: 103–14.

Grabowski, H.G. and Vernon, J.M. (1992) Brand loyalty, entry, and price competition in pharmaceuticals after the 1984 Drug Act, *Journal of Law and Economics*, 35: 331–50.

Grabowski, H.G. and Vernon, J.M. (1996) Longer patents for increased generic competition in the US: The Waxman-Hatch Act after one decade, *PharmacoEconomics*, 10 (suppl. 2): 110–23.

Harris, C.M. and Scrivener, G. (1996) Fundholders' prescribing costs: the first five years, *British Medical Journal*, 313: 1531–4.

Hill, S.R., Mitchell, A.S. and Henry, D.A. (2000) Problems with the interpretation of pharmacoeconomic analyses: a review of submissions to the Australian Pharmaceutical Benefits Scheme, *Journal of the American Medical Association*, 283: 2116–21.

Howells, J. and Neary, I. (1995) *Intervention and Technological Innovation: Government and the Pharmaceutical Industry in the United Kingdom and Japan*. London: Macmillan.

International Federation of Pharmaceutical Wholesalers (IFPW) (2001) *Annual Report 2000*. http://www.ifpw.com/00an_rpt.pdf (accessed 31 July 2001).

Kaitin, K.I., Bryant, N.R. and Lasagna, L. (1993) The role of the research-based pharmaceutical industry in medical progress in the United States, *Journal of Clinical Pharmacology*, 33: 412–17.

Kanavos, P. (1998) *Determinants of Market Structure in the International Biopharmaceutical Industry*. Paris: OECD Biotechnology Unit.

Maynard, A. (1993) The regulation of the pharmaceutical industry, in M.F. Drummond and A. Maynard (eds) *Purchasing and Providing Cost-effective Health Care*. London: Churchill Livingstone.

Maynard, A. and Bloor, K. (1997) Regulating the pharmaceutical industry, *British Medical Journal*, 315: 200–1.

Mossialos, E. (1997) An evaluation of the PPRS: is there a need for reform?, in Institute of Economic Affairs (ed.) *Should Pharmaceutical Prices be Regulated?* London: IEA Health and Welfare Unit.

Mrazek, M. and Mossialos E. (2000) Increasing demand while decreasing costs of generic medicines, *Lancet*, 356: 1784–5.

Organisation for Economic Co-operation and Development (1992) *The Reform of Health Systems: A Review of Seven OECD Countries*, OECD Health Policy Studies No. 2. Paris: OECD.

Organisation for Economic Co-operation and Development (1994) *The Reform of Health Systems: A Review of Seventeen OECD Countries*, OECD Health Policy Studies No. 5. Paris: OECD.

Randy Stround Consulting Inc. (1995) *Drug Submission Evaluation: International Comparison of Performance Standards and Performance: Canada, USA, UK, Australia, Sweden, European Community*. Ottawa: Health Canada.

Reekie, W.D. and Buxton, M.J. (1994) Cost-effectiveness as a guide to pricing a new pharmaceutical product, *South African Medical Journal*, 84: 421–3.

Rigter, H. (1994) Recent public policies in the Netherlands to control pharmaceutical pricing and reimbursement, *PharmacoEconomics*, 6 (suppl. 1): 15–21.

Robinson, R. and Dixon, A. (1999) *Health Care Systems in Transition: United Kingdom*. Copenhagen: European Observatory on Health Care Systems.

Ryan, M., Yule, B., Bond, C. and Taylor, R.J. (1996) Do physicians' perceptions of drug costs influence their prescribing?, *PharmacoEconomics*, 9: 321–31.

Saltman, R., Figueras, J. and Sakellarides, C. (1998) *Critical Challenges for Health Care Reform in Europe*. Buckingham: Open University Press.

Scherer, F.M. (1996) *Industry Structure, Strategy and Public Policy*. New York: Harper Collins.

Selke, G.W. and Schröder, H. (1997) Recent proposals for changing pharmacy margins in Germany, *Pharma Pricing Review*, 2: 230–3.

Siegel, J.E., Torrance, G.W., Russell, L.B. *et al.* (1997) Guidelines for pharmacoeconomic studies: Recommendations from the Panel on Cost Effectiveness in Health and Medicine, *PharmacoEconomics*, 11: 159–68.

Slater, A.E. (1997) Regulating the price of the UK's drugs: second thoughts after the government's first report, *British Medical Journal*, 314: 365.

Wyatt, S., Bertin, G. and Pavitt, K. (1985) Patents and multinational corporations: results from questionnaires, *World Patent Information*, 7: 196–212.

Zweifel, P. and Crivelli, L. (1996) Price regulation of drugs: lessons from Germany, *Journal of Regulatory Economics*, 10: 257–73.

chapter eight

Regulating entrepreneurial behaviour in social care

Julien Forder

Introduction

In the context of increasing spending on social services and demographic predictions of a significant future ageing of the population in many European countries, reform of social services has become a priority agenda item. Arguably, reform is motivated by cost-containment worries, although other factors are also relevant, including concerns about poor coordination and the balance between institutional and home-based care, ideological factors and concerns about distribution and equity (Glennerster and Le Grand 1995).

The increased use of market mechanisms to structure and govern transactions in social care is central to reforms in many European countries. The rhetoric portrays market governance arrangements as freeing up entrepreneurial activity, leading to improvements in quality and cost-cutting innovations. It is argued that markets create the appropriate incentives for stakeholders. Although there is still a wide diversity of structures in European social care, markets or market-like governance arrangements have become more prominent, with a separation and decentralization of funding and supply of social care. After some years of experience of marketization, however, particularly in the United Kingdom and other western European countries, the initial pro-market rhetoric is now being questioned. The central concern is that, although markets work well under textbook conditions, these conditions may not hold in social care (Bartlett and Le Grand 1993; Bartlett *et al.* 1994). The relevant policy question, then, is how the often mentioned shortcomings of public hierarchies fare in comparison with actual social care markets and their limitations.

This chapter considers in more detail the hypothesized relationship between entrepreneurial behaviour and market-like governance arrangements. It then goes on to describe the social care systems in several European countries in terms of their governance arrangements.

Entrepreneurial behaviour

Within the context of increasing fiscal pressure and changing political perceptions regarding the efficiency of public-sector culture, the policy goals of increasing productivity, innovation, user outcomes and cost-cutting – or what we might summarize as improving efficiency – have become relevant for decision-makers. Although a conceptual definition of these goals can be freestanding, much of the thinking about them relates specifically to the means by which transactions (relating in our case to social care) are undertaken (Wistow *et al.* 1994; Glennerster and Le Grand 1995; Lewis and Glennerster 1996).

In particular, there is a view that traditional bureaucracy arrangements stifle innovation and cost-cutting, and that the introduction of market-like arrangements will facilitate the attainment of these goals. This policy rhetoric has roots in neo-liberal and 'New Right' ideologies, which draw on public choice critiques of government and public bureaucracy (Niskanen 1971; Bucannon and Tollison 1984; Cullis and Jones 1987). The conceptual basis of this tradition is neoclassical economics and, in particular, the predicted optimal welfare consequences of using (textbook) perfectly competitive markets rather than collective action (Varian 1978). The literature on government failure (e.g. Wolf 1979) and the problem of collective action (Buchanan and Tullock 1965; Downs 1967) assert that non-market behaviour will be inefficient. New Right normative rhetoric takes this theorem to imply that markets are the *best* way to promote efficiency and are 'natural' mechanisms; alternative arrangements such as government bureaucracy merely distort the working of markets and create inefficiency.

Assuming providers wish to maximize surpluses – either directly because profits are sought or indirectly as a means to serve other goals – then competition is not needed to promote entrepreneurial behaviour. For example, for-profit monopolists would cut costs and innovate to maximize profits. Organizations with other motives and goals, however, whose attainment is little affected by the amount of surplus made, will be unresponsive to market incentives. Then, only the threat of business failure will be an effective sanction in forcing entrepreneurial-like behaviour. Competition will push down revenue and so force these providers to cut costs, innovate relative to demand, or fail. Generally, competition is *sufficient* but not *necessary* for entrepreneurial behaviour.

What kinds of social care system promote entrepreneurial behaviour? To address this question, we need a conceptual framework able to (a) characterize different social care systems in ways that are relevant to this purpose and (b) consider the nature of relationships between different social care systems and entrepreneurial behaviour. The economics of organization offers a useful framework, with the concept of governance structures at its heart (Williamson 1985, 1986; Milgrom and Roberts 1992; Miller 1992).

Governance structure

Williamson (1994: 102) defined a governance structure as 'the institutional matrix within which the integrity of a transaction is decided'. It comprises the institutions, conventions, rules and regulations that shape interaction between stakeholders as they undertake transactions. Using transactions rather than production as the unit of analysis, the literature identifies market and hierarchy archetypes and also intermediate forms (Coase 1937; Williamson 1975, 1979, 1985; see also Granovetter 1985; Dow 1987; Perrow 1990; Hamilton and Feenstra 1995). Governance structures can be distinguished in four ways: by the way control rights and property rights are distributed among stakeholders; by the nature of the mechanism for allocating resources (e.g. the reimbursement arrangements); by supply-side regulation arrangements; and by the types of contract agreed on between stakeholders. As we shall see, most policy reforms can be conceived as changes along these dimensions.

In what follows, I describe each of these four dimensions and also consider how choices along each dimension relate to the promotion of entrepreneurial behaviour. The latter draws on the theoretical literature on the economics of organization. The essence of the argument is that entrepreneurial behaviour is closely concerned with the power of incentives (see, in particular, Williamson 1985).

'High-powered' incentives promote behaviour such as cost-cutting and innovation regarding product specification/characteristics. Williamson uses the term 'high-powered incentives' with reference to a stakeholder who has 'residual claimant' status – that is, a stakeholder who 'either by agreement or under the prevailing definition of property rights, appropriates a net revenue stream, the gross receipts and/or costs of which stream are influenced by the efforts expended by the economic agent' (Williamson 1985: 132). Incentives are of highest power when a stakeholder keeps all of the residual financial spoils created by his effort; when the terms of the exchange (i.e. the payment structure) are negotiable but determined in advance and fixed by agreement; and when demand is responsive to the characteristics of the product on offer (i.e. responsive to innovation). In general, and consistent with the policy rhetoric, market governance structures create high-powered incentives, which, in turn, facilitate entrepreneurial behaviour.

Control and property rights

Control rights confer the authority to make transaction-relevant decisions (Coleman 1990). Property rights are 'the bundle of rights over the use and the income to be derived from property and the ability to alienate an asset or a resource' (North 1990: 47). Market governance structures have a real separation between purchasers and providers; control rights over the relevant processes are dispersed across these and other relevant stakeholders.

Although markets can be differentiated from hierarchies by the nature of control rights, the characteristics of property rights serve to differentiate *types* of market. *Private markets* have dispersed property rights; providers are residual claimants because they own the production assets, and hence have rights to any (residual) income flow from those assets. Purchasers are also private and can dispose of their income as they wish (within broad, mainly legal, limits). *Public markets* have both public-sector purchasers and providers. Providers, therefore, do not have claims to residuals as a result of ownership of production assets. In fact, social care providers are generally salaried, and thus have lower powered incentives (Wistow *et al.* 1996).[1]

Quasi-markets have a mix of public purchasers and private providers. In such markets, therefore, production processes generally involve relatively high-powered incentives (although powerful purchasers can reduce these incentives contractually if they wish). In social care, these arrangements usually involve local authorities using public funds to purchase care from voluntary and private, for-profit providers (Bartlett and Le Grand 1993; Bartlett *et al.* 1994, 1998; Wistow *et al.* 1994, 1996).

Unlike markets, hierarchical governance structures have centralized, unified configurations of control rights. Managers are responsible for both needs planning ('purchasing') and production, making relevant decisions centrally and passing to subordinates instructions concerning the implementation of these decisions. In archetypal hierarchies, employees generally lack both (significant) property *and* control rights and so have little incentive to be entrepreneurial. In private hierarchies, managers may have higher-powered incentives (having property and control rights) and the effects, in principle, can be transmitted to employees. In practice, however, many problems limit this effect. Finally, managers in public hierarchies are much less likely to have claims to residuals and, therefore, public hierarchies will have even lower-powered incentives in theory.

Reimbursement arrangements

Where control rights are shared, as in markets, the purchaser and provider need to agree on the terms of the transaction. Although some form of retrospective reimbursement contract is possible, it is usual for prices to be negotiated in advance and then fixed for the duration of the contract. *Prospective payments* are those that are not contingent on the production costs of the service. Hierarchies have central control over reimbursement rates. Prices tend to be determined retrospectively within the organization, or resource allocation is by quota rather than by price.

In practice, prices and price structures will be determined according to the distribution of market power among stakeholders, unless some regulatory control is exercised over prices (e.g. a minimum wage or a price ceiling). *Price regulation* is sanctioned politically or legally and is different from the case of powerful purchasers exerting their influence over price.

Supply-side regulation

Some control over the supply characteristics of services may be vested with regulatory bodies, as with price regulation. In social care, regulation to protect users usually involves (legally sanctioned) control over production process factors, such as staffing ratios and qualifications, certifications regarding care facilities, and so on. To the extent that these regulatory powers remove control rights from providing stakeholders, they have ramifications for the nature of entrepreneurial behaviour.

Contracts

Contracts define control rights among stakeholders, explicitly specify commitments and the contingencies for which they apply, and also represent the agreements among stakeholders concerning reimbursement structures. Unlike third-party regulation, parties involved in a transaction *voluntarily* agree to contracts. Generally, they are subject to the provisions of contract law, but this need not be the case and 'contracts' can be simply the representation of the agreement among stakeholders. In most cases, contracts can be renegotiated at any time.[2]

Contracts as such do not promote entrepreneurial behaviour, as they are only representations of stakeholders' choices of governance structure (Buchanan 1986). Nonetheless, the use of the term 'contracting' in most of the social care policy literature is synonymous with market-like governance. Thus, we distinguish between tightly specified arms-length contracts and much more generally specified relational contracts (Dore 1983; MacNeil 1985; Sako 1992) in describing different forms of market governance. In social care, the combination of users' vulnerability, their need for protection and purchasers' mistrust of private providers has meant the use of relatively tight contract specifications, at least initially after the introduction of social care markets (for the United Kingdom, see Wistow *et al.* 1994, 1996).

Entrepreneurial behaviour and social care systems in Europe

Three of the four dimensions that describe governance structures are also relevant to the issue of promoting entrepreneurial behaviour: property and control rights, reimbursement arrangements and supply-side regulation. Social care reform in Europe can be understood as a change along these dimensions. Privatization and decentralization are real policy counterparts of the first dimension. The adoption of new payment structures, particularly prospective payment systems, relates to the second dimension. Finally, the establishment of new independent monitoring and review bodies reflects supply-side regulation, the third dimension.

Figure 8.1 shows forms of social care organization according to (a) the ownership of the purchasing function and (b) the ownership (property rights) of the means of provision. This is then further broken down by whether control rights are arrayed hierarchically or whether they are dispersed as in a market.

Figure 8.1 Forms of formal social care organization in western European countries

Purchasing				Provision		
				Public	Private	
					Non-profit	For profit
Hierarchy	Public organization			Public bureaucracy		
Hierarchy	Private organization				Voluntary bureaucracy	
(Quasi-) market	Public organization			Internal market	Contracting-out	Contracting-out
(Quasi-) market	Private	Organization			Voluntary brokerage	
(Quasi-) market	Private	Individual	Social insurance/ assistance		Vouchers	Vouchers
(Quasi-) market	Private	Individual	Personal income	User payments	Private market	Private market

United Kingdom

The drive towards the unbridling of entrepreneurial behaviour, or 'enabling' as it was called, was the central characteristic of the reform of the British social care system in the early 1990s (Griffiths 1988; Ridley 1988; Wistow *et al.* 1994; Lewis *et al.* 1995). The White Paper, *Caring for People*, which set out the main policy groundwork for the subsequent 1990 National Health Service and Community Care Act, endorsed the vision of Margaret Thatcher's adviser, Sir Roy Griffiths, which was of 'authorities as arrangers and purchasers of care services rather than monopolistic providers' (Secretaries of State 1989: 17).

Before the implementation of the reforms in 1993, the social care system had two main governance structures. The first involved central and local tax funding administered by the local authority. The local authority allocated budgets to its social services department (SSD) to fund services supplied mainly by SSD providers and, to a very limited extent, by external providers. Most local authority social services departments operated a traditional hierarchical bureaucracy, with spending and service-need decisions undertaken by managers who were also directly responsible for provision. Funding went straight to the internal provider (some of which was then re-routed to the independent sector) on the basis of retrospective supply levels, and individual stakeholders were salaried. This configuration of control rights and reimbursement created very low-powered incentives, a feature that was at the heart of the subsequent policy critiques (Audit Commission 1986; Griffiths 1988).

The second governance structure, in particular in contrast to the first, was essentially a private market with price regulation (a voucher system). For institutional and residential care, individuals could purchase places from independent (non-public) sector providers using a dedicated social assistance benefit. This benefit paid only up to a fixed ceiling and so prices were *de facto* regulated in the market. The high-powered nature of incentives is reflected in the very high responsiveness of provision to changes in demand. Because the benefit entitlement was rather loose – eligibility required only minimum financial conditions and a care need that could be sanctioned by a local general practitioner – demand-led supply increased substantially.

The reforms in 1993 substantially reconfigured the governance arrangements. They involved stopping the residential care social assistance payment to new users, thus removing the publicly supported vouchers. At the same time, the role of purchaser and provider were made distinct and separate within the local authority. Thus, a quasi-market was created. Public-sector (local authority) purchasing stakeholders would act on behalf of (new) users who were assessed as eligible, buying their assessed package of care but not having provision responsibilities. Control over provision would pass to provider stakeholders, either public or private. In both residential and home care, the scale of local authority funding has increased rapidly, as has the proportion going to the independent sector (Department of Health 1998).

Within the quasi-market structure, the reform legislation gave local authorities a good deal of discretion in determining their own local arrangements. At present, the nature of the purchaser–provider separation of control remains different in many cases for transactions with public-sector providers compared with transactions with private providers (Audit Commission 1997; Forder *et al.* 1997). In cases of public provision, managers in authorities exercise control over purchasing and, at the same time, much of the provision. Only comparatively low-level provision decisions are ceded to providers. Moreover, reimbursement is largely retrospective in these cases (Forder *et al.* 1997). The distinction between quasi-market and hierarchy is therefore rather blurred. In the extreme, these arrangements can (still) be regarded as public bureaucracies.

The separation of purchasers from private-sector providers has been much more distinct. Most local authority purchasers have used their considerable contracting power to impose prospective, fixed-price reimbursement on providers (Walsh 1995; Lewis and Glennerster 1996; Wistow *et al.* 1996). At least initially, relatively formal arms-length contractual relationships were used with detailed specifications and service delivery conditions. As purchaser–provider relationships have matured, the governance of transactions has changed, with decision-making becoming more integrated or obligatory (Sako 1992). The 1998 White Paper on social care (Secretary of State 1998) advocates this partnership model as the 'third way' between the extremes of pure market and pure bureaucracy.

There is currently little price regulation in the social care market, but supply-side regulation of standards is significant. Consistent with the recommendations of the 1998 White Paper, new Commissions for Care Standards are being set up. These Commissions will consolidate the previous social care registration and inspection arrangements into a national standards framework, and will broaden their scope to cover both public and private providers. The focus of regulation is set to shift from process indicators to user outcomes.

There is some recent evidence in the United Kingdom that market arrangements generate lower production costs under market governance compared with more hierarchical forms (Forder 1999, 2000). Regarding purchaser innovation, the change in governance has been argued to remove some of the perverse incentives for the use of residential rather than home care (Secretaries of State 1989).

Nevertheless, there is also some indication of information problems in social care. In social care with its complex, multidimensional and dynamic character, the potential for stakeholders (particularly providers) to exploit information advantages is significant (Forder 1997). The transaction costs of addressing these problems can be large, and the theory suggests that high-powered incentives and entrepreneurial behaviour can exacerbate these costs. Thus the above evidence, in providing some support for these hypotheses, raises some questions about the policy goals of promoting entrepreneurial behaviour.

Little quantitative evidence currently exists regarding the balance of use of partnership modes. But anecdotal findings suggest its increased use, particularly in response to information problems and other market failures. Thus, policy-makers seem to be developing beyond the entrepreneurial behaviour rhetoric described above.

Germany

Social care reform in Germany is mainly concerned with the funding of care rather than its provision. Its centrepiece is the 1994 extension of the social insurance system to cover long-term care.

Pre-1994, funding was mixed and somewhat fragmented, with many people relying on their own income and supported, where required, by social assistance (Wasem 1997). Services were delivered either by municipal bureaucracy or by traditional non-profit organizations that formed a virtual cartel in welfare markets. Although these non-profit organizations could charge prospectively determined fees and were residual claimants, the combination of a non-profit constraint, objectives that were only weakly responsive to (small) changes in surplus and poor competition meant that there was little incentive to diversify or introduce innovative new services. Schunk (1998) argues that the various internal interests within the organization blunted external responsiveness to incentives (see also Cyert and March 1963).

The present funding structure for social care in Germany comprises public funders and individual private payers. Public funding takes two forms: non-means-tested care insurance – which pays out either cash benefits or benefits-in-kind as chosen by the claimant – and means-tested social assistance (Wasem 1997). Seventy-seven per cent of people entitled to home care benefits by the care insurance have opted for the cash benefit (and an additional 12 per cent for a mixture of cash and in-kind), even though its buying value is only around half that of the in-kind benefits (Busse 2000).

Provision of institutional care services has a mainly non-profit structure. In the mid- to late 1990s, more than half of provider agencies were run by the non-profit sector. About 30 per cent were run by commercial (for-profit) agencies and the remainder were public (usually operated by the municipality). The care insurance scheme gives priority to private providers (not legally discriminating against for-profit organizations) over public organizations (Schunk 1998).

So what are the main forms of governance in the German social care system? Private payers or individuals drawing on social assistance are their own primary purchaser, undertaking care planning and purchasing functions themselves. For informal services, individuals can take a cash-benefit option from the social insurance system and make their own service arrangements. In these cases, therefore, a private market (with public support) is in operation, with dispersed control and property rights.

In relation to formal services, the publicly administered care insurance fund can be regarded as the purchaser working on behalf of individuals who opt to take benefits-in-kind. The insurer contracts with provider organizations, specifying the terms and prices under which the services offered by the provider organization are eligible for reimbursement. Prices are prospectively determined and, once set, are binding for the period of the contract; they cannot be increased to cover any increases in real costs (Schunk 1998). Clearly, this pricing system creates high-powered incentives for providers. The more centralized and public character of purchasing in this case means that the system is best considered a quasi-market. Funding is public, commissioning is by the care insurance agency, and contracted provision is by a mix of non-profit and for-profit providers (and to a lesser extent, public providers).

Differences with the British system relate to Germany's stronger emphasis on the individual as *purchaser* for state-funded services, which underlines the importance of private-market governance for publicly supported care in the German system (Evers 1997). The demand side of the social care market potentially generates high-powered incentives and, in turn, entrepreneurial behaviour. Social insurance purchases are more centralized, but the prospective pricing and binding regulation of contract prices should certainly not mean any lessening of incentives compared with the rest of the social care market. In relation to the stimulation of entrepreneurial behaviour, the increased use of private, for-profit providers on the supply side reflects stiffer competition and organizations that are more responsive to financial incentives.

France

In France, the funding structure for home care is a mix of public means – funds from the social assistance system (administered by local government *départements*) and the social insurance fund (Caisse Nationale d'Assurance Vieillesse) – and individual self-funding. The provision structure comprises mainly non-profit organizations or *associations* (a small for-profit provision element exists) and also public organizations (local municipalities) (Davies *et al.* 1998).

In France, it is typical for the non-profit *association* to be the purchaser of home care services as well as the provider. The financing agency defines general terms of service delivery in the form of a *convention*, but it is the non-profit *association* that undertakes the purchasing. This form of organization is a voluntary sector bureaucracy; control rights are hierarchical and all property rights are private sector. The *convention*, with its prospective nature, is an instrument to potentially create incentives for the *associations*. But the system is not very competitive. With predominantly non-profit-related objectives, this governance structure is unlikely to demonstrate much entrepreneurial behaviour.

Newer types of *association* also act as purchasers on behalf of users, but relinquish the provider role. They help users determine their service needs but then purchase from other private-provider organizations. In effect, this is a hybrid purchaser arrangement with a mix of private organization and individual stakeholders, termed 'voluntary brokerage' in Figure 8.1. Use of this arrangement also reflects moves by French policy-makers to direct funds to individuals.

Residential care provision is also through a mix of public and private organizations, although for-profit organizations play a greater role than in the case of home care. The funding structure comprises a social component and a health component. The former – the cost of board and lodging – is met by the users and their families (under the provisions of *obligation alimentaire*, the legal requirement that a family meets the living costs of an elderly relative's care) and also by the social assistance scheme in the case of low income. Purchasing is either by the individual or by the municipality. Individual purchasing from private providers is a private-market system. When individual purchasers are funded by social assistance, the system is more precisely a voucher system. Purchasing by the public authorities can be described as contracting-out if there is a purchaser–provider separation or, otherwise, a public bureaucracy.

With parallels to German social insurance, France in 1995 introduced an experimental social security allowance, the Prestation Expérimentale Dépendance, which can be received by users as in-kind service benefits (through payments to providers) or as a cash benefit paid directly to the elderly person. Unlike the German system, the allowance is means-tested and tax-based rather than funded by social insurance. This experiment represents a restructuring of the commissioning function with more importance given to user choice, a move away from brokerage by public and non-profit organizations. Where cash benefits are concerned, rather than a voucher system, the system more closely approximates a private market with income transfers.

The implications for entrepreneurial behaviour of this experimental system are like those of the German system. Nonetheless, French public services have traditionally avoided private entrepreneurialism, with a long history of bureaucratically organized provision. This culture is likely to continue to influence social care governance systems, although the implications for care of more limited entrepreneurial behaviour are unclear for the reasons alluded to above, and need not be negative.

Denmark and Finland

Denmark has very high levels of public provision of institutional care and funding is almost exclusively public. Funds are raised by local taxation and supplemented by grants from central government (out of general taxation) (OECD 1996). In the main, therefore, the governance system is a public-sector hierarchy, although the Scandinavian model has traditionally devolved these hierarchies geographically to very local levels, with improved local responsiveness as a result.

More recently, there have been several initiatives that have involved the use of private provision (although still exclusively purchased by the local municipality). First, voluntary respite services for carers have been introduced, although they work closely with public providers. Second, there has been some contracting-out of standard home care services to private companies, together with a modest amount of leasing of municipal nursing homes. Third, policy changes have allowed individuals to self-fund 'top-up services' beyond the standard minimum provided under public financing (Pederson 1998).

These contracting-out initiatives are as yet of modest size. Pederson (1998) cites resistance from public providers, local municipalities and users. Public employees fear adverse effects on working conditions should ownership change. Public service professionals also fear a loss of discretion as a result of standardization that can result from detailed service specifications in a contracting culture. Local users and the general public are also said to be resistant to the ideology of profit in welfare services. Finally, local government members are reticent about losing responsibilities. But a move in the direction of quasi-market governance clearly suggests that ideas relating to entrepreneurialism are appearing on the policy agenda.

Consistent with the Scandinavian model, in Finland the production of social services is almost entirely by local municipalities, with funding shared by local and central government. Like the other Nordic countries, this principle of universal collective funding of social care is now coming under pressure. In 1993, changes in regulations allowed municipalities to levy charges for the services they provide. Although from the outset these charges were relatively modest, there were intentions to increase the cost share met by charges to around a third, particularly for home care (Martimo 1998). Overall, then, in both Denmark and Finland, a quasi-market fringe is developing around the core of the traditionally dominant public hierarchy, and represents an incipient unbridling of entrepreneurial behaviour.

Spain

Spain's expenditure on formal social services, at less than 1 per cent of gross domestic product in the early 1990s, is relatively low compared to the OCED average (OECD 1996). The level of residential care is similarly low, with over two-thirds of homes privately owned. Overall, the purchasing function is undertaken by public authorities using 'agreements' between public purchasers and providers. Care planning is administered by a combination of regional governments and also by the National Institute for Social Services, a part of the Ministry of Labour and Social Affairs. Local governments are also involved in social care, especially in the planning and management of services. The funding structure is a combination of collective public subsidies (tax-based) and individual payments in the form of charges. For the typical residential care site, the charge made to the individual user covers less than a third of the cost and can be met by social assistance and pension provisions. The residential care system fits with the quasi-market contracting-out structure.

Day and home care services are mainly provided by local authorities, although there is a growing involvement of religious and other non-profit organizations (OECD 1996). Tax funding meets most of the costs of these services for low-income individuals, and administration of commissioning and purchasing is mainly by the local authority.

In Spain, as in other southern European countries, social care is centred around the family and is relatively informal. In this way, it can be very cognisant of, and responsive to, the needs of the individual. Continuing economic development and associated changes in cultural perceptions might be expected to mean a greater role for formal care services. These changes will present a challenge in maintaining this responsiveness and flexibility or in stretching the concept of informal entrepreneurial behaviour.

Conclusions

Markets, with varying degrees of regulation and private sector provision, are increasingly important features of many European social services systems. Decentralization of funding structures has also accompanied the drive of marketization, especially in the form of cash benefits and vouchers to users or client-led brokerage by local authorities. The pro-market rhetoric emphasizes the 'high-powered' incentives created by markets, which can improve productivity and investment, cut costs and sharpen targeting. It is argued that markets can unbridle entrepreneurial behaviour.

Changes in the policy landscape in European social care in the 1980s and early 1990s reflect the beliefs that promoting entrepreneurial behaviour is possible and that it would attend to the perceived efficiency failures of the previous systems. A breaking up of traditional bureaucratic organization was a fundamental feature of the reforms and occurred in many western European systems. At the same time, public funding of long-term care was being moved away from the social assistance route and individual purchasing, diminishing the role of private markets. Instead, quasi-market arrangements were being adopted with public financing and public purchasers, be they local government or social insurance funds. Entrepreneurialism in relation to providers was certainly increased. But the centralization of purchasing from individual to broker organizations is inconsistent with the drive towards entrepreneurial behaviour and, perhaps, demonstrates concern on the part of decision-makers regarding the characteristics of social care users, especially their vulnerability and their understanding of the significant complexities of the market.

In practice, several conditions need to exist for provider entrepreneurial activity in markets to be directed in a mutually beneficial way, rather than in a way that exploits purchasers and users. Economic theory holds that healthy competition and good information flows are important prerequisites. When these conditions are absent, and especially when bureaucracies are well managed, the comparative advantage of markets claimed by their proponents is called into question.

There are several implications for the structure and regulation of social services. Putting aside funding issues, the regulation of social care needs to attend to information issues and the alignment of incentives between purchaser and provider. More flexible and innovate forms of contracting may provide the answer. Developing relational contracting (Williamson 1985; Kreps 1996), fostering trust between stakeholders and adopting mutual and adaptive solutions to problems have significant potential (Sako 1992; Taylor and Hoggett 1994; Fukuyama 1995; Lyons and Mehta 1997).

In social care especially, there now appears to be a period of assessment regarding the comparative merits of markets and (loosely regulated) entrepreneurial behaviour. If public bureaucracy constituted a first phase in policy thinking about social organization, and quasi-markets characterize the second phase, then arguably we are now entering a new phase that can be described as the third way (Blair 1998; Giddens 1998).

Notes

1 Nonetheless, when providers in public systems have significant control rights and operate with payment structures that are contingent on outputs, they can appropriate incomes that can be influenced through their own efforts. Examples include performance-related pay, piece rates, employee share ownership schemes, and so on. Incentives will be attenuated, in comparison to cases where stakeholders are conferred residual claimant status by ownership, but this demonstrates that entrepreneurial behaviour does not depend on separate ownership.

2 Even legally binding contracts are subject to renegotiation. Most legal systems will enforce the renegotiated contract, not the original, so the new version could simply have a clause that waives the original penalty clauses (Hart 1995).

References

Audit Commission (1986) *Making a Reality of Community Care*. London: HMSO.

Audit Commission (1997) *The Coming of Age: Improving Care Services for Older People*. London: Audit Commission.

Bartlett, W. and Le Grand, J. (1993) The theory of quasi-markets, in J. Le Grand and W. Bartlett (eds) *Quasi-markets and Social Policy*. Basingstoke: Macmillan.

Bartlett, W., Propper, C., Wilson, D. and Le Grand, J. (eds) (1994) *Quasi-markets in the Welfare State*. Bristol: SAUS Publications.

Bartlett, W., Roberts, J. and Le Grand, J. (1998) The development of quasi-markets in the 1990s, in W. Bartlett, J. Roberts and J. Le Grand (eds) *A Revolution in Social Policy: Quasi-market Reforms in the 1990s*. Bristol: Policy Press.

Blair, T. (1998) *The Third Way: New Politics for the New Century*, Fabian Pamphlet No. 588. London: The Fabian Society.

Bucannon, J. and Tollison, R. (eds) (1984) *The Theory of Public Choice II*. Ann Arbor, MI: University of Michigan.

Buchanan, J.M. (1986) *Liberty, Market, and State*. Brighton: Wheatsheaf.

Buchanan, J.M. and Tullock, G. (1965) *The Calculus of Consent*. Ann Arbor, MI: University of Michigan.

Busse, R. (2000) *Health Care Systems in Transition: Germany*. Copenhagen: European Observatory on Health Care Systems.

Coase, R. (1937) The nature of the firm, *Economica*, 4: 386–405.

Coleman, J.S. (1990) *Foundations of Social Theory*. Cambridge, MA: Harvard University Press.

Cullis, J. and Jones, P. (1987) *Microeconomics and the Public Economy: A Defence of Leviathan*. Oxford: Blackwell.

Cyert, R. and March, J. (1963) *A Behavioural Theory of the Firm*. Englewood Cliffs, NJ: Prentice-Hall.

Davies, B., Fernandes, J. and Sanders, R. (1998) *Community Care in England and France*. Aldershot: Ashgate Arena.

Department of Health (1998) *Community Care Statistics: Residential Personal Social Services for Adults, England*, Bulletin 1998/37. London: Department of Health.

Dore, R. (1983) Goodwill and the spirit of market capitalism, *British Journal of Sociology*, 34: 459–82.

Dow, G. (1987) The function of authority in transaction cost economics, *Journal of Economic Behaviour and Organization*, 8: 13–38.

Downs, A. (1967) *An Economic Theory of Democracy*. New York: Harper & Row.

Evers, A. (1997) *Long-term Care for the Elderly: Britain and Germany Compared*. London: Anglo-German Foundation.

Forder, J. (1997) Contracts and purchaser–provider relationships in community care, *Journal of Health Economics*, 16: 517–42.

Forder, J. (1999) *Market Power and Mental Health*, PSSRU Discussion Paper. London: London School of Economics.

Forder, J. (2000) *Governance Issues in Social Care: Comparative Transaction and Production Costs*, PSSRU Discussion paper. London: London School of Economics.

Forder, J., Hardy, B., Kendall, J., Wistow, G. and Knapp, M. (1997) *Broad Mixed Economy Mapping*, MEOC Discussion Paper. London/Leeds: London School of Economics/ University of Leeds.

Fukuyama, F. (1995) *Trust*. London: Penguin.

Giddens, A. (1998) *The Third Way: The Renewal of Social Democracy*. Cambridge: Polity Press.

Glennerster, H. and Le Grand, J. (1995) The development of quasi-markets in welfare provision in the United Kingdom, *International Journal of Health Services*, 25: 203–18.

Granovetter, M. (1985) Economic action and social structure: the problem of embeddedness, *American Journal of Sociology*, 91: 481–510.

Griffiths, R. (1988) *Community Care: Agenda for Action*. London: HMSO.

Hamilton, G. and Feenstra, R. (1995) Varieties of hierarchies and markets: an introduction, *Industrial and Corporate Change*, 4: 51–91.

Hart, O. (1995) Firms, contracts and financial structure, *Clarendon Lectures in Economics*. Oxford: Oxford University Press.

Kreps, D. (1996) Markets and hierarchies and (mathematical) economic theory, *Industrial and Corporate Change*, 5: 561–95.

Lewis, J. and Glennerster, H. (1996) *Implementing the New Community Care*. Buckingham: Open University Press.

Lewis, J., Bernstock, P. and Bovell, V. (1995) The community care changes: unresolved tensions in policy and issues in implemenation, *Journal of Social Policy*, 24: 73–94.

Lyons, B. and Mehta, J. (1997) Contracts, opportunism and trust: self-interest and social orientation, *Cambridge Journal of Economics*, 21: 239–57.

MacNeil, I. (1985) Relational contracts: what we do and do not know, *Wisconsin Law Review*, 483–525.

Martimo, K. (1998) Community care for frail older people in Finland, in C. Glendinning (ed.) *Rights and Realities: Comparing New Developments in Long-term Care for Older People*. Bristol: Policy Press.

Milgrom, P. and Roberts, J. (1992) *Economics, Organization and Management*. Englewood Cliffs, NJ: Prentice-Hall.

Miller, G. (1992) *Managerial Dilemmas: The Political Economy of Hierarchy*. Cambridge: Cambridge University Press.

Niskanan, W. (1971) *Bureaucracy and Representative Government*. Chicago, IL: Adline.

North, D. (1990) *Institutions, Institutional Change and Economic Performance*. Cambridge: Cambridge University Press.

Organisation for Economic Co-operation and Development (1996) *Caring for Frail Elderly People: Policies in Evolution*. Paris: OECD.

Pederson, L. (1998) Health and social care for older people in Denmark: a public solution under threat?, in C. Glendinning (ed.) *Rights and Realities: Comparing New Developments in Long-term Care for Older People*. Bristol: Policy Press.

Perrow, C. (1990) Economic theories of organization, in S. Zukin and P. DiMaggio (eds) *Structure of Capital: The Social Organization of the Economy*. Cambridge: Cambridge University Press.

Ridley, N. (1988) *The Local Right: Enabling Not Providing*, Policy Study No. 92. London: Centre for Policy Studies.

Sako, M. (1992) *Prices, Quality and Trust: Inter-firm Relations in Britain and Japan*. Cambridge: Cambridge University Press.

Schunk, M. (1998) The social insurance model of care for older people in Germany, in C. Glendinning (ed.) *Rights and Realities: Comparing New Developments in Long-term Care for Older People*. Bristol: Policy Press.

Secretaries of State (1989) *Caring for People: Community Care in the Next Decade and Beyond*, Cm 849. London: HMSO.

Secretary of State (1998) *Modernising Social Services: Promoting Independence, Improving Protection, Raising Standards*. London: The Stationery Office.

Taylor, M. and Hoggett, P. (1994) Trusting in networks? The third sector and welfare change, in P. 6 and I. Vidal (eds) *Delivering Welfare – Repositioning Non-Profit and Co-operative Action in Western European Welfare States*. Barcelona: Centre d'Iniciatives de l'Economia Social.

Varian, H. (1978) *Microeconomic Analysis*. New York: W.W. Norton.

Walsh, K. (1995) *Working with Contracts*. Birmingham: University of Birmingham.

Wasem, J. (1997) A study on decentralizing from acute care to home care settings in Germany, *Health Policy*, 41: S109–S129.

Williamson, O. (1975) *Markets and Hierarchies*. New York: Free Press.

Williamson, O. (1979) Transaction cost economics: the governance of contractual relations, *Journal of Law and Economics*, 22: 233–61.

Williamson, O. (1985) *The Economic Institutions of Capitalism*. New York: Free Press.

Williamson, O. (1986) *Economic Organization: Firms, Markets and Policy Control*. Brighton: Wheatsheaf.

Williamson, O. (1994) Transaction cost economics and organization theory, in N. Smeltzer and R. Swedberg (eds) *The Handbook of Economic Sociology*. Princeton, NJ: Princeton University Press.

Wistow, G., Knapp, M., Hardy, B. and Allen, C. (1994) *Social Care in a Mixed Economy.* Buckingham: Open University Press.

Wistow, G., Knapp, M., Hardy, B. *et al.* (1996) *Social Care Markets: Progress and Prospects.* Buckingham: Open University Press.

Wolf, C. (1979) A theory of non-market behaviour: framework for implementation analysis, *Journal of Law and Economics*, 22: 107–40.

chapter nine

Regulating the entrepreneurial behaviour of third-party payers in health care

Igor Sheiman and Jürgen Wasem

Introduction

A key aspect of health care reform in several European countries has been to strengthen 'market mechanisms' and 'entrepreneurial behaviour' while still maintaining the notion of risk pooling and solidarity. This chapter deals with the relationship between regulation and entrepreneurial behaviour at the level of health care payers. First, we address conceptual issues – mechanisms of entrepreneurial behaviour of health care payers, public expectations and concerns about new roles of payers, and the main areas of regulation. Subsequently, we review the major regulatory institutions and instruments that are needed to ensure equity, efficiency and effectiveness, given available evidence about various types of entrepreneurial behaviour among third-party payers.

Conceptual issues

Two intriguing economic ideas have caught the attention of health policy-makers in several western and eastern European countries. One is that health care payers should become economically motivated health care purchasers who collect information on consumer needs, plan the most cost-effective medical interventions and contract selectively with the most efficient health care providers. The second idea is that a more competitive environment in which purchasers contract with both consumers (insured) and health care providers should be encouraged. These two interrelated ideas are at the core of various different models of regulated competition or managed competition (van de Ven 1990, 1994; Enthoven 1991).

It should be noted that here the notion of 'market principles' does not refer to a highly competitive market, but rather to the relatively new development in health care of a planned or internal market. This entails the intentional development of a market by the exercise of state power. It involves decentralization of the planning process, as well as 'the partial replacement of bureaucratic administrative mechanisms with market-derived incentives' (Saltman and von Otter 1992: 17).

Creating competitive incentives among payers

In the theory of regulated competition, the transformation of payers into health care purchasers and the resulting competition should create market pressure to make payers' behaviour more entrepreneurial. Four major mechanisms can be identified.

Consumer choice

Consumers acquire the ability to choose among various health care payers – health insurance institutions or general practitioner (GP) fundholders – who control the budget, purchase services of other providers and act to some extent as insurers. Insurance institutions, interested in attracting new members, are encouraged to become more responsive to consumer needs by using entrepreneurial tools, such as offering new 'products' or better prices, consumer protection and quality assurance programmes.

Setting premiums or adding supplementary benefits

These parameters are expected to influence the decision of consumers to switch from one health insurance institution to another and also make insurers cost-concious. The extent to which these parameters play a role in specific health insurance systems, and the impact of these parameters on insurance institutions, depends on the design of the system and the regulatory framework (Schneider 1994).

In private health insurance markets, differences in premiums have a long tradition. In social health insurance systems, they are rather rare in most countries (Normand and Busse 2001). If such differences are allowed, economic theory contends that they will influence decisions by insurers.

Provider contracting

A health insurer has some discretion as to how to organize its interaction with health care providers: the kinds of contract it will sign, the providers with which it wants to contract, how it will remunerate providers, the kind of referral systems (e.g. gatekeeping) it will implement, and so on. The minimum requirements for the implementation of contracting are: (a) a shift from collective (with associations of providers) to mostly individual contracting (with individual providers) and (b) a shift from contracting with all providers who wish to participate to selective contracting through mechanisms of competitive tendering (Saltman and Figueras 1997).

Increased risk-bearing

In social health insurance systems, as in private health insurance markets, payers may act as entrepreneurs responsible for covering the risks of subscribers' costs. Such payers must bear financial responsibility for the variation in health care costs for insurees (expected versus actual costs). Insurers are funded on a capitation basis, with a limit on their financial responsibility for possible variation of costs (van de Ven 1990). Risk-bearing makes payers inclined to look for ways to lower the cost of purchased care and hence to become more entrepreneurial. These new entrepreneurial activities by health purchasers need not make them commercial entities in which profit is the sole indicator of performance. Rather, they remain quasi-public organizations, but with more freedom to contract and higher degrees of risk-bearing.

Payers in non-competitive environments

Entrepreneurial behaviour of health payers can also be encouraged in a non-competitive environment, in which the market structure of health purchasing is monopsonic, with one dominant payer. In this case, a payer is required by regulation to use certain entrepreneurial instruments, such as contracts with providers or performance-related methods of provider payment. Government pressure is expected to compensate for the lack of market pressure.

This type of administrative pressure on health payers can be relevant in countries with integrated health systems (with no separation of health purchasers and providers). It is particularly appropriate in the countries of central and eastern Europe (CEE) and those of the Commonwealth of Independent States (CIS) with a traditional command-and-control approach to health management (Goldstein *et al.* 1996; Klugman and Schieber 1996).

A set of entrepreneurial instruments, used by payers, is not directly related to the health purchasing market structure. For example, selective contracting, at least in theory, can be required by the government in countries with a monopsonic market structure. With a formal procedure of competitive tendering in place, the monopsony of health purchasers may co-exist with a competitive model of health provision. In the same way, a competitive model of health purchasing may co-exist with a non-competitive model of health care provision. Competing purchasers may or may not contract selectively with health providers. The institutional constraints to selective contracting may exclude competitive contracting and make purchasers look for other ways to attract members. Thus the competitive model encourages entrepreneurial behaviour by health purchasers, but does not necessarily ensure the use of a full set of entrepreneurial tools.

Potential policy dilemmas

The entrepreneurial behaviour of health purchasers has generated concerns about its impact on the equity, accessibility and efficiency of health care provision. One concern is that competitive purchasers have a strong incentive to select risks – that is, to attract healthy members ('good risks') and to keep out the less healthy ('bad risks'). This risk selection can become a major aspect of entrepreneurial behaviour by health purchasers unless specific regulatory measures are undertaken to avoid it. Experience from the United States is perhaps the best indicator of the potential monetary impact of risk selection: estimates of competitive insurers' profits due to risk selection range from 20 to 34 per cent of premiums for hospital and specialist care (van de Ven and Van Vliet 1992). Thus competitive purchasers tend to erode social solidarity in health financing (Saltman and Figueras 1997) unless specific regulations ensure equity.

There is also concern about a potential conflict between the short-term interests of competing health purchasers and long-term health policy objectives. Purchasers may be more interested in contracting with service providers that look more attractive to 'good risks' or, for the same reason, to select more costly options of medical interventions with unclear clinical outcomes. They may be reluctant to pay for additional costs of training primary care providers or for experimental medical interventions designed to lower health costs in the long run. Also, preventive measures that would result in health gains or a reduction of health care costs in the long run could be unattractive to health purchasers.

A further potential conflict with health policy objectives is that selective contracting may impede the continuity of health care for many patients who have started their treatment with one physician but finish it with another, because their first physician was not re-awarded the contract. The same is true if insured persons switch health insurers (for instance, because of lower premiums) and the new insurer does not contract with the same network of providers.

Every country starting market or quasi-market health reforms faces the issue of how to avoid sudden dramatic shifts in the system of health care provision, for example through changes in the volume and structure of services across medical facilities in the region, and closures of hospitals due to the failure to contract. These changes are always politically sensitive, as they can damage access to medical care and they touch the interests of many actors in the health sector.

An important area of public regulation is how to ensure accountability. It has two major dimensions: on the one hand, health care purchasers have to be accountable to the general public (represented by public authorities, such as parliament, the Ministry of Health or a supervisory authority), while on the other hand, purchasers have to be accountable to their clients. The more health policy relies on competition among health insurance institutions, the greater the need for accountability. Choosing among institutions reflects choices between designs of benefit packages and contractual relations with providers. To make these choices rational, additional regulation is needed.

The issue of health purchasers' accountability to consumers is most relevant in private health insurance based on voluntary consumer choice, with a lower degree of risk pooling than in the social health insurance model. In this case, products sold must match the individual or group expectations of the subscribers who buy them with their own money, but who are not informed enough to make rational choices. The common examples of regulatory concern in private health insurance are whether the products have real value; whether consumers can easily understand and compare products; whether complaints are handled in a fair and prompt fashion; whether the access to and availability of services from providers are assured and adequate; and whether insurers have internal operating policies and procedures to prevent fraud (Turnbull 1997).

In sum, the need for regulation can be seen partly as an inherent characteristic of a entrepreneurial health purchasing model – its potential tendency to conflict with health policy objectives – and partly as a requirement for a transitional period when strengths and weaknesses of this model are not quite clear and a safety net is needed to neutralize potential losses in terms of equity, efficiency and accountability.

Institutional framework of regulation and supervision

Regulation of third-party payers is a multi-level process. The *general regulatory framework* comprising the basic 'rules of the game' forms the basis for regulation. These are issues such as how often the insured are allowed to switch from one insurance institution to another, who may contract with whom and under what conditions, whether any authority will be empowered to approve contracts, how premiums (or contribution rates) are set, whether there is an obligation for insurance institutions to accept every applicant and how risk selection can be avoided. The general framework is usually set up in the form of laws covering, for example, health insurance or health care institutions.

Individual regulatory acts fulfil the requirements of the general regulatory framework. For instance, if the general framework states that contracts between payers and providers need approval by a tariff authority, then there must be a procedure established for such approvals. Or, if there is a regulation for a risk-adjustment mechanism, then this mechanism must be specified and performed on a regular basis.

Supervision of the implementation of regulatory acts is necessary in a competitive setting with entrepreneurial behaviour. It cannot be taken for granted that funding institutions will 'automatically' behave according to the regulations, because at least sometimes they might gain competitive advantage if they do not follow the regulations (such as not accepting bad risks for membership). Supervision is therefore necessary to increase the likelihood that they follow regulations.

In most countries, designing the general regulatory framework is the responsibility of parliament, which may mean, in fact, that it follows the proposals of the government. In any case, individual regulatory acts are the responsibility of government agencies. These are usually the Ministry of Finance and the

Ministry of Health, but in some countries (such as Kazakhstan and the Russian Federation) the major regulatory agency is the central (federal) mandatory health insurance (MHI) fund.

The involvement of the Ministry of Health in the regulatory process of health insurance is a controversial issue in many CEE and CIS countries with an emerging Bismarck model. In the initial transition to the new model, there was a tendency to limit the role of the Ministry, fearing that it would limit the potential of insurers as independent payers. Also, health insurance bodies tended to build up their own industry by separating off that part of the whole system of health care provision that was funded by health insurers. In the Russian Federation, for example, regional health authorities and MHI funds tried to control as many financial resources as possible and therefore looked for ways to build their own system of health care provision. Regulatory acts were passed that tried to control the resulting fragmentation of the entire health system (Sheiman 1997).

The general tendency in CEE and CIS countries is to integrate or at least to coordinate more closely the regulatory activity of the Ministry of Health and the MHI fund. After a few years of regulatory mismatch – and sometimes even heated conflicts – between two governmental agencies, they have chosen to work closer on MHI regulation. In the Czech Republic, for example, the loss of control over health expenditure has required tougher regulation and a major role of the Ministry (National Economic Research Associates 1995; Busse *et al.* 2000). In the Russian Federation, the Ministry and the federal MHI fund now work closely on developing a uniform package of medical benefits and coordinate their regulatory roles.

As far as regulation of private health insurers is concerned, the Ministry of Finance and/or the Ministry of Commerce are mainly responsible, whereas the Ministry of Health is not, even though there often is an impact on health policy as well. In some countries, such as Germany and the Netherlands, the Ministry of Health is concerned with relations between private health insurers and health care providers.

Supervision is conducted through various government agencies, mostly the Ministry of Finance and the Ministry of Health. In some countries, the Ministry of Finance is also responsible for licensing health insurers. Sometimes this creates serious problems because, owing to its nature, the Ministry of Finance tends to focus on financial issues of insurers' performance with little or no supervision of their compliance with health policy objectives. In some countries, where the major role of licensing and supervision falls under the Ministry of Finance, there is a tendency for closer coordination between this Ministry and other health agencies. In the Russian Federation, for example, the federal MHI fund is seeking a new role for itself as a licensing and supervising agency to complement the activity of the Ministry of Finance (Semenov 1997).

In many countries, supervision is carried out by a mix of health-related agencies and special government institutions. In Germany, for example, official supervision of statutory sickness funds is the responsibility of small special units within the Ministries of Health of the *Länder*, and also of state insurance inspectors. Most countries have both local and central (federal) supervisory agencies.

In Germany, these supervisory agencies exert their influence and power over statutory sickness funds by a broad scale of legally defined instruments, including the right to:

- be informed and react to information before the sickness funds make any formal decisions;
- take an equal part in decision-making themselves by consensus, and reject possible non-consensual options of sickness funds; and
- in extreme cases replace decision-making by sickness funds by government order.

Thus, the regulation of sickness funds in Germany is a special mix of guidance and consultancy, supervision and inspection, information and control, permission and interdiction (Affeld 1997). Similar arrangements are being established in countries with the emerging health insurance model, although specific institutions and regulatory procedures differ from country to country (Marrée and Groenewegen 1997).

Areas of regulation

Regulation to ensure equity

A major task in establishing a regulatory framework for competition concerns equity. Health care costs are distributed among persons very unevenly. For instance, in the United States, it has been shown that 30 per cent of health costs are caused by 1 per cent of the population, whereas 50 per cent of the population cause less than 3 per cent of health care expenditure (Luft 1996). For equity reasons, regulators in most competitive (social) health insurance systems in Europe do not allow insurers to charge high premiums to those high-cost individuals. Instead, community rating (as in Switzerland) or income-related contributions (as in Germany) or a mixture of the two (as in the Netherlands) are prescribed by the regulator. As a result of this regulation, however, high-cost individuals become 'bad risks' for the insurers, because expenditures for these enrolees are much higher than the revenues from these people (Pauly 1984). If insurers engage in 'risk selection' and manage to avoid having bad risks in their portfolio, they could gain an advantage in competition. Additional regulation, therefore, is required to avoid risk selection.

One common regulatory instrument has been mandatory open enrolment – individual rights of the insured to periodically choose or change membership in social health insurance institutions. Related to this is regulation that obliges health insurance institutions to accept all applicants for membership. Some countries with an emerging competitive health-purchasing model have sought to ensure these rights and obligations (Czech Republic, Netherlands, Switzerland). Others, such as the Russian Federation, have declared the right of open enrolment, but the actual choice is usually made by employers who pay contributions for their employees and by local governments for the unemployed. Although the individual can formally apply for membership to any insurance company, the specific procedure that allows consumers to choose among insurers does not exist (Sheiman 1997).

Regulation in Germany does not include universal open enrolment. Whereas some social health insurance institutions are obliged to accept everybody, other health insurance institutions have a choice as to whether to accept everybody or only to accept certain categories of people. Those social health insurance institutions allowed to restrict membership to certain categories manage, on average, to have a better risk structure of their insured.

A second regulatory instrument consists of introducing a risk-adjustment mechanism for equalizing risks among insurers. The idea is to pool income-related health insurance contributions (or community rated premiums) in a central insurance fund and then to allocate them to competing health insurers according to a risk-adjusted capitation formula. The objective of this mechanism is to remove, or at least reduce, incentives for insurers to avoid insuring higher-risk groups.

Risk-adjustment mechanisms have been introduced in a variety of countries in recent years, the technical design of which differs a great deal. Important issues that have to be taken into account when designing such a risk-adjustment mechanism include (cf. Rice and Smith 2001):

- the 'risk factors' to be included in the risk-adjustment mechanism;
- the extent of the risk to be taken by health insurers; and
- whether risk equalization should be done at regional level (e.g. Switzerland) or at national level (e.g. Germany and the Netherlands).

A typical example in western Europe is that of Switzerland, where a risk-adjustment mechanism was introduced in 1993. Each health insurance institution in Switzerland collects its premiums from its insured. A risk-adjustment formula, with the age and gender of the insured as risk adjusters, is applied to each insurance institution; those institutions with a 'better' risk structure have to pay into the risk-adjustment system, while those with a below-average risk structure obtain funds from it. Thus the financial consequences with regard to differences in the distribution of the insured between age groups and gender are neutralized.

A major concern for the introduction of the risk-adjustment mechanism in Switzerland was solidarity and equity, because it was seen as unfair that those insurers who were insuring the young could offer lower premiums than those who were insuring the elderly. Another concern was efficiency: the mechanism should retain strong incentives for all insurance institutions to reduce health care costs. Analysis after 5 years of implementation showed that the main effects, which the Swiss Government wanted to achieve, were realized (Spycher 1999); nevertheless, there are still incentives for risk selection because age and gender are insufficient as risk adjusters.

An alternative solution is to impose a special regime of funding for high-cost cases (catastrophic risks) to reduce the incentives of insurers to select risks. Regulation in many countries (Estonia, Latvia, Kazakhstan, Russian Federation) takes away catastrophic risks from health insurers and has the government directly cover these risks.

Risk adjustment is not only an issue with regard to health insurance. It is always relevant when an agent with funding responsibilities has some discretion to select risk and is driven at least partly by entrepreneurial incentives. In the United Kingdom, for instance, under the fundholding scheme (1991–99) GP fundholders may have had an interest in attracting some patients but not others. General practitioner fundholders received a budget to finance three major areas of activity – staffing, drugs and those hospital and community health services that fundholders could purchase directly on behalf of their patients. The first two areas were budgeted mostly on a practice's past prescribing patterns and historical levels of staffing. In the early stage of the reform, budgets for hospital care were also historically based. Later, fundholder allocations were determined by negotiations with health authorities around an 'activity-based capitation benchmark' based on age and sex characteristics and also on the practice's historic activity. The presumption was that local factors (risk-adjusters) should be included in budgetary decisions through the negotiations.

In the first years of the fundholding scheme, there was no evidence of risk selection (Glennerster *et al.* 1998), which can be attributed to several factors. First, this was related to the open-ended process of setting budgets. General practitioners could negotiate for additional resources to cover higher costs of expensive patients on their lists, which reduced the incentive to exclude such patients. Second, regulation allowed health authorities to monitor changes in GPs' lists of patients and to investigate the sources of savings by fundholders. Third, there was a limit on payment for inpatient care and community care by fundholders, with the most costly referrals reimbursed directly by district health authorities. With all these factors limiting the incentives for risk selection in the short term, there was a strong possibility of more aggressive 'cream-skimming' in the future. For example, practices with less negotiating capacity for additional funds will most likely be tempted to be more selective regarding their list of patients. Thus, improvements in risk-adjustment regulation are needed that allow better links between budgets and risk characteristics of patients (National Economic Research Associates 1995).

Regulation of contracting

In countries with market-oriented reforms in a social health system, two different strategies of regulation on contracting usually co-exist. The first is to encourage and even pressure payers to contract selectively through a set of required rules and procedures for contracting. In most countries in Europe, there are obstacles to selective contracting, the most important being opposition from the medical profession. For decades, the prevailing pattern of resource allocation has been either totally non-contractual (direct provision of care by the government in most countries with the Beveridge model) or contractual, but with all physicians and hospital associations (in countries with the Bismarckian model). The second strategy consists of setting some limits on free contracting, mainly through contract approval procedures and the setting of a regulatory framework for reimbursement of health providers. This strategy is designed to ensure equity and efficiency.

Usually these two strategies conflict, resulting in purchaser dissatisfaction and calls for deregulation. The role of regulators is to find an optimum balance between freedom and regulation. The first strategy is implemented through a set of formal requirements for the contractual process, including the following.

- *The requirement to follow a specific procedure of contracting.* For example, in the early stages of the 1991 reform of the British National Health Service (NHS), the government approved competitive contracting. According to this procedure, purchasers assess needs and issue a statement describing these targets for providers, including expected volume of care, quality requirements and outcomes of care. Providers bid for contracts with the specifications of their capacity to meet the purchasers' requirements. The applications are then compared by the purchaser. This makes competitive bidding a mandatory procedure (Secretaries of State for Health 1989).
- *The requirement to negotiate on cost characteristics.* The purchaser is to look for the optimum balance of volume, cost and quality. Negotiated rates of payment become more important than fixed rates. Providers are selected through comparative costs across specialities and diagnosis.
- *The requirement to have open information for both purchasers and providers.* From the beginning, the purchaser is required to be as open as possible to attract more providers for the negotiating process. Providers are also to make all parameters of their applications open, including expected costs. This regulation is needed to facilitate the purchasing function and also to pressure providers to evaluate their costs relative to potential competitors (Culyer and Posnett 1990).
- *The requirement to follow specified rules of costing and pricing.* In the United Kingdom, the government passed regulation on principles and methods of costing and pricing. The regulation is designed so that there is a common basis for competitive contracting (Grant and Collini 1996).
- *The requirement to follow framework contracts* to ensure minimum standards of quality of care. The government may prescribe some form of service specification. In the Russian Federation, for example, emphasis is put on clinical standards that specify the minimum requirements for the process and outcomes of care for each diagnosis, so the range of options regarding the set of quality characteristics is relatively small (Kemerovo Department of Health 1995).
- *The right of purchasers to monitor and evaluate implementation of contractual provisions.* This includes the requirement for contracted medical facilities to provide all necessary clinical and economic information, and also to allow purchasers access to facilities for monitoring and evaluation of providers' performance.

The second strategy regarding the contracting process has a tendency to change as a reaction to reform implementation. The case of NHS reform in the United Kingdom provides a useful lesson about changing priorities regarding regulating the interaction between health purchasers and providers.

The broad consensus of research on the new role of health purchasers (district health authorities and GP fundholders) has been that they have shifted the balance of power away from hospital providers towards the patient's GP. General practitioner fundholders can pick hospitals that are more responsive in terms of quality requirements and waiting times. Thus hospitals must increasingly compete for patient referrals by GP fundholders. In addition, hospitals have become more patient-oriented owing to the competitive bidding process (Glennerster *et al.* 1998).

Nevertheless, there was controversy over the rising transaction costs of the contracting process, medical outcomes under increased competition and an emerging two-tiered system (one for patients of GP fundholders and another for those of non-fundholders). There was also concern about fragmentation of purchasing functions between GP fundholders and district health authorities: the former place their contracts on individual patients' needs, the latter on community-wide public health needs (Robinson and Le Grand 1994; Ham and Shapiro 1995).

With the new Labour government in 1997, regulation in the United Kingdom became reoriented more towards cooperation between health purchasers and providers, with a focus on joint planning. A key element of the government's new strategy, begun in April 1999, has been the statutory requirement for health authorities to work closely with all relevant agencies (hospital trusts, GPs, community health councils, voluntary bodies, professional medical organizations, etc.) to produce a plan for maintaining and improving the health of the local community. Contracting is increasingly incorporated into the joint planning process, and is implemented in the context of health targets and health care utilization targets developed by different levels of government. Alliances are supposed to remove many of the tensions that previously existed during contract negotiation. Thus contracting is increasingly becoming the final point in the planning process, with the involvement of many actors.

The contracting function is also modified owing to the formation of 480 primary care groups (covering a population ranging from 50,000 to 250,000) and the involvement of these groups in the purchasing decisions of health authorities (Higgins 1999). The planning function of these groups ('voice strategy') is combined with the pressure on other providers through contracting ('exit strategy') to achieve organizational efficiency (Glennerster *et al.* 1998).

These changes in the regulation of contracting and the 'internal market' in the United Kingdom can be regarded as an inevitable reaction to maturing quasi-market relationships in the system. After several years of reform, it has become clear that, in the long run, there are no winners if purchasers and providers act only in their own interests, because the market is 'closed' with only finite resources available within it. Changes should be jointly planned, so that true benefits can be gained for all parties.

Similar modifications in the contracting process are currently under way in the Russian Federation. The original pattern of contracting between health insurers and providers, with a focus on the independent decisions of the parties, is gradually giving way to more coordinated actions within the general framework of the planning process. In 1998, the government set the procedure of developing a package of medical benefits (both federal and regional), which provides for joint planning work by regional health authorities and mandatory health insurance funds, as representatives of insurers. Local insurers are expected to base their contracting decisions on cost and utilization targets. There is early evidence of more coordinated actions by insurers and providers.

In other countries that are attempting to make purchasing more entrepreneurial, a restrictive strategy of contracting regulation still prevails. In Germany at present, almost all negotiated contracts of sickness funds must be given to official supervisory units of federal or state governments, either for information or official approval or for real agreement in substance. The major criterion for evaluating the contract is its impact on cost containment. For example, the supervisory unit can refuse to approve a contract between the insurance fund and the local medical facility for investment in the further development of some services if there is an excess capacity for a similar service in the neighbouring local area and if this capacity can be used. The reason for this is that the contract is in conflict with cost containment (Affeld 1997).

In 1989 in Germany, sickness funds were given the freedom to cancel contracts with inefficient hospitals. Collective arrangements with hospital associations do not close the opportunities for the selection of providers and competitive tendering. Insurers can contract selectively under the general rules specified by the collective contract. But the collective nature of contracting still prevails. Compared to contracting as currently practised in the United Kingdom, German purchasers are more limited by regulation (Saltman and Figueras 1997). Today, sickness funds are calling for deregulation of their relationship with health care providers so that there are more opportunities for them to compete with each other.

There are reasons to believe that collective contracting is still needed and will most likely co-exist with individual contracting. Insurers, providers and government also feel a need to negotiate collective arrangements that constrain or even discipline the market of individual contracting. Collective contracts offer a general binding framework in which local negotiations between third-party payers and providers can take place. So collective contracts do not necessarily contradict individual contracts, and sometimes even work as a prerequisite for individual contracting.

Regulation of health purchasing in a non-competitive environment

The prevailing approach to regulating the entrepreneurial behaviour of health purchasers depends on whether the market is competitive or non-competitive. There are two broad groups of countries with a different market environment of health purchaser activity. The first has a monopsonic (single purchaser) model that excludes consumer choice. This group includes countries with a well-established health insurance model (for example, France) as well as countries with an emerging health insurance model (Estonia, Hungary, Kazakhstan, Latvia, Lithuania, Slovenia). They have one health insurance agency, with regional branches in their catchment areas that do not compete with each other. The second group of countries (Czech Republic, Germany, Netherlands, Slovakia) has a model with multiple insurers that can be encouraged to compete.

In the first group of countries, there is the issue of how to encourage entrepreneurial behaviour of purchasers in a non-competitive market environment when market forces do not affect their performance. In the second group, the scope for the use of entrepreneurial mechanisms is broader and the emphasis is on market pressure. Regulation of the purchasing process tends to focus on how to neutralize the negative consequences of market-driven health purchasing.

In a non-competitive environment, it is usually the government that places pressure on health purchasers to act in a more entrepreneurial way. The regulatory strategy is to activate the role of health payers and make them prudent purchasers. A critical aspect is that regulatory agencies set clear objectives and targets relating to health care provision for payers. In a more specific way, this strategy means widening the functions of payers beyond traditional reimbursement of services. Purchasers should be involved in planning health delivery and use purchasing instruments to change the structure of health care provision in the interests of patients.

This strategy is not self-evident in many countries. In the Russian Federation, for example, regulatory agencies consider health care planning and restructuring to be the responsibility of health authorities and local governments, while insurers pay provider bills and control quality. Regulation reflects this narrow understanding of the role of insurers and, therefore, limits the potential of independent payers to ensure more efficient use of health resources. The absence of a clear-cut strategy to enhance the role of insurers makes them mostly indifferent payers, which leads to continued excess hospital capacity, a relatively low role of primary care provision and other structural distortions in health care provision (Sheiman 1997).

Countries with a Bismarckian model typically attempt to activate the role of health payers through a statutory requirement to make contracting the prevailing pattern of their relationships with health providers. The outcome of this strategy differs, mainly owing to different amounts of control by health insurers over health care revenue, and also to the level of integration of purchasing policy. In the Czech Republic, Hungary, Latvia, Lithuania and Slovenia, most public money is controlled by insurers, while the role of health authorities in funding is limited to public health and major investments. Purchasing of health care is integrated, which allows for better planning of medical service delivery (both strategic and operational) with a focus on cost containment. In Kazakhstan, Kyrgyzstan, the Russian Federation and some other CIS countries, however, insurers control only a limited portion of health care revenue (30–35 per cent). The major part of health funding is allocated by health authorities on a non-contractual basis, with little coordination of funding decisions among actors. This allows providers to receive most of the money for the input rather than for actual output of performance. The regulation does not clearly specify the role of health insurers as a major purchaser. Therefore, contracting becomes more an exercise for managers rather than an entrepreneurial tool with a real impact on health providers.

In theory, entrepreneurial behaviour of health purchasers in non-competitive environments can also be encouraged through the regulatory requirement to contract selectively. The evidence of selective contracting in this group of countries is marginal, with the exception of the United Kingdom, which is a special case. The British Government has pressured district health authorities to select the most cost-effective providers, and has formed their views on what constitutes a good contract. But, in addition to the actual and potential managerial incentives (organizational survival, job security or promotion), there has been at least some market pressure through competition with traditional payers and among GP fundholders. The latter push a monopsonic purchaser, like a health authority, to perform better (Glennerster *et al.* 1998).

A better example is the case of Kazakhstan, a country with no competition among purchasers. In 1998, the government introduced a formal requirement for most governmental agencies to contract selectively through a tendering mechanism. This mechanism began in 1999 in Almaty City. Local hospitals and polyclinics (outpatient care settings) bid competitively for contracts for broad specialty groups. Some were contracted for only a reduced workload. Competitive tendering has allowed excessive hospital capacity to decrease.

As unlikely as it might seem, the obstacles to selective contracting are similar, if not the same, in countries with competitive and non-competitive environments, namely opposition by the medical profession, resistance to reducing excessive capacity and traditions of collective contracting.

Another mechanism to encourage entrepreneurial behaviour in a non-competitive environment can be to encourage purchasers to use prospective provider payment methods, like global budgets, capitation and fundholding. In this case, a purchaser works within the general planning framework, negotiating with providers on volume and quality of care, risk sharing arrangements and, in some forms of contract, rates of reimbursement. This work requires better entrepreneurial skills than retrospective payment for the actual volume of care at fixed rates. Most countries in Europe with well-established health funding systems (irrespective of the prevailing model of health purchasing) are increasingly using global budgets, sophisticated block contracts or cost-and-volume contracts as a method of inpatient care reimbursement (Saltman and Figueras 1997). Thus purchasers have to play a more active role in the specification and selection of the pattern of health care provision.

Countries with an emerging health insurance model have a tendency to start with a mixture of retrospective methods of payment and traditional item-by-item funding of medical facilities. For example, insurers in the Czech Republic, Hungary and the Russian Federation use, or have used, various versions of retrospective payment for inpatient care. They have encouraged hospitals to increase workload and have contributed to the higher internal efficiency of hospitals. Nevertheless, the problem of structural inefficiency has worsened in most cases owing to the growth of inappropriate admissions and a lack of constraint on using costly methods of care. In the Czech Republic, for example, following the introduction of a retrospective payment system, health expenditure increased by almost 40 per cent in 2 years (Marrée and Groenewegen 1997). Thus there is evidence of a need for tougher regulatory requirements for health insurers to use less open-ended provider payment schemes in this group of countries.

In non-competitive environments, the administration costs of purchasers are regulated. In some CEE and CIS countries, such as the Czech Republic, Poland, the Russian Federation and Slovakia, a ceiling for administration costs has been established as a percentage of social health insurance revenue (in the range 2–7 per cent). Having an efficient health insurance administration should not be confused with minimizing costs of administration 'at any price'.

Arranging prudent contracts with health care providers requires better trained and, therefore, more expensive personnel, as well as investments in management information.

Thus there is some evidence of government pressure on health purchasers to act in a more entrepreneurial way and to make health care provision more entrepreneurial. Nevertheless, the evidence is not sufficient to draw conclusions and it is unclear whether pressure from the state can fully compensate for the market mechanism.

Regulation to ensure 'real' competition

All the above-mentioned areas of regulation are also relevant for countries that have an emerging competitive structure to their health purchasing arrangements. Some additional regulatory activity is needed to ensure workable competition by health care purchasers.

Regulate the entry of new actors

Regulation in all countries requires government approval of participation by health payers, mostly through the formal licensing procedure of health insurance institutions. Apart from requirements regarding the financial viability of these institutions, licensing regulation sets the strategic framework of payers' activity so that they comply with health policy objectives.

In countries with well-established social health insurance models, start-up regulation focuses on ensuring cost containment and equity. A set of requirements is intended to encourage an active role for health insurers and a more efficient use of resources in the health sector. For example, in Germany and the Netherlands, sickness funds must submit an operational plan to the licensing or supervisory agency that reflects not only expected internal operations (equipment investment, staffing, etc.) but also the interactions with health providers. This plan should demonstrate both managerial capacity and specific health care purchasing decisions, such as expected volumes of inpatient care and substitution strategies.

In the United Kingdom before April 1999, GPs applying for the status of fundholder required approval by the Department of Health. The Department also set requirements for developing the budgets of GP fundholders and procedures for budget negotiation and approval by health authorities.

Regulate mergers between health insurance institutions

Mergers have an ambiguous impact in an environment intended to be competitive. On the one hand, the economies of scale with regard to administration suggests that larger insurance institutions may be attractive. On the other hand, mergers can lead to a situation in which there are not enough insurance institutions for real competition. Regulation is needed, therefore, to clearly define conditions under which mergers between social health insurance institutions are allowed.

Even in countries with a well-established health insurance model, dealing with mergers in a competitive environment is a new challenge. In most cases, a regulatory framework for dealing with mergers of insurers has not been established. In the United Kingdom, the Ministry of Health regulates mergers of both providers (hospital trusts) and purchasers (health authorities and GP fundholders). Regulation is based on the presumption that competitive solutions are favourable. But where intervention is needed (for example, to integrate purchasing decisions of GP fundholders and health authorities, or to lower administration costs), there are clear aims and explicit criteria so that stakeholders can predict the outcome (NHS Executive 1994).

Facilitate the consumer's choice of health purchaser

In addition to the above-mentioned open enrolment procedure, additional regulation is needed with regard to transparency of information. Public regulation is a necessary tool to make sure that certain minimum standards of information are given to the insured.

The minimum requirement for consumer choice is that subscribers must contribute to insurance funds themselves (together with employers and the government) and therefore have incentives to obtain more value for their money. This requirement is not met in most of the CEE and CIS countries, which have started a transition to a social health insurance model and have declared this new model to be competitive. In the Russian Federation, for example, employers make a contribution to the regional mandatory health insurance fund for their employees and local governments pay for the non-working population. Residents do not pay for their insurance and thus do not have a strong interest in selecting their health insurance company. Around 400 such companies with licences to provide mandatory health insurance compete, mostly to attract employers. In big cities, they compete for contracting with the best health providers and thereby indirectly compete for patients. However, this kind of competition was relevant only in the initial stage of the reform implementation (1993–94) (Sheiman 1997). If the system is based totally on payments by the employer and the government's choice of insurer, there is not enough market pressure on insurers to lower the cost of a medical benefits package.

Regulate the allocation of funds to health purchasers

The use of a risk-adjusted capitation formula for funding health care purchasers is the major instrument to facilitate the operation of a competitive insurance market. It is usually discussed in the context of government policy for ensuring equity of coverage in a health care system with multiple payers. But a risk-adjustment mechanism is also a major tool to ensure efficiency and effectiveness of health care provision. Properly designed and implemented, risk-adjustment systems encourage competition between payers based on cost and quality rather than on risk selection. The process of risk-adjusting insurers focuses attention on minimizing the cost of providing care and administration costs. Health care purchasers are motivated to look for more cost-effective medical interventions and select the most efficient providers. Therefore, regulation on the use of risk-adjustment is critical for operating efficient markets.

Regulate to encourage the collection of information

The experience of some countries with existing and emerging health markets, such as the United Kingdom and the United States, has revealed a natural imbalance in the information available to purchasers and providers for an efficient purchasing process (Maynard 1994). This imbalance can only be corrected by regulatory acts and investment in the collection of information. In the United Kingdom, for example, the government encourages the collection of information on consumer attitudes towards providers (through district health commissions and general practitioners) and also on the relative effectiveness of different medical interventions and organizational settings (Glennerster *et al.* 1998).

Conclusions

A set of entrepreneurial mechanisms on the purchasing side ranges from relatively traditional instruments used in non-competitive environments (planning purchasing decisions, contracting, performance-related methods of provider payment in the context of cost-containment strategies) to market-driven mechanisms such as selective contracting, variation of rates of premiums and packages of medical benefits. Some of the traditional entrepreneurial mechanisms have a long history of use in countries with well-established health insurance systems. Their introduction is particularly relevant for CEE and CIS countries, which are in transition from a command-and-control model to a model based on separating purchasers and providers. Nevertheless, the use of these instruments also requires regulation to ensure that they remain consistent with health policy objectives.

The focus of entrepreneurial mechanisms in a competitive structure of health purchasing depends strongly on the prevailing values in society and also on the starting point of new developments. In western Europe, cost containment and a search for better cost–benefit ratios of health expenditures are overriding public goals, while there is still a broad consensus that risk-pooling and solidarity be maintained. In CEE and CIS countries, where cost containment is less relevant due to chronic underfunding of health systems, a competitive health purchasing model is usually seen as a strategy for patient protection. Concerns about equity are not as strong as in western Europe because, in the process of transition, freedom of choice and freedom of entrepreneurship have become prevailing values.

The impact of entrepreneurial mechanisms in a competitive structure of health purchasing is less clear. The scope of their use is still limited in most countries for many reasons, the most important being concerns about risk selection and opposition by the medical profession to selective contracting. It is therefore difficult to make definite judgements on the initial steps, and attempts to introduce these mechanisms are not always coherent. Evidence from the United Kingdom gives some grounds for positive outcomes in terms of a higher degree of competition among providers and increased responsiveness to local needs, although these outcomes are questioned by many opponents of the reform. In other countries, the emerging competitive model of health purchasing is more a design than an actual process. Selective contracting by competing insurance funds is more a formal exercise than a prevailing approach to relationships with providers.

Conceptual reasoning, as well as some empirical evidence, suggest that 'more markets' and 'more entrepreneurial activities' do not mean 'less regulation'. It is true that, in comparison to a non-entrepreneurial setting, the type of public intervention will change: there will be less direct public financing and management and more of setting a framework for actors and supervising them. This, however, may be even a greater challenge.

There is no clear evidence of the impact of regulation to ensure equity. Risk-adjustment mechanisms, as well as other regulatory instruments, are reducing the degree of risk selection but are still far from solving the issue.

The substance of regulatory activity has a tendency to change as a reaction to the emerging issues of purchaser and provider interaction. The case of the United Kingdom shows that the maturing of quasi-market relations shifts the focus of regulation from competition to more cooperation between purchasers and providers, and also to coordination of different purchasers. The role of joint planning is increasing. The participation of primary care providers in purchasing decisions by health authorities co-exists with their market pressure on hospital and community care. Thus the actual purchasing activity gains new dimensions unknown in traditional market mechanisms.

In western Europe, the experience of prudent buying is rather new, and this is even more true in CEE and CIS countries. Here, most funders still behave as reimbursing institutions and not as managers of care. In the near future, in most European countries, it is likely that the entrepreneurial mechanisms of health purchasing will be developing in mostly non-competitive environments, with a monopsonic payer acting as a more informed purchaser. The pressure of the government to operate in a more entrepreneurial way will probably compensate for the lack, or absence, of market pressure. Thus, the focus of regulation will still be on how to improve entrepreneurial mechanisms through supervision and evaluation.

References

Affeld, D. (1997) *Regulations for Sickness Funds and Health Insurance Companies Activities in Germany*. Workshop on Regulating Health Insurance Companies in Russia. Federal Fund of Mandatory Health Insurance, Moscow, 16–18 September.

Busse, R., Struck, P., Marshall, T., Pyrmula, R. and Petrakova, A. (2000) *Health Care Systems in Transition: Czech Republic*. Copenhagen: European Observatory on Health Care Systems.

Culyer, A. and Posnett, J. (1990) Hospital behaviour and competition, in A. Culyer, A. Maynard and J. Posnett (eds) *Competition in Health Care: Reforming the NHS*. London: Macmillan.

Enthoven, A. (1991) Internal market reform of the British National Health Service, *Health Affairs*, 10: 60–70.

Glennerster, H., Cohen, A. and Bovell, V. (1998) Alternatives to fundholding, *International Journal of Health Services*, 28: 47–66.

Goldstein, E., Preker, A., Adeyi, O. and Chellaraj, G. (1996) *Trends in Health Status, Services, and Finance: The Transition in Central and Eastern Europe*, Vol. 1, Technical Paper No. 341. Washington, DC: World Bank.

Grant, K. and Collini, E. (1996) *The Evolution of Management in the UK National Health Service, 1948–1995*. London: Institute for Health Sector Development.

Ham, C. and Shapiro, J. (1995) The future of fundholding (editorial), *British Medical Journal*, 310: 1150–1.

Higgins, J. (1999) *Restructuring the Whole System: The Newsletter of the Health Services Management Unit*. Manchester: University of Manchester.

Kemerovo Department of Health (1995) *Quality Assurance in Health Care*. Kemerovo: Department of Health (in Russian).

Klugman, J. and Schieber G. (with the assistance of Heleniak, T. and Hon, V.) (1996) Health reform in Russia and Central Asia, in J.M. Nelson, C. Tilly and L. Walker (eds) *Transforming Post-communist Political Economies*. Washington, DC: National Academy Press.

Luft, H.S. (1996) Modifying managed competition to address cost and quality, *Health Affairs*, 15: 21–38.

Marrée, J. and Groenewegen, P.P. (1997) *Back to Bismarck: Eastern European Health Care Systems in Transition*. Aldershot: Avebury.

Maynard, A. (1994) Can competition enhance efficiency in health care? Lessons from the reforms of the U.K. National Health Service, *Social Science and Medicine*, 39: 1433–45.

National Economic Research Associates (1995) *Risk-Adjustment and its Implications for Efficiency and Equity in Health Care Systems*. London: Pharmaceutical Partners for Better Healthcare.

NHS Executive (1994) *The Operation of the NHS Internal Market: Local Freedoms, National Responsibilities*, HSG(94)55. London: HMSO.

Normand, C. and Busse, R. (2002) Social health insurance financing, in E. Mossialos, A. Dixon, J. Figueras and J. Kutzin (eds) *Funding Health Care: Options for Europe*. Buckingham: Open University Press.

Pauly, M.V. (1984) Is cream-skimming a problem for the competitive medical market?, *Journal of Health Economics*, 3: 87–95.

Rice, N. and Smith, P.C. (2002) Strategic resource allocation and funding decisions, in E. Mossialos, A. Dixon, J. Figueras and J. Kutzin (eds) *Funding Health Care: Options for Europe*. Buckingham: Open University Press.

Robinson, R. and Le Grand, J. (eds) (1994) *Evaluating the NHS Reforms*. London: King's Fund.

Saltman, R.B. and Figueras, J. (1997) *European Health Care Reform: Analysis of Current Strategies*, WHO Regional Publications, European Series No. 72. Copenhagen: WHO Regional Office for Europe.

Saltman, R.B. and von Otter, C. (1992) *Planned Markets and Public Competition*. Buckingham: Open University Press.

Schneider, M. (1994) *Complementary Health Schemes in the European Union*. Augsburg: BASYS.

Secretaries of State for Health (1989) *Working for Patients*, Cm 55. London: HMSO.

Semenov, V. (1997) [Insurance company – real guarantees are needed] (in Russian). *Meditsinskij Vestnik*, 18: 4–5.

Sheiman, I. (1997) From Beveridge to Bismarck: health finance in the Russian Federation, in G. Schieber (ed.) *Innovations in Health Care Financing*. Proceedings of a

World Bank Conference, 10–11 March 1997. World Bank Discussion Paper No. 365. Washington, DC: World Bank.

Spycher, S. (1999) *Wirkungsanalyse des Risikoausgleichs in der Schweizer Krankenversicherung*, Zusammenfassung der Studie im Auftrag des Bundesamtes für Sozialversicherung. Bern: Büro für arbeits- und sozialpolitische Studien.

Turnbull, N. (1997) *How Can State Regulators Ensure Health Insurance Companies are Accountable to Consumers?* Workshop on Regulating Health Insurance Companies in Russia. Federal Fund of Mandatory Health Insurance, Moscow, 16–18 September.

van de Ven, W. (1990) From regulated control to regulated competition in the Dutch health care system, *European Economic Review*, 34: 632–45.

van de Ven, W. (1994) Forming and reforming the market for third-party purchasing of health care (editorial), *Social Science and Medicine*, 39: 1405–12.

van de Ven, W.P.M.M. and Van Vliet, R.C.J.A. (1992) How can we prevent cream skimming in a competitive health insurance market?, in P. Zweifel and H.E. Frech (eds) *Health Economics Worldwide*. Dordrecht: Kluwer.

Where entrepreneurialism is strong but not changing

chapter ten

The regulatory environment of general practice: an international perspective

Peter P. Groenewegen, Jennifer Dixon and Wienke G.W. Boerma

Introduction

Regulation serves to try to reconcile the goals of individuals and health care organizations on the one hand and those of society on the other. Although governments are usually chiefly responsible for shaping the regulatory environment, they are not the only players. Professional bodies also have considerable influence – they instil professional values, set standards and, in many cases, monitor achievement against standards. The key actors subject to regulation in health care include professionals working in the public or private sector, public providers and private-sector organizations that are funders or providers of care. A variety of tools are available to influence, or regulate, the behaviour of these actors at different levels of the health care system. As the pendulum of health sector reform in the last decade has swung away from public funding and ownership of health care in centrally planned bureaucracies, towards a mixed model of care with a greater role for private provision, there has been an upsurge of interest in how governments might best regulate, rather than plan, health care to achieve desired objectives.

In the context of regulation and entrepreneurship in health care, primary care deserves special attention. Primary care has been defined as first-contact care for new health problems, person-focused rather than disease-focused, comprehensive and coordinated care (Starfield 1996). An effective system of primary care does not emerge spontaneously within a health care system. It must be financed, planned and regulated in such a way that primary care providers are able and willing to take responsibility for the health of the population under their care. Sufficient resources need to be allocated to primary care relative to secondary care to enable adequate access to primary care services for the population. The supply and location of primary care staff, the quality of care and access to care need to be planned, monitored and regulated. One prominent theme has been to encourage greater freedom for professionals in primary care (for example, by giving them a budget for secondary care, as in the United Kingdom, or by effectively privatizing primary care, as in central Europe), while at the same time introducing financial incentives to avoid possible negative effects of such freedom.

This chapter focuses on general practice as the central discipline within primary care. The general practitioner (GP) is the key professional in primary care because he or she is generally the first point of contact for health problems or health-related problems. In health care systems where GPs are gatekeepers to secondary care, they are important because they almost entirely control entry by patients to specialist health care. Primary care is usually delivered in the community by a range of professional staff, sometimes organized in integrated health centres or, in central and eastern Europe, 'polyclinics'. General practitioners are the key primary care group, since they typically manage and, in some countries, also own the organization in which they work. Additionally, GPs may hire and manage other staff, such as practice nurses or assistants.

Entrepreneurship and primary care

In countries with social insurance systems, such as France and Germany, GPs are self-employed and working under contract, while in national health care systems, GPs can be either self-employed (as in the United Kingdom) or salaried (as in Finland and Portugal). In the countries of central and eastern Europe, GPs used to be state employees but are increasingly becoming self-employed (Boerma and Fleming 1998).

In many health care systems, then, GPs are not only professional care-givers but also small-scale entrepreneurs. Taken literally, an entrepreneur is 'a person who undertakes an enterprise or business, with the chance of profit or loss' (Allen 1990). More generally, doctors aim to realize their personal goals. These might be assumed to be of an economic nature (profit, income in relation to (time) investments) and of a social nature (social approval, status) (Delnoij 1994; Groenewegen 1996). It is clear that realizing one's personal economic goals, first of all, is not restricted to self-employed doctors. Within employment contracts, salaried doctors also try to achieve their individual economic goals. In addition, irrespective of employment status, economic gain may not be the first aim of health care providers. Health care providers also value their status in terms of approval as professionals by their patients and peers (Saltman and Young 1983).

Thus, although in a strict sense entrepreneurial behaviour would have to be restricted to GPs who work in independent practice and thus have the opportunity to maximize profits, tensions between personal interests and professional values also exist when GPs are salaried employees. We have therefore broadened our discussion to designing appropriate incentive structures for all GPs.

A fundamental goal of all health care systems must be to improve the welfare of the population served. As a central feature of primary care, GPs are responsible for the health of the population they serve. This implies that regulation is required to ensure availability of appropriately trained and supported GPs and access to other kinds of care via the GP. It also implies the need to design an appropriate payment system that encourages continuity of care. Regulation of this kind might affect both the personal goals of GPs and the welfare of patients.

Many recent health care reforms, both in western and in eastern Europe, have introduced financial incentives that have increased the potential for tension between the personal interests of GPs and professional and societal values. In some countries, there has been significant devolution of budgetary powers to GPs, and incentives have been introduced to spend less than the budget allocated. In central Europe, many GPs have become independent contractors rather than employees of the state. This increased potential for conflicting goals can only be balanced if there is an increase in effective regulation at the same time by the government or by professional bodies.

The regulatory environment in primary care

Regulation of general practice has different levels of application, from the macro-level of the health care system as a whole, to intermediate levels of regional or local organization, to the micro-level of the individual GP's practice (see Figure 10.1).

The health care system, the macro-level, provides the context of the regulatory environment and the limits as to what can be achieved through regulation. National standards, rules and incentives are set at this level, which influence the broad scope of duties of GPs. For example, in some countries GPs serve the entire population, while in others primary care for children or for women is more specialized, carried out by paediatricians and gynaecologists, respectively (Boerma et al. 1997). In addition, in the administration of health care systems, there are usually intermediate structures such as regional authorities or health insurance funds, which in turn, steer the behaviour of health care professionals and organizations.

Explicit professional values and standards may also serve to regulate the behaviour of GPs. Values are largely set by professional bodies and, in some European countries, professional organizations of GPs also set standards of care. Through the mechanism of peer approval, professional standards are likely to motivate GPs to work in the interest of their patients' health and well-being (although not always in line with patients' preferences). Many countries, notably those in western Europe, have strong, active professional associations of

Figure 10.1   Levels of application of regulation and lines of accountability

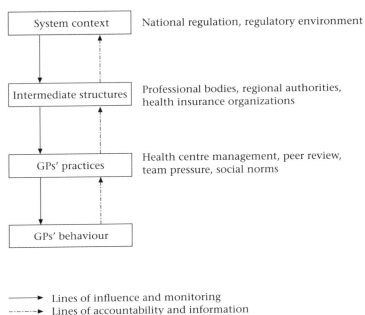

Lines of influence and monitoring
Lines of accountability and information

physicians, and some specifically for GPs. Because of the historical dominance of the state in central and eastern Europe, professional bodies are relatively weak, and those specifically focused on GPs are either absent or in the early stages of development. The quality of leadership in, and the activities of, professional bodies are crucial in upholding professional values. These are reinforced by medical education and especially specialty training, which is obligatory throughout the European Union although not uniformly well developed. In other countries, specialty training of GPs is optional or practically nonexistent, and the length varies considerably.

Additional types of behavioural incentive, usually applied by the government or by sickness funds, are financial in kind. These might motivate GPs to act as entrepreneurs in the narrow sense (to make a profit) and act in the best interests of patients at the same time, for example by increasing vaccination rates (if a fee-for-service incentive for vaccinations is operating). They might also result in a GP reducing the volume of care for a patient to preserve a budget or profit, or just the opposite, leading to over-provision of care, as might be the case in fee-for-service medicine.

At the micro-level, social controls inside the practice group and the incentives provided by micro-budgets tend to influence GPs' behaviour. General practice across Europe is organized in many ways, but one of the most obvious differences is the number of GPs working in an organizational unit. The organization of the practice, and in particular team size, may have an influence in weighing personal interests and professional values, which probably have the strongest influence on GPs' behaviour when they work in small groups. For example, when GPs work in a single-handed practice, they are more dependent on their patients and are more inclined to give in to a patient's demands, even if it is not in the interest of the health of the patient (Freidson 1970). When GPs work in large groups, the strength of group norms concerning professional values is usually weaker and the individual GP's behaviour is less visible. Because of this, personal interests could influence the behaviour of GPs more when they work single-handedly or in large groups than when they work in small groups. Depending on other incentives and regulations, these personal interests may be predominantly economic, fostering entrepreneurial behaviour.

Taking all levels of regulation together, there are stark differences in both the amount and content of regulation surrounding general practice across Europe, for example regarding the types of rules and incentives used. Independent of the actual regulator, regulatory elements to help to develop an effective system of primary care – that is, ensuring availability and access to the whole population, together with continuity of care, comprehensiveness and integration within other levels of care (Starfield 1996; Boerma and Fleming 1998) – might include the following:

- permits for new practices and incentives to work in underserved areas – to improve equity in the geographical distribution of GPs and primary care facilities;
- personal lists of registered patients for GPs – to encourage them to be responsible for a defined population;
- elements of capitation in the payment system for GPs – to promote more cost-effective management of resources and greater continuity of care;
- a gatekeeping role (defined as whether or not patients can see a specialist only after referral by their GP) – to encourage appropriate, and prevent unnecessary, specialist care;
- facilitation of peer review – to bring about effective external and internal monitoring of the quality of care provided.

The regulatory environment of primary care in different health systems

Issues of regulation differ strongly among tax-based, national health service systems, social insurance systems, and transitional systems in central and eastern Europe. This reflects variations in history, culture and economic circumstances, although important differences exist within these three types of system as well (Marrée and Groenewegen 1997; Grielen et al. 2000). In addition, the definition of a GP itself, while rather uniform in western Europe (especially in the countries of the European Union, where qualifications are mutually recognized), differs in the CEE countries.

A number of organizational features have a direct bearing on the capacity and likelihood of entrepreneurship (such as employment status) or are more broadly relevant for the balance between personal and professional incentives. Table 10.1 shows, across a wide range of European countries, the extent to which GPs are self-employed, as opposed to salaried employees of

Table 10.1 Characteristics reflecting regulation of the market for GPs' services (employment status, payment system, personal list system and gatekeeping) by type of health care system

Country	Percentage of GPs self-employed[a]	Payment system[b]	Personal list	Gatekeeping
National health service				
Denmark	100	capitation + fee-for-service	yes	yes
Finland	2	salary	no	no
Greece	30	salary (if self-employed, fee-for-service)	no	no
Iceland	25	salary + fee-for-service (if self-employed, capitation + fee-for-service)	no	yes
Italy	98	capitation	yes	yes
Norway	58	fee-for-service (if employed, salary)	no	yes
Portugal	1	salary	yes	yes
Spain	4	salary	yes	yes
Sweden	1	salary	no	no
United Kingdom	99	capitation + fee-for-service	yes	yes
Social insurance				
Austria	99	fee-for-service	no	no
Belgium	97	fee-for-service	no	no
France	97	fee-for-service	no	no
Germany	100	fee-for-service	no	no
Ireland	91	capitation	yes (lower incomes)	yes
Luxembourg	98	fee-for-service	no	no
Netherlands	93	capitation + fee-for-service	yes	yes
Switzerland	99	fee-for-service	no	no
Transitional countries[c]				
Belarus	0	salary	no	no
Bulgaria	1	salary	no	no
Croatia	0	salary	no	yes
Czech Republic	33	salary (if self-employed, fee-for-service)	no	no
Estonia	1	salary	no	no
Hungary	12	salary (if self-employed, capitation or fee-for-service)	no	no
Latvia	3	salary	no	no
Lithuania	0	salary	no	no
Poland	0	salary	no	no
Romania	6	salary	no	no
Slovenia	1	salary	yes	yes
Ukraine	0	salary	no	no

[a] The percentage of GPs who are self-employed was established in a European survey in 1993 and 1994 (Boerma and Fleming 1998).
[b] Predominant payment system; if more than 25 per cent but less than 50 per cent has a different payment system, this is noted in brackets.
[c] Since the collection of these data, there have been considerable changes in the transitional countries, particularly the Czech Republic, Estonia, Hungary and Poland.

Sources: Boerma *et al.* (1993, 1997), Boerma and Fleming (1998)

a public or private payer, and how they are paid. For each country and by broad type of health care system, the table also indicates the presence or absence of two main features of effective primary care – whether GPs have a personal 'list' of registered patients and whether they have a 'gatekeeping' role.

Table 10.2 shows the percentages of GPs who said they had had general practice postgraduate training. This percentage varies widely, even in those countries where this training is compulsory. This variation depends on the date on which compulsory GP training was introduced and the rules applying to those who were in practice at that time. Table 10.2 also shows the percentage distribution of the size of the organizational units of general practice. Especially in social insurance based health care systems, a large percentage of GPs are in single-handed practice, although this proportion is decreasing in most countries. In most former communist countries, GPs still practised in very large groups when the data were collected.

Trends in health care reform

National health service systems

In these tax-funded systems, the state generally exercises a large measure of control over the income of GPs and the way that primary care is organized (Westert 1997). Governments typically control the number, distribution, hours of work and fee schedules or salaries of GPs. However, control over the actual quality of care has been limited historically, and the incentives for increasing activity or quality of care have been weak.

Room for entrepreneurial behaviour has thus been small, particularly relating to the income of GPs or the primary care organization, and many of these systems have been slow to improve the responsiveness of care and, in some cases, efficiency. A key dimension of state control that influences entrepreneurial behaviour is the extent to which GPs are allowed to increase their personal income. In countries where the income of GPs is firmly controlled – such as where GPs are salaried – the potential for entrepreneurial activity is lowest. With independent GPs there are more opportunities, although these are not necessarily related to a direct increase in personal income.

Governments and payers have generally been more active than professional bodies in regulating behaviour. An important reason for increasing the scope for entrepreneurship during the last decade has been to improve the quality, responsiveness and efficiency of the service. A notable trend has been the growing separation of purchaser and provider functions, and devolution of budgets to primary care organizations.

The case of the United Kingdom

There are many rules and incentives that shape primary care in the National Health Service (NHS). For example, the overall number of GPs is regulated

Table 10.2   Characteristics indicating the chances of professional social control (percentage of GPs with postgraduate training and partnership size or group size) by type of health care system

Country	Postgraduate training (%)[a]	Single-handed practice	2–5 in practice	6–10 in practice	More than 10 in practice
National health service					
Denmark	99[b]	30	56	14	0
Finland	34	8	38	28	27
Greece	67	45	24	15	17
Iceland	82[b]	15	39	37	10
Italy	11	86	12	1	1
Norway	45	25	64	7	4
Portugal	65	12	28	25	35
Spain	27	24	28	21	28
Sweden	96[b]	2	63	28	7
United Kingdom	71[b]	16	55	27	2
Social insurance					
Austria	54[b]	93	7	0	0
Belgium	71	69	28	2	1
France	16	59	40	0	1
Germany	75	67	33	0	0
Ireland	45	54	43	3	0
Luxembourg	35	61	39	0	0
Netherlands	66[b]	46	51	3	0
Switzerland	86	73	27	0	0
Transitional countries					
Belarus			No data available		
Bulgaria	15	10	8	15	67
Croatia	57	37	37	9	17
Czech Republic	90[b]	43	30	9	18
Estonia	12	25	21	9	45
Hungary	33	56	33	8	3
Latvia	49	17	51	6	26
Lithuania	16	33	51	2	14
Poland	19	78	21	1	0
Romania	26	32	55	6	8
Slovenia	45	21	27	23	30
Ukraine	unknown	22	20	23	35

[a] Percentages are based on answers to a survey questionnaire; they do not necessarily refer to a regular postgraduate training programme for general practice.
[b] Postgraduate training for general practice is obligatory.

Sources: Boerma *et al.* (1993), Boerma and Fleming (1998)

centrally by government, and there are rules on where GPs can practice, the extent to which they can attract private fees and exactly how they are paid within the NHS. General practitioners are not salaried, but work independently on contract to the NHS. Most GPs (and the proportion is growing) are in group practice, with two or three partners, working with a multidisciplinary team and with an average registered list per GP of around 1800 patients.

In the late 1980s and early 1990s, there were moves to increase entrepreneurship by the then Conservative government. The GP fundholding scheme (Mays and Dixon 1996; Goodwin 1998) was introduced in 1991. General practitioners in large practices could opt for a capitated budget to cover laboratory tests, outpatient care and some inpatient care, prescription drugs and staff costs (Dixon and Glennerster 1995). This devolution of budgetary power to GPs allowed them to generate and keep surpluses to buy extra patient care, and provided an incentive to purchase and provide cost-effective care.

By 1997, when over 50 per cent of the population in England was registered with a fundholding practice, there was concern that the transaction costs of a large number of small purchasers were avoidably high, and that fundholding had resulted in unacceptable inequities in access to care among practices. The White Paper *The New NHS* (Secretary of State 1997) and the subsequent NHS Act of 1999 required all GP practices to join primary care groups, each covering a population of around 100,000 (rather than between 10,000 and 20,000 as in fundholding) and to be responsible for a budget covering the costs of most care not provided in primary care. Competition between GPs is discouraged, and primary care groups must collaborate with local stakeholders under a statutory duty of partnership when developing a local 'health improvement plan', which, in turn, influences how the primary care groups' funds will be spent.

Another influence on the position of GPs as entrepreneurs has been a gradual increase by the state in shaping and monitoring the standards of clinical care provided in general practice. In 1990, for the first time, the national GP contract spelled out the type of services that GPs were expected to provide under the National Terms and Conditions of Service under the NHS. This move was bitterly opposed by the profession. In 1999, 'clinical governance' was introduced, requiring that GPs and other members of the medical profession follow a national strategy to improve the quality of clinical care (Secretary of State 1998). Guidelines have been published by the National Institute for Clinical Excellence on the effectiveness of eight new treatments, and guidance has also been published by the government on the care of coronary heart disease, cancer and mental health. The publication of national guidelines aims to provide details on best practice in the organization of care and treatment of patients, and a new national body has been set up to assess progress. The profession has also taken steps to tighten up clinical performance by the introduction of mandatory 'revalidation' of professionals (Irvine 1999).

On the one hand, these themes represent more freedom in purchasing services and making savings on the budget and, on the other hand, less freedom as a result of increased external scrutiny of clinical performance. Independent evaluation of fundholding generally showed that financial incentives did not produce entrepreneurial behaviour that was detrimental to patient care (Goodwin 1998), probably because the incentives were too weak (Le Grand *et al.* 1998). In the United Kingdom, the themes mentioned are likely to be developed more fully over time, towards a system that will look more like fully fledged managed care (Dixon *et al.* 1998).

Social insurance systems

In social insurance systems, GPs are usually self-employed with a contract to the sickness funds. Only in the Netherlands do GPs have a personal list, a role as gatekeeper and payment based on capitation. The organizational scale of general practice is rather small, with the majority of GPs in single-handed practice.

Both the power and the responsibility to regulate is divided among government, insurance organizations and providers' organizations. Because of this division of power, the role of GPs has not changed substantially in social insurance systems during the past decade of health reforms. Where there is debate about the role of GPs, it is about introducing previously mentioned key elements in general practice such as a patient list system, or a GP as the gatekeeper to secondary care services. Only in Belgium has a small step been taken towards a list system. Other countries, such as France and Germany, have concentrated on piecemeal approaches to control costs, such as by capping the budgets for ambulatory care, regulating fees and tightening up on prescribing in general practice.

The case of the Netherlands

In the Netherlands, general practice is in a strong position. Independent GPs have a contract with the sickness funds. This contract is necessary to be able to treat statutorily insured patients. General practitioners have a personal list system and they are the gatekeepers to specialist care. Average list size is approximately 2300. Formally, the gatekeeping role applies to the statutorily insured, but *de facto* this role also applies to the privately insured. General practitioners receive a capitation fee from the sickness funds but are paid on a fee-for-service basis for privately insured patients (Groenewegen and Delnoij 1997).

Only those physicians who have completed a 3-year programme of postgraduate training in family medicine can be certified to work as GPs. Requirements for re-certification, obligatory every 5 years, include proof of having practised during this period for a minimum number of hours per week and of at least 40 hours per year spent on approved continuing medical education.

The contract between GPs and sickness funds is rather general. One of the obligations is to provide care to the listed patients 24 hours a day. The funds have the obligation to control the specific providers with whom they have a contract. In the past, this was limited to routine financial checks to prevent fraud. Currently, the funds give feedback to the contracted GPs about their referrals and the volume of prescriptions. This may lead to a discussion and outliers will be asked to justify their behaviour.

Professional self-regulation for GPs is well developed in the Netherlands, being monitored by the National Association of GPs. Professional development (for example, development of standards of good practice for a range of conditions) is the task of the College of General Practice (Grol *et al.* 1993). Both organizations cooperate in supporting continuing medical education. Although many GPs work single-handedly, they group together to provide after-hours coverage (van de Rijdt 1994). More and more of these so-called 'locum groups', consisting of 8–10 GPs, also engage in other activities such as peer review. Changes in the past decade have been in the direction of more professional control, rather than more entrepreneurship, despite policy changes in the direction of introducing more market elements in Dutch health care. These policy changes (following the Dekker Committee's report in 1987) have had profound consequences for the sickness funds (van de Ven 1997) though not for the role of GPs. Although the sickness funds have the possibility of contracting selectively with individual GPs, in practice they do not because of high transaction and information costs and because the logical unit of contracting is not the individual GP but the locum group.

The case of Belgium

For its population, Belgium has a very large number of GPs: approximately one GP for every 600 inhabitants, which is three- to four-fold the number in the Netherlands. General practitioners are in independent practice and are paid on a fee-for-service basis. There is no personal list system and people have free access to specialists. By law, Belgian GPs are obliged to take part in a collaborative group to cover after-hours duties. In other respects, they are free to establish a practice in any location. It was recently made possible for elderly patients to be listed with a GP of their choice. If they do so, they are exempted from the co-payments that exist for all other citizens. This is in line with the conclusion of Ros *et al.* (2000) that the steering of demand for health services should be done either through cost-sharing or though GP gatekeeping. No individual contract exists between the GP and the sickness funds; there is only a general contract. The funds' control over the GPs is still limited to controlling the accuracy of bills.

Belgium and the Netherlands provide an interesting contrast. Policy in the Netherlands is geared towards strengthening the professional values of GPs, resulting in low levels of competition among GPs. The risk of a low level of activity and a high referral rate, commonly associated with capitation payment, is countered by stimulating professional values (de Maesseneer *et al.* 1999). Entrepreneurship is effectively restricted by the organization of general practice and by cooperation among professional organizations, sickness funds and the government. In Belgium, the situation is quite different. Owing to strong competition and the small scale of general practice, GPs have incentives to do what patients demand, whether or not it is necessary from a professional point of view. This is illustrated by the extremely high proportion of home visits by GPs (approximately half of all contacts, probably a world record) (de Maesseneer *et al.* 1994).

Transitional systems

In most CEE countries there is an inclination, if not an apparent move, towards independent practitioner status for GPs. There is the potential for, and there actually exists in some cases, marked entrepreneurial activity. The extent to which professional organizations or the state can regulate this behaviour is limited and uneven. There is not yet a new and stable balance between freedom from old bureaucratic rules and the regulation that is necessary to stimulate professional norms. A few years ago, at the time of the international survey on practice profiles in Europe (Boerma *et al.* 1997), primary care physicians in most of these countries were still in salaried service, working in rather large organizations (the polyclinics). With the exception of Croatia, and to a lesser extent Slovenia, GPs have no strong primary care position.

The case of Belarus

The Belarus health care system is in an early stage of transition and the main features of the old system can still be identified: funding and provision by the state, dominated by specialist care. The competence of primary care doctors and the range of equipment at their disposal are low and, consequently, their range of (particularly curative) services is limited. The status and income of primary care physicians is low and their professional identity weak. The central responsibility for planning, funding and providing medical services is with the Ministry of Health. There is no health insurance fund or other organization that could contract independent providers, and relevant legislation is absent.

Professional regulation is largely missing. Apart from the traditional state-controlled 'Medical Chamber', physicians are not organized. If the government would be willing to share responsibilities in the future with non-governmental organizations, this would require the creation of organizations of professionals that could be self-regulating partners. However, there is no tradition of non-governmental organizations in the country.

The case of the Czech Republic

Virtually the opposite situation to that of Belarus is seen in the Czech Republic. Since the 'Velvet Revolution' in November 1989, the country has quickly introduced a market economy and democratic structures. Health care has been changed profoundly in an attempt to cope with the deteriorating health status of the population. Decentralization and privatization have been key elements in health care reform. By 1999, more than 95 per cent of primary care physicians were working in independent practice. The system distinguishes between GPs for adults (one per 1780 persons over 15 years) and GPs for children and adolescents (one per 1170) (Busse 2000). General practitioners do not hold a gatekeeping position. Practically speaking, all specialists are accessible without a referral, although some, such as gynaecologists and internists, are more involved than others in the provision of first-contact care.

Professional regulation is still weak, as is the position of GPs, although there are several associations that defend the professional and economic interests of GPs. Competence could be improved and practices are often not well equipped. There are only few requirements for physicians (such as postgraduate training in family medicine) to establish a GP practice; the same is true for (re-)certification. The result is competition to make a living and insufficient attention to cost-effectiveness and quality of care.

There is currently growing awareness that more specific legislation and regulation are needed in human resources planning to improve the quality of care, strengthen primary care and counteract inefficient competition among providers.

Conclusions

Accountable entrepreneurs

The general trend in the past decade has been towards introducing market forces in health care, competition and an increased scope for entrepreneurship. Evidence suggests, however, that the aims of primary care are easier to reach in a less competitive and more regulated environment (Starfield 1996; Groenewegen and Delnoij 1997; Delnoij *et al.* 2000).

The conditions favouring the development of effective primary care (available and accessible to the whole population, with continuity of care, comprehensiveness and integration within the broader health care system; Starfield 1996; Boerma and Fleming 1998) probably fit in better in a regulatory environment that emphasizes a social justice ethos rather than an autonomy ethos. In this respect, it is important to have accountable GPs who are responsible for a defined population for which they serve as coordinators and gatekeepers to specialized care.

Growing responsibilities of GPs

Despite the differences in employment status, means of payment, formal position and work setting, there are also important similarities in the regulatory environment of primary care within the differing health care systems. In tax-based national health systems, there has been a tendency to devolve budgetary responsibilities to independent primary care providers. In countries with salaried GPs, there is a tendency to create a personal doctor–patient relationship by introducing free choice of GPs and a list system.

In most social insurance systems, the self-employed GPs are paid on a fee-for-service basis and have no gatekeeping function. If there is a debate in these systems about the future role of general practice, systems with gatekeeping GPs and personal patient lists are taken as examples to follow. Great diversity exists in the transitional countries, ranging from the *status quo* to complete privatization of primary care. As a general tendency across all health care systems in Europe, we see a gradual increase in responsibility, financially or professionally, assigned to GPs.

Stepwise approach in central and eastern Europe

An important aspect of entrepreneurship among European GPs is the trend towards independent GPs in the CEE countries. In the course of the first post-communist decade, GPs are now able to be self-employed, although the number who have actually switched from state employment to independent practice differs from country to country. There is a lack of knowledge and experience, both from would-be independent GPs (such as how to set up and run a practice) and from government agencies (such as how to regulate independent practice). The question is what both sets of actors can learn from the western European experience.

In our opinion, a stepwise approach to changes in transitional countries is preferable to rapid, large-scale changes. Sudden privatization of primary care introduces competition among GPs where professional values have not developed to serve as a countervailing power to personal interests. In trying to keep a balance between private and social interests, state regulation could seek to increase responsibility at lower levels, and create small groups of better qualified GPs while maintaining their salaried status. Professional values should be developed by means of retraining and vocational training programmes, through the introduction of peer review and the development of professional standards and protocols. When a professional infrastructure has developed and professional values influence behaviour, the next step to self-employed status can be taken.

References

Allen, R.E. (ed.) (1990) *The Concise Oxford Dictionary of Current English*, 8th edn. Oxford: Oxford University Press.

Boerma, W.G.W. and Fleming, D.M. (1998) *The Role of General Practice in Primary Health Care*. London: The Stationery Office.

Boerma, W.G.W., De Jong, F.A.J.M. and Mulder, P.H. (1993) *Health Care and General Practice across Europe*. Utrecht: NIVEL.

Boerma, W.G.W., van der Zee, J. and Fleming, D.M. (1997) Service profiles of general practitioners in Europe, *British Journal of General Practice*, 47: 481–6.

Busse, R. (2000) *Health Care Systems in Transition: Czech Republic*. Copenhagen: European Observatory on Health Care Systems.

de Maesseneer, J., de Prins, L. and Heyerick, J.P. (1994) Het huisbezoek in Belgie; analyse van een wereldrecord [The home visit in Belgium; analysis of a world record], *Huisarts en Wetenschap*, 37: 552–6.

de Maesseneer, J., Bogaert, K., de Prins, L. and Groenewegen, P.P. (1999) A literature review, in S. Brown (ed.) *Physician Funding and Health Care Systems – An International Perspective*. London: Royal College of General Practitioners.

Delnoij, D.M.J. (1994) *Physician payment systems and cost control*. Thesis, NIVEL, Utrecht.

Delnoij, D.M.J., van Merode, G., Paulus, A. and Groenewegen, P. (2000) Does general practitioner gatekeeping curb health care expenditure?, *Journal of Health Services Research and Policy*, 5: 22–6.

Dixon, J. and Glennerster, H. (1995) What do we know about fundholding in general practice?, *British Medical Journal*, 311: 727–30.

Dixon, J., Holland, P. and Mays, N. (1998) Developing primary care: gatekeeping, commissioning and managed care, *British Medical Journal*, 317: 125–8

Freidson, E. (1970) *Profession of Medicine: A Study of the Sociology of Applied Knowledge.* New York: Harper & Row.

Goodwin, N. (1998) GP fundholding, in J. Le Grand, N. Mays and J. Mulligan (eds) *Learning from the NHS Internal Market: A Review of the Evidence.* London: King's Fund.

Grielen, S.J., Boerma, W.G.W. and Groenewegen, P.P. (2000) Unity or diversity? Task profiles of general practitioners in central and eastern Europe, *European Journal of Public Health*, 10: 249–54.

Groenewegen, P.P. (1996) Het gedrag van hulpverleners en patienten: toepassingen van de methode van de sociologische modelbouw [The behaviour of health care providers and patients: applications of the method of sociological modelling], *Tijdschrift voor Sociale Gezondheidszorg*, 2 (suppl., Medical Sociology): 4–9.

Groenewegen, P.P and Delnoij, D.M.J. (1997) *Wat zou Nederland zijn zonder de huisarts? De positie van huisartsen in relatie tot aard en kosten van de zorg [Where Would the Netherlands be Without GPs? The Position of GPs in Relation to the Nature and Costs of Care].* Utrecht: Elsevier/De Tijdstroom.

Grol, R., Jacobs, A., Baker, R. and Wensing, M. (1993) *Quality Assurance in General Practice: The State of the Art in Europe.* Utrecht: Nederlands Huisartsen Genootschap.

Irvine, D. (1999) The performance of doctors: the new professionalism, *Lancet*, 353: 1174–7.

Le Grand, J., Mays, N. and Dixon, J. (1998) The reforms: success or failure or neither?, in J. Le Grand, N. Mays and J. Mulligan (eds) *Learning from the NHS Internal Market: A Review of the Evidence.* London: King's Fund.

Marrée, J. and Groenewegen, P.P. (1997) *Back to Bismarck: Eastern European Health Care Systems in Transition.* Aldershot: Avebury.

Mays, N. and Dixon, J. (1996) *Purchaser Plurality in UK Health Care: Is a Consensus Emerging and is it the Right One?* London: King's Fund.

Ros, C.C., Groenewegen, P.P. and Delnoij, D.M.J. (2000) All rights reserved, or can we just copy? Cost sharing arrangements and characteristics of health care systems, *Health Policy*, 52: 1–13.

Saltman, R.B. and Young, D.W. (1983) Hospital cost containment and the quest for institutional growth: a behavioral analysis, *Journal of Public Health Policy*, 4: 313–34.

Secretary of State for Health (1997) *The New NHS – Modern, Dependable*, White Paper. London: The Stationery Office.

Secretary of State for Health (1998) *First Class Service*, White Paper. London: The Stationery Office.

Starfield, B. (1996) Is strong primary care good for health outcomes?, in J. Griffin (ed.) *The Future of Primary Care.* London: Office of Health Economics.

van de Rijdt, T. (1994) *Huisartsengroepen, groei en grenzen: een onderzoek naar nieuwe vormen van professionele organisatie [GP Groups, Growth and Boundaries: A Study of New Forms of Professional Organization].* Tilburg: Tilburg University Press.

van de Ven, W. (1997) The Netherlands, in C. Ham (ed.) *Health Care Reform.* Buckingham: Open University Press.

Westert, G.P. (1997) State control and the delivery of health care: a preliminary study in eleven European countries, *Environment and Planning, C: Government and Policy*, 15: 219–28.

chapter eleven

Regulating entrepreneurial behaviour in oral health care services[1]

Dorthe Holst, Aubrey Sheiham and Poul Erik Petersen

Introduction

Dentistry as an institution

Historically, the image of dentists has been that of tradespeople whose dental skills were regarded as a mechanical art and who advertised their services and worked from a shop (Davies 1980). By its nature, the profession is characterized by relative independence. Apart from certain specialist areas, an individual practitioner can offer the client a full range of services. Surgical and other equipment are usually not easily shared, and the exclusivity of the relationship with the patient makes the provision of oral health care a predominantly personal service. The relatively strong national dental associations in western Europe have supported the independence of private practitioners.

As a profession, dentists have traditionally opposed third-party control and have managed to maintain a high level of autonomy. In Europe, the profession has been able to influence the numbers entering university dental schools and has managed to resist 'peer review' in the form of audit, which is becoming more commonplace in general medical practice (Silvester *et al.* 1999). Auxiliary dental health care workers, including nurses, hygienists and therapists, have been successfully subordinated as employees or as subcontractors.

Currently, more than two-thirds of Europe's dentists are private practitioners. Therefore, most dentists are used to managing a small health business and are thus entrepreneurs. In the Nordic countries, 30–50 per cent of dentists are salaried employees in public service. Most salaried dentists concentrate their efforts on clinical aspects and not on business and management, since the financing and management of the services is not their primary role. In recent years, as a response to shrinking budgets, salaried dentists have felt the need to develop skills to improve the efficiency of their services.

Oral health services are expensive. In Germany, for example, the mouth is the most expensive part of the body to treat. In many European countries, oral health costs rank third or fourth as a percentage of overall health care costs. In 1995, the estimated total per capita expenditure on oral health services was 3–9 per cent of total health expenditure.

Dentistry is recognized as an independent specialty of medicine, yet its *modus operandi* has few parallels with medicine. Most oral health care is provided as an outpatient service, and hospital oral health care is very limited. Among the reasons suggested for this are: (a) the elective nature of most dental treatment; (b) the highly individualistic nature of solo dental practice; (c) the relatively restricted use of dental auxiliaries; (d) the chronic rather than life-threatening nature of most dental diseases; (e) the minimal interest in and development of hospital-centred treatment in general dentistry; and (f) the relatively slow advances in oral health sciences compared to medicine (Willcocks and Richards 1971).

Far from being unique, the rise of dentistry can be seen as part of a broad movement involving the expansion of the entire service sector in industrial society. The dual image of dentistry as both a service and a health profession (more like medicine) is a dilemma for the profession in its struggle for identity and choice of future strategies. On the one hand, most oral health care services are simple, low-cost, repetitive and preventive, which to some extent can be carried out by dental auxiliaries (Hancock 1993). On the other hand, there are several oral conditions that require highly skilled specialized clinicians. The profile of dental needs indicates that the oral health care delivery units should be big enough to provide both the simple routine preventive and maintenance care and also complicated surgery and reconstruction.

Regulatory models

The oral health care sector includes examples of three different regulatory models: (1) the professional, self-regulatory model, (2) the technocratic public model and (3) the market-based model (Saltman and Figueras 1997). The self-regulatory principle assumes that control over the oral health care system is by the dental profession. This control is exerted through education and training that ensures standardized skills. It is also exerted through a strong professional code of ethics that emphasizes dental practice based on a patient's needs. Within this model, government has a role in providing restrictions to entry to the profession through educational requirements, licensing and entry restrictions from the outside. A number of European Union (EU) directives apply to dentistry, including the Medical Devices Directive 93/42/EEC, which relates to prostheses and appliances made by dental technicians and most materials and equipment used in dentistry. Within the EU, governments have lifted restrictions, and EU-licensed dentists are free to practise anywhere within the EU. Directives 686/78/EEC and 687/78/EEC regulate undergraduate and specialist dental training and the mutual recognition of diplomas within EU countries, respectively. An additional role of government is found in countries that rely partly on a 'technocratic model' of regulation. In such countries, there is regulation of access to services in terms of pricing and distribution of services.

While European health care reform in general has attempted to generate more independent, self-regulating and self-managing behaviour at lower levels within the health care system, dentistry has already been predominantly dominated by small entrepreneurial businesses.

Delivery models in Europe

Even though dentistry has many common features in most European countries, the political history of the countries has a direct impact on the structure and organization of oral health care services (Costlan 1979; Yule 1986, 1989; Widström and Eaton 1997; Anderson *et al.* 1998a,b).[2]

In countries based on the Bismarckian model, oral health care is mainly financed through compulsory social insurance, which includes dental treatment. Oral health care has the following features.

- Provision relies mainly on private dental practitioners.
- The government sets the legal and regulatory framework within which many of the independent agencies organize the flow of funds between the patients and employers on the one hand and the dental professionals on the other.
- The insurance system is governed by law and managed by negotiation among professional organizations.
- The agreements cover most restorative dental care.
- There are also private insurance schemes in which patients pay their dentist directly and are reimbursed from the insurance company.
- Cost-sharing generally consists of the consumer's payment of a fixed percentage of expensive porcelain or gold restorations and fixed prostheses.

In central and eastern European (CEE) countries, the former system for oral health care closely followed the general provision of health care. The main features of the oral health care system were as follows.

- Comprehensive care was provided free of charge to the whole population.
- Dentists were salaried public employees who operated from local or company-based polyclinics or hospital dental departments.
- Oral health facilities were publicly owned and the distribution of personnel, clinics, treatment and materials was planned.
- A small part of expensive services, mainly prosthetic services, was covered by patient co-payment.
- Some private practice existed in several CEE countries, entirely paid for by patients on a fee-for-service basis.

In Beveridge countries, financing of oral health care used to be predominantly through taxation and oral health care services were traditionally provided through publicly owned and managed institutions. A key element of this approach is the universal or near-universal access to oral health care. In the United Kingdom, the National Health Service (NHS) contracts with independent practitioners. The contract regulates prices and treatment profiles, average income and pensions; otherwise the service is unregulated. 'The Nordic model' was established in principle and to some extent in practice earlier (1910–20) than Beveridge's 'White Paper'. Originally, the model consisted of salaried services for children, but otherwise had completely private practitioners. Later, the Nordic model also covered oral health care for adults (with the exception of Norway). Since 1994, regional national health agencies in Ireland have contracted with private practitioners to provide oral health care for low-income and unemployed people (approximately 35 per cent of all adults).

In southern Europe, the emphasis has always been on private provision and financing of oral health care, with a residual government health service for specific groups who are unable to afford care from private practitioners. In a few regions, preventive and treatment programmes have been started for children and some risk groups (O'Mullane 1997). In Greece, health insurance agencies have started to make contracts with dentists for their members.

Recent changes in oral health care in European countries

To obtain a reasonably clear picture of the main changes oral health care is undergoing in European countries, reforms are analysed along two dimensions: funding and the provision of services (Figure 11.1). Taking funding first, at one end the funding dimension comprises government revenues, mainly tax funding. At the other end, funding is out-of-pocket or is purchased by private health insurance, mainly unregulated by government. In the middle of the axis, payroll social security insurance is found, which is government-regulated and managed by agencies of health insurers or professions. The provision dimension ranges from government health services to completely independent private practitioners. Between these extremes there are private practitioners who contract with public authorities.

The dimensions can be combined into a typology with four categories. In category (a), oral health care services are mainly provided by government salaried personnel combined with private financing. This is not a common combination. In some of the CEE countries, however, such as in the Baltic States and Romania, dentists still working in the public service charge adults for the cost of treatment. Category (b) comprises public oral health care services with complete or nearly complete public funding. Typically, services for children and adolescents in the Nordic countries and all services in the CEE countries fall into this category. Category (c) includes oral health care services that are predominantly delivered by private practitioners and funded by public insurance. Several European countries are in this category. In category (d), oral health care is primarily privately funded and delivered by independent private practitioners. Oral health care for adults in Norway and most oral health care in Italy, Portugal and Spain are examples of this category. In this case, individuals pay for services either directly or through private insurance companies.

Figure 11.1 Recent changes in the delivery of dental services in some European countries according to two dimensions: provision and financing

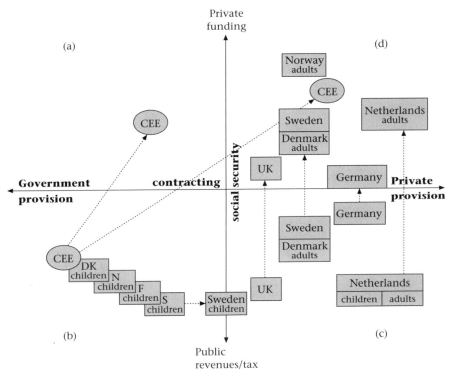

Figure 11.1 illustrates changes and their direction in a number of countries. The picture, although crude, shows that in some countries little change has occurred, whereas in others great strides towards privatization have taken place. The most common movement is from mainly public funding towards more private funding, namely higher cost-sharing by the consumer. In the Nordic countries, this has resulted in higher expenditures borne by the patients. In the Netherlands, the exclusion of oral health care services for adults from the national health insurance has led people to purchase additional insurance through sickness funds and private health insurance companies. Except for the CEE countries, there is little movement along the provision dimension. Those countries that traditionally relied on integrated public services for segments of the population still do so. Figure 11.1 shows a shift in Sweden, with the pioneering county of Stockholm allowing purchaser–provider split, free choice and contracting. In Germany, co-payments for a range of oral health services were increased from 1997 to 1998. Generally, cost-sharing of oral health care services does not apply to children and other priority or disadvantaged groups.

The CEE countries have moved away from integrated public services, free at time of service, to decentralized, privately owned dental offices. Collective preventive programmes have been terminated for either political or economic reasons.[3] Consumers have compulsory health insurance, which reimburses part of the expenses for certain restorative treatments. Oral health services are now to be demanded like most commodities, which are available at a certain price. Prices have gone up and services have therefore become less economically accessible to consumers. Equity in finance and access is still the fundamental government policy; pluralistic insurance systems may have compromised this objective.

In the United Kingdom, primary oral health care was virtually unaffected by the internal market. In the Nordic countries, the basic principles of the delivery system of oral health care have not changed, although there have been a number of changes to deal with specific problems.

Changes in oral health care policies seem to follow one or both of two processes:

- *They are part of major health care reforms.* This was the case in the United Kingdom when the NHS was introduced. Health care reforms can also be part of fundamental political reforms, as in the CEE countries.
- *Oral health care is affected by political opportunism.* This occurred, for example, when oral health care services were excluded from the national health insurance in the Netherlands. A recent proposal in Sweden (July 1999) by the Secretary of State for Health to again include oral health in the national health insurance package is understood as a political showcase.

It should be noted that health care reforms often affect oral health care services late in the process of reform implementation. Legislation on oral health care in Denmark, Norway and Sweden fits this description (Holst 1997).

In summary, the basic features of dentistry in Europe may explain why the sector is less affected by health reform in countries that have otherwise engaged in comprehensive health care reform.

- The oral health sector is already characterized by many of the features of the entrepreneurial policies of health care reform in Europe.
- The sector is relatively small in terms of budget. The potential for political, regulatory and financial gains by further changes is small.
- Traditionally, users of oral health care services make few complaints, even about economically inaccessible and unavailable services.
- By and large, there are a sufficient number of dentists to satisfy demand for oral health care services (Anderson *et al.* 1998b). There is little reason for politicians to establish unpopular distributive regulation of the provision of services, even though there is an uneven geographical distribution of dentists, for example, in Norway, the United Kingdom and other parts of Europe.

Entrepreneurial behaviour and regulation

Given the small-scale entrepreneurial nature of the oral health sector in Europe, it is justifiable to ask what the potential entrepreneur's role is and how entrepreneurial forces could be further developed by adequate incentives. The same question can be asked of public services. There are few research results available to answer these questions. The approach here, therefore, is a blend of scattered observations and some qualified reasoning. Six issues have been selected that will serve to illustrate accountability, incentives and activities and the need for regulation in the sector.

Decentralization

A common component of health care reform has been to generate more independent, self-regulating and self-managing behaviour at lower levels of the health care system. Private dental practice is completely decentralized, with the exception of contracted general oral health services in the United Kingdom. In the Nordic countries, as a consequence of health care reform, governments have decentralized several functions within the public services to the regional level (Norway in 1984 and Sweden in 1987). In Denmark and Finland, responsibility has been decentralized to the municipalities since 1972.

In the CEE countries, the current transition of oral health care systems to decentralized public and private services appears to have a number of consequences:

- polarization of dentists with respect to income (rich dentists working in new private sector versus relatively poor dentists working in outdated facilities and for low salaries);
- lack of modern equipment and shortage of dental materials;
- decreased use of services, higher demand for radical treatment (tooth extractions) and potential negative consequences to the oral health status of children and adults; and
- termination of organized oral health programmes, particularly school-based preventive oral care activities.

These observations are based on many simultaneous processes. Some are a result of the transition process; others are due to the fundamental lack of resources. Decentralization allows more flexible decision-making, which leads to variations at the local level in the day-to-day management of services. It is too early to know whether decentralization will lead to a better allocation of resources according to need, or whether fragmented services with higher transaction costs and greater inequality will be the result.

There has been too little evaluation of the adequacy and efficiency of oral health services, especially under greater decentralization. There is a role for government initiatives in monitoring and evaluating such developments.

Prevention: whose responsibility? Short- and long-term consequences

The oral health care sector is renowned for efforts to prevent oral disease. With today's knowledge and technology, it is considered unethical not to engage in preventive work, either on an individual or on a collective basis. Over the last 40 years, governments, professional organizations and industry have joined together in health education programmes and preventive activities for better oral health. Improvements in economic standards and living conditions have enabled populations to take an active part in improving their general health and oral health.

Despite obvious differences in preventive efforts and activities among European countries, oral health is improving in most countries. This is puzzling to the researchers and administrators of oral health care. In some countries, prevention has been the responsibility of private practitioners and consumers, with educational support from government or professionals. Dental insurance fees only occasionally include preventive services. The scale of fees is supposed to be neutral – that is, not to provide an incentive to the provider to prefer one service over the other. Nevertheless, fee scales have usually not worked neutrally and prevention has been the loser. In the Nordic countries and the United Kingdom, for example, government and professional policies strongly advocated prevention as a first priority, primarily as a duty of the public service, but also as a moral obligation to the private sector. The virtue of the public service is its structural ability to organize prevention; on the negative side is its inability to evaluate the effectiveness of prevention.

Unfortunately, there are few empirically based predictions of the long-term consequences of good oral health (Bronkhorst *et al.* 1994). The market for simple and high-tech dental treatment and dental prevention is growing. Even though the evidence for supplier-induced oral health services is uncertain (Grytten 1992), the asymmetry of dental knowledge between the consumer and the provider will require strong ethical attitudes and behaviour by the dental profession and more external regulation.

The success of prevention may need the development of government policies to protect consumers in oral health care markets. Professional self-control may not be sufficient.

Financing oral health care: from third-party to one-party payment systems

Most adult oral health care in Europe is paid for directly by patients. Third-party payers, governments and insurance companies in western European countries have lower budgets for oral health care. In eastern European countries, health insurance has been given a funding role in health care, although a lack of funds and individual assets may push oral health care further down the list of priorities.

Oral health is improving in many European countries irrespective of public or private funding. It is therefore relevant to investigate the role of a third-party payer in achieving better oral health. Is it reasonable to expect a public third-party payer to place greater emphasis on equity at the expense of efficiency, and private funding to take the opposite perspective?

It is necessary to clarify the concept of oral health and the mechanisms by which funding and type of funding could contribute to improve oral health.

In this context, it is most fruitful to define oral health as the level of untreated and treated oral disease in a population. At the time of consumption, money cannot reduce the level of disease, but may nevertheless reduce the consequences and barriers to treatment and lessen the costs. From a long-term perspective, third-party funding of preventive services may reduce future disease rates by preventing serious consequences of untreated disease. Because of the irreversibility of common oral diseases, improved oral health outcomes can only be expected in younger cohorts.

Third-party funding provides an incentive on the demand side to purchase care by reducing its price. There are four aspects of funding that should be taken into consideration:

- *The nature of expenditure in oral health care*. In countries where oral health services are demanded at fairly regular intervals, most oral health care is consumed at a relatively low cost. Approximately 10 per cent of patients carry high costs. Administrative costs are high in handling low-cost reimbursement (Holst and Grytten 1998).
- *Moral hazard in the consumption of oral health care services financed by a third party*. Both consumers and providers may be tempted to overuse necessary and unnecessary services. Cost-sharing can be a tool to ration the demand for care. Selective cost-sharing may improve efficiency by using price signals to channel demand in desired directions. Excluding cost-ineffective services from the benefit package increases efficiency in both public and private funding.
- *Supplier-induced demand, one of the threats to efficiency of third-party payment systems that has attracted most attention* (Grytten *et al.* 1990; Grytten 1991, 1992). Supplier-induced demand occurs when a dentist recommends or provides services that differ from those that the patient would have chosen if he or she had had the same information and knowledge as the dentist.
- *Equitable distribution of oral health and access to services*. Although funding may not be decisive for achieving higher levels of oral health in populations, reduced variation among individuals may be enhanced by third-party funding. However, tension exists between efficiency – gained through market forces and competition – and equity.

As stated above, the main trend in oral health care funding is towards more private funding. Government policies are implicit and woven into claims to contain costs. While cost containment is directed to the supply side in other health care services in western European countries (Kutzin 1998), cost containment in dentistry is mainly directed to the demand side of the market by increasing patient charges. The costs of adult oral health care for public payers have been contained by increasing patient charges. Germany has addressed macro-efficiency objectives by implementing expenditure caps and cost-sharing in oral health care services. As a result, the reimbursement to patients of complex treatments like crowns, bridges and partial dentures is only 50–60 per cent of the costs. Dental implants, for example, are not included in the benefits (Anderson *et al.* 1998a).

Since public and social security funding are declining rapidly, there is a clear opportunity for private insurance of oral health care services. In the Netherlands, within a few years, expenditure on adult oral health care through additional dental insurance increased by twice the amount cut by the government. In the more affluent countries, where data are available, increased patient charges seem to have had a marginal effect on utilization rates. In Norway, for example, the increased cost-sharing did not decrease yearly utilization of oral health services, where 65–75 per cent of adults demand annual check-ups (Holst and Grytten 1998). This is explained by the relatively low annual cost per person and increasing income for large segments of the population. In less affluent countries, demand is expected to decrease with cost-sharing.

Governments should monitor the extent of equal access to necessary oral health services and protect individuals against the costs of infrequent, expensive and debilitating conditions.

Paying for services

The classical way of paying an entrepreneur for oral health care is fee-for-service, which is the dominant payment system in European dentistry. The challenge to governments, health administrators and insurers has been whether – and eventually how – to regulate fees. In most countries where third-party payers have contributed to the funding, fee scales have been developed administratively or negotiated between relevant partners to control and contain costs. Fee-for-service as a payment system in oral health care has been shown to be very productive, but is fraught with many potential disadvantages. As in other areas of health care, providers seem to use considerable entrepreneurial energy in evading regulations and obtaining their target income.

Price regulation was recently lifted in Norway (1997) and Sweden (1999) to stimulate entrepreneurial creativity and competition. Price development is being monitored by the authorities. So far, the average increase in prices has been considered acceptable in Norway (Grytten and Skau 1999).

While fee-for-service may induce both necessary and unnecessary services, capitation may compromise necessary prevention and treatment. A comprehensive evaluation study in the United Kingdom showed little gain of efficiency when capitation was compared with fee-for-service (Lennon *et al.* 1990).

Fee-for-service was preferred in most countries when there was a considerable need for treatment in the population and too few dentists to meet the need. The improved oral health among children and young adults has led to a change in preference to payment by capitation. Paradoxically, a progressive policy of capitation in the United Kingdom led to excessively high earnings by NHS dentists. Attempts by the government to retrieve the excess resulted in large withdrawals of dentists from the NHS and the expansion of private dentistry.

Contracting mechanisms bind third-party payers and providers to explicit commitments, and generate the economic motivation to fulfil those commitments. A new dental contract in the United Kingdom (1994) aimed to improve the oral health of the nation by encouraging patients to visit their dentists regularly and for dentists to practise preventive care. The mechanism to achieve this aim was to make adults sign a 2 year rolling contract with a dentist, who was given a 'continuing care' payment to enable him or her to undertake basic preventive work. The same principle was built into the reformed health insurance for oral health care in Sweden in 1999. Dentists were encouraged to sign a contract with patients for 1–2 years. Compared to contracting between third-party payer and provider, contracts between patients and providers may stimulate patients' awareness of price and interest in preventing future need for treatment.

Unfortunately, very little research is carried out on payment systems and payment mechanisms in oral health care in Europe. It is important to evaluate the behaviour of consumers, providers and funders under these new systems so that appropriate regulation can be developed if necessary.

Delegating and specializing

European dental entrepreneurs reluctantly delegate duties to auxiliaries. Compared to medicine and dentistry elsewhere, they make less use of auxiliaries and specialize less. In Canada, Japan and the United States, for example, there are 5–6 times more dental auxiliaries per capita than in the United Kingdom (Hancock 1993). In New Zealand, dental therapists are under dentists' control but work independently and refer difficult cases to dentists. They virtually manage the entire children's oral health service. In a number of countries, including Canada, Denmark and the Netherlands, the provision of dentures is largely the responsibility of denturists. Many countries now extend the availability of orthodontic care through the employment of orthodontic auxiliaries. Dental hygienists are not trained in all European countries and only in restricted numbers in other countries (Widström and Eaton 1997, Anderson *et al.* 1998b).

Research has shown that regular attention by preventive auxiliaries can keep rates of disease very low in children and adults. Including independent dental hygienists in the dental team can increase efficiency in the public oral health services with no loss of quality (Wang and Riordan 1995).

In terms of cost-effectiveness, it appears to make little sense for dentists to spend much of their time carrying out work that could be done effectively by someone with less training, carrying out a narrower range of relatively simple routine work at a lower cost. Delegating would enable dentists to deploy those skills from which they would derive much greater job satisfaction. From an economic point of view, this raises questions about why income-oriented practitioners and administrators of public services do not spontaneously take advantage of the cost-reducing potential represented by auxiliaries. Part of the answer is revealed by evaluation data that show that efficient use of auxiliaries by private dentists requires a major capital investment and a reorganization of the whole practice flow to accommodate a much larger patient load. Unless reorganized, single practices may therefore not easily employ auxiliaries. Corporate dental clinics (such as that of Boots Chemists in London) are an example of a new structure of oral health care. Such corporations provide easily accessible clinics and employ dentists and hygienists.

The organized public oral health services have been surprisingly reluctant to employ dental hygienists, mainly because they were regarded as a professional threat to the dentists. Reduced budgets and increasing difficulties in recruiting dentists have necessitated expanding dental teams in the public oral health services in the Nordic countries. Governments in some of the Nordic countries have recently licensed dental hygienists to work independently.

Governments have a clear role in balancing the number of trained dentists and auxiliaries.

Organization of dental practices

A combination of professional skills and entrepreneurialism is necessary to manage a dental practice. Dental education equips graduates with information and professional skills. Entrepreneurial skills are acquired during practice. These will vary among practitioners and delivery systems. Managing a single-handed practice can be lonely and limiting. It also has many challenges, including financial viability, basing the practice on evidence, consumer expectations, organizational control and lifelong competence.

Oral health care is increasingly seen as a business by non-dental entrepreneurs who use venture capital to purchase practices. The corporate practice of dentistry, which links administrative and business professionals to dental professionals, is a recent challenge in a number of countries. In essence, these private firms – for example, Dental Bodies Corporate in the United Kingdom – organize and run chains of practices. These groups arose for the following three reasons:

- not all dentists enjoy the daily management of a dental practice (Bejerot 1998; Silvester *et al.* 1999);
- patients expect some accreditation or approval that they are attending a licensed practice; and
- there are economic and managerial benefits from linking practices to corporations and chains.

For general dental practitioners, one of the largest financial commitments is sufficient funding to develop a practice. An important benefit of these chains is their ability to limit an individual's liability.

Corporate organizations vary in the level and nature of management services they provide and in their overall business arrangements and sophistication. In general, when acquiring a dental practice, all the tangible assets of the practice are acquired, while the dentist retains the patients. Agreements explicitly state which management services are to be provided. Dentists enter an employment contract and are paid a percentage of the revenue. Some organizations employ all support staff and manage all aspects of the practice except patient treatment. Management service plans are organized with the aim of building large caseloads, with continuing growth at perhaps 10 per cent a year (Editorial 1999).

Corporate organizations are viewed with scepticism by dental organizations, as they are seen as a threat to professional autonomy. From an economic perspective, corporate dentistry may develop monopolistic behaviour, leading to increasing rather than decreasing prices. On the positive side, such organizations may develop safe working conditions and quality-assured treatment procedures.

While the publicity from such corporations may be very positive, their long-term future is not yet secure. The perceived advantages of these chains may not be in the best interests of either the public or the profession as a whole. An important aspect to note is that corporate organizations are mainly driven by the expectations of their investors, not the needs of the patients and practitioners. Even those that are publicly traded will find it difficult to keep growth and share values high for investors to be happy.

There is a clear role for health authorities to monitor and consider appropriate regulation of this new service sector.

Is there a need to regulate entrepreneurialism in dentistry?

The present regulation of dentistry in Europe reflects historical and political traditions and values. Like the medical professions, the dental profession has been given a self-regulatory role that in many ways has forced it to use a set of acceptable professional ethical standards. During the 1990s in the CEE countries, dentistry in general was deregulated, and in the Nordic countries, prices and dental practice were deregulated. The question health authorities must ask is whether the new balance between actors meets societal expectations, or whether additional regulation is necessary in the light of a free European market for providers and consumers, and a transnational flow of funds, third-party payers and dental products. There may be areas in which additional regulation is necessary to protect consumers against the results of market imperfections, such as too-high prices, induced demand, chain monopolies and inadequate clinical quality and skills.

In the wake of competitive policies, there is a need to develop appropriate regulation. However, there seems to be much uncertainty as to how such regulation should be designed. One approach is a policy on 'clinical governance', which has been launched in the United Kingdom. Clinical governance is a formal structure to ensure that dentists practise ethical behaviour, and includes the system and the manner of governing clinical affairs. It has been defined as a framework through which NHS organizations are accountable for continuously improving the quality of their services and safeguarding high standards of care by creating an environment in which excellence in clinical care will flourish (Department of Health and Social Security 1999). This requires an explicit means of setting clinical policy and an equally explicit means of monitoring it (Department of Health and Social Security 1998; Lugon and Secker-Walker 1999). Previously, health authorities in the United Kingdom did not regard clinical effectiveness as their own responsibility. Under the standards of clinical governance, however, this will become a requirement (Ferguson 1999).

The priorities for additional regulation to steer newly created entrepreneurial incentives in directions that are clinically, financially and socially productive are:

- provider behaviour within chains of dental clinics;
- dental education institutions and lifelong learning of the necessary skills;
- patients' rights and consumer protection (protection of socially deprived, low-income and handicapped groups or those with chronic diseases); and
- control of marketing, dental equipment and dental materials.

There are areas of concern for dentistry in Europe that are not covered either by national dental organizations or by educational institutions. These include:

- the structure of dental practice – whether the single practice can or should survive;
- incentives for delegating work – the profile of oral health services invites a discussion of the distribution of work and of a more specialized oral/dental physician;
- increased focus on integrated health promotion – that is, on a self-reliant, competent, active consumer in a health-promoting community; and
- the harmonization of basic education, and its appropriate revision and reform, according to new knowledge and evidence about the necessity and the efficiency of care.

With the drive to implement both clinical and corporate governance, the dental profession needs to thoroughly debate the advantages and disadvantages that any changes may bring. Failure to think through all the issues may well create additional and far more complex problems than those that currently exist.

Future trends/conclusion

Trends in oral health care provide an interesting case study of what could happen in health care when levels of disease decrease. The oral health care sector is considered to be a growth industry (Grytten and Lund 1999) and the sector is growing faster, in real terms, than the economy as a whole. The reasons for this are the growth in gross national product, in dental insurance and in the number of dentists per capita (Waldman 1987; Grytten and Lund 1999).

This growth has occurred despite the dramatic decline in dental caries in children and young adults over the past 25 years. Nevertheless, there is increased utilization of oral health care and there are demands by some planners for more dentists. The improvement in oral health, paradoxically, appears to lead to demand for maintenance and cosmetic treatment among adults. The main factors relate to the increased concern of dentists to sustain demand. Five possible explanations should be considered.

1 With a lower severity of disease, dental treatment is more acceptable. That, together with the long-established health education messages to visit dentists regularly, may increase utilization.
2 Public expectations have increased. People want healthy teeth and a good appearance. Entrepreneurs have capitalized on this, concentrating on questionable preventive 'packages' and selling oral health aids such as brushes

and rinses. Many dentists work in 'drop-in' centres where no prior appointment is required, thus reducing barriers to oral health care.

3 Dentists constantly redefine need. Instead of being mainly concerned with caries, the emphasis has shifted to periodontal disease, malocclusion, tooth wear and cosmetic dentistry. Some of these conditions are of questionable importance for health gain. In addition, there is the presence of supplier-induced demand (Grytten *et al.* 1990).

4 More adults are retaining more teeth and each new adult cohort has more teeth. Previously, many older adults had few or no natural teeth and, therefore, needed less treatment.

5 Payment systems, particularly child and adult capitation systems, encourage dentists to have patients return for follow-up visits to ensure their capitation fee. Increased privatization of dentistry has led to the marketing of preventive and cosmetic dentistry.

The asymmetry of knowledge has been a barrier for potentially rational consumers. At least two important changes have occurred that may balance the actors in the oral health care market. First, consumers today are generally better educated and therefore possess greater power as consumers of most goods, including oral health care. Second, treatment profiles of oral health care show a fundamental change from treatment based on pain, inflammation and disease to services dominated by preventive, aesthetic, maintenance and rehabilitation care. Improved oral health and new service profiles offer a greater role for consumers. Consumers can assess the value of these services, and the utility of such treatment in relationship to their cost. In this new context, consumers can choose and take responsibility for their choice.

Some fundamental questions remain about the organization of oral health care services. How should social conditions in oral health care be shaped or regulated to ensure that the professional behaviour of dentists at the micro-level is also beneficial at the macro-level? The traditional structure of delivery of oral health services may not survive the demands of society for much longer.

Dentistry faces new demands and possibilities in the twenty-first century. There will be fewer self-regulatory mechanisms, which are now challenged in the United Kingdom, for example, by government bodies such as the National Institute for Clinical Excellence and the Commission on Health Improvement. These new mechanisms, with evidence-based oral health care and clinical governance, will turn the tide for dentistry. In the future, consumers should be protected and providers adequately regulated. Health care reforms should encourage funders to be cost-conscious, providers to be efficient and ethical, and consumers to be rational.

Notes

1 The World Health Organization has adopted the terms 'oral health care' and 'oral health care services' instead of 'dental care' and 'dental care services'. These terms are now being used by educational institutions, research groups and public health organizations in most European countries.

2 A recent EU study illustrated the difficulties of a cross-sectional design to interpret associations between the characteristics of oral health care systems and oral health outcomes (O'Mullane 1997).
3 There is serious concern about the expected negative effects of stopping preventive programmes, such as in Hungary and Romania (Petersen *et al.* 1994; Petersen and Tanase 1997; Szöke and Petersen 2000). At the same time, an evaluation in the former German Democratic Republic of the effects of stopping water fluoridation and other preventive programmes did not result in an increase in caries (Künzel 1998). This suggests the need to assess preventive programmes at the community level, and also shows that monitoring of oral health conditions is important.

References

Anderson, R., Treasure, E.T. and Whitehouse, N.H. (1998a) Oral health care systems in Europe, Part I. Finance and entitlement to care, *Community Dental Health*, 15: 145–9.

Anderson, R., Treasure, E.T. and Whitehouse, N.H. (1998b) Oral health care systems in Europe, Part II. The dental workforce, *Community Dental Health*, 15: 243–7.

Bejerot, E. (1998) *Dentistry in Sweden – Healthy Work or Ruthless Efficiency?* Arbete och Hälsa, Vetenskaplig Skriftserie. Lund: Arbetslivsinstitutet.

Bronkhorst, E.M., Truin, G.J. and Wiersma, M.T. (1994) *Future Scenarios on Dental Health Care: A Reconnaissance of the Period 1990–2020*, Scenario report commissioned by the Steering Committee on Future Health Scenarios. Dordrecht: Kluwer Academic.

Costlan, J. (1979) *Oral Health Services in Europe*. WHO Regional Publications, European Series No. 5. Copenhagen: WHO Regional Office for Europe.

Davies, J. (1980) *The Social Context of Dentistry*. London: Croom Helm.

Department of Health and Social Security (1998) *A First Class Service: Quality in the New NHS*. London: The Stationery Office.

Department of Health and Social Security (1999) *Clinical Governance: Quality in the New NHS*. London: The Stationery Office.

Editorial (1999) DMSO and dentistry, *Journal of the American Dental Association*, 130 (suppl., February): 1–8.

Ferguson, A-L. (1999) Legal implications of clinical governance, in M. Lugon and J. Secker-Walker (eds) *Clinical Governance: Making it Happen*. London: Royal Society of Medicine Press.

Grytten, J. (1991) The effect of supplier inducement on Norwegian dental services: some empirical findings based on a theoretical model, *Community Dental Health*, 8: 221–31.

Grytten, J. (1992) The Norwegian dental care market: empirical studies on accessibility and supplier inducement in the adult population. Thesis, Department of Community Dentistry, University of Oslo.

Grytten, J. and Lund, E. (1999) Future demand for dental care in Norway: a macroeconomic perspective, *Community Dentistry and Oral Epidemiology*, 27: 321–30.

Grytten, J. and Skau, I. (1999) Konkurranse og tilbudsinduksjon i den private tannhelsetjenesten, *Norske Tannlegeforenings Tidende*, 109: 15–31.

Grytten, J., Holst, D. and Laake, P. (1990) Supplier inducement: its effect on dental services in Norway, *Journal of Health Economics*, 9: 483–91.

Hancock, R. (ed.) (1993) *Education and Training of Personnel Auxiliary to Dentistry*. London: Nuffield Foundation.

Holst, D. (1997) Dental services in the Nordic countries, in C. Pine (ed.) *Community Oral Health*. Oxford: Butterworth-Heinemann.

Holst, D. and Grytten, J. (1998) Forbruk av tannpleie og tannhelse i et velferdsperspektiv, in P-O. Burén and R. Lagercrantz (eds) *Tandhälsan. Samhällsekonomi och det personlige ansvaret*, Antologi, Välfärdsprosjektets Skriftserie No. 12. Stockholm: Socialdepartementet.

Künzel, W. (1998) *Eine Studie zur Entwicklung der Mundgesundheit*. Heidelberg: Hüthig Verlag.

Kutzin, J. (1998) The appropriate role for patient cost sharing, in R.B. Saltman, J. Figueras and C. Sakellarides (eds) *Critical Challenges for Health Care Reform in Europe*. Buckingham: Open University Press.

Lennon, M.A., Worthington, H.V., Coventry, P., Mellor, A.C. and Holloway, P.J. (1990) The Capitation Study. 2. Does capitation encourage more prevention?, *British Dental Journal*, 168: 213–15.

Lugon, M. and Secker-Walker, J. (1999) Organizational framework for clinical governance, in M. Lugon and J. Secker-Walker (eds) *Clinical Governance: Making it Happen*. London: Royal Society of Medicine Press.

O'Mullane, D. (ed.) (1997) *Efficiency in Oral Health Care: The Evaluation of Oral Health Systems in Europe*, Final Report. Cork: BIOMED1.

Petersen, P.E. and Tanase, M. (1997) Oral health status of an industrial population in Romania, *International Dental Journal*, 47: 194–8.

Petersen, P.E., Danila, I. and Dalean, A. (1994) Oral health status among schoolchildren in Romania, 1992, *Community Dentistry and Oral Epidemiology*, 22: 90–3.

Saltman, R.B. and Figueras, J. (1997) *European Health Care Reform: Analysis of Current Strategies*, WHO Regional Publications, European Series No. 72. Copenhagen: WHO Regional Office for Europe.

Silvester, S., Calnan, M., Manley, G. and Taylor-Gooby, P. (1999) *Public or Private? Dental Practitioners' Beliefs, Values and Practices*. Canterbury: Centre for Health Services Studies, University of Kent.

Szöke, J. and Petersen, P.E. (2000) Changing oral disease pattern of children in Hungary, *Community Dentistry and Oral Epidemiology*, 28: 155–60.

Waldman, H.B. (1987) Changing disease patterns of dental disease in children and the use of dental services, *Journal of Dentistry in Children*, 54: 89–92.

Wang, N.J. and Riordan, P. (1995) Recall intervals, dental hygienists and quality in child dental care, *Community Dentistry and Oral Epidemiology*, 23: 8–14.

Widström, E. and Eaton, K.E. (1997) *Systems for the Provision of Oral Health Care, Workforce and Costs in the EU and EEA: A Council of European Chief Dental Officers' Survey*. Helsinki: Stakes.

Willcocks, A.J. and Richards, N.D. (1971) Dental manpower and dentistry as an institution, in N.D. Richards and L.K. Cohen (eds) *Social Sciences and Dentistry: A Critical Bibliography*. The Hague: World Dental Federation.

Yule, B. (1986) *Financing of Dental Care in Europe: Part I*. Copenhagen: WHO Regional Office for Europe.

Yule, B. (1989) *Financing of Dental Care in Europe: Part II*. Copenhagen: WHO Regional Office for Europe.

Index